SOUTH KOREA

SOUTH KOREA

CONTENTS

DISCOVER 6

Welcome to South Korea 8
Reasons to Love South Korea 10
Explore South Korea 14
Getting to Know South Korea 16
South Korea Itineraries 20
South Korea Your Way 30
A Year in South Korea 50
A Brief History 52

EXPERIENCE SEOUL 58

Central Seoul 64

Beyond the Center 90

EXPERIENCE SOUTH KOREA 106

Gyeonggi-do Province 108

Gangwon-do Province 128

Chungcheong-do Province 150

Jeolla-do Province 170

Busan 202

Gyeongsang-do Province 220

Jeju Island 244

NEED TO KNOW 266

Before You Go 268
Getting Around 270
Practical Information 274
Index 276
Phrase Book 282
Acknowledgments 286

Left: Bongeunsa Temple, Seoul
Previous page: Seoraksan National Park
Front Cover: Hyangwonjeong Pavilion, Seoul

DISCOVER

Panoramic view of downtown Seoul

Welcome to South Korea..........................8

Reasons to Love South Korea...............10

Explore South Korea....................14

Getting to Know South Korea...............16

South Korea Itineraries...........................20

South Korea Your Way............................30

A Year in South Korea..............................50

A Brief History...52

WELCOME TO SOUTH KOREA

South Korea has gained international attention throughout history, most recently with the rise of Korean pop culture. But beyond the K-dramas and K-pop beats lies a country of trendsetting cities and timeless traditional culture. Explore majestic mountain ranges and mouthwatering cuisine, enjoy a raucous *noraebang* session or soak up the sacred silence of a Buddhist temple. Whatever your dream trip includes, this DK travel guide is the perfect companion.

1 *Dolharubang* statue on Jeju Island.

2 Cycling under pretty spring blossom.

3 Traditional bibimbap in Jeonju.

4 Myeong-dong shopping street at night.

Squeezed between China and Japan, South Korea packs a lot into a small peninsula. Some 70 per cent of the country is mountainous, its spine formed by the rugged Baekdudaegan range, which directs the courses of rushing rivers and provides a playground for hikers. On the west coast, fertile plains give way to thousands of tiny islands, while dramatic tides retreat to reveal mudflats as far as the eye can see. Meanwhile, on subtropical Jeju Island, volcanic Mount Hallasan looms over lava tubes, tuff cones, and powdery white-sand beaches.

For all of Korea's natural blessings, though, it's the country's culture that most excites, from its perfect K-pop melodies to food that's full of big, bold flavors. Get swept up by Seoul's intoxicating energy, reveling in its world-class arts scene and nightlife. Go table to table on an epic eating spree in Jeonju, Korea's culinary capital. Explore the lasting influence of the Joseon Dynasty as you walk the centuries-old walls of Suwon Hwaseong Fortress. Or find inner peace during a stay at one of the country's many mountain temples.

There's so much to see and do in Korea that it can be hard to know where to start. We've broken the country down into easily navigable chapters, with detailed itineraries, expert local knowledge, and colorful, comprehensive maps to help you plan the perfect trip. Whether you're sticking to Seoul or covering the entire country, this DK travel guide will ensure that you see the best Korea has to offer. Enjoy the book, and enjoy South Korea.

REASONS TO LOVE SOUTH KOREA

Infectious K-pop tunes and captivating culture. Refined royal palaces and unusual museums. Boisterous nights of barbecue and quiet hikes in nature. There are endless reasons to love South Korea; here are just a few.

1 K-EVERYTHING
K-pop and K-drama has captured the world's imagination. Experience it firsthand in neighborhoods like Seongsu (p99), Seoul, or spend time exploring the locations of on-screen dramas.

2 HIKING
Answer the mountains' call with a visit to Seoraksan National Park (p136), or savor a long ramble past volcanic formations on the subtropical Jeju Olle Trail (p255).

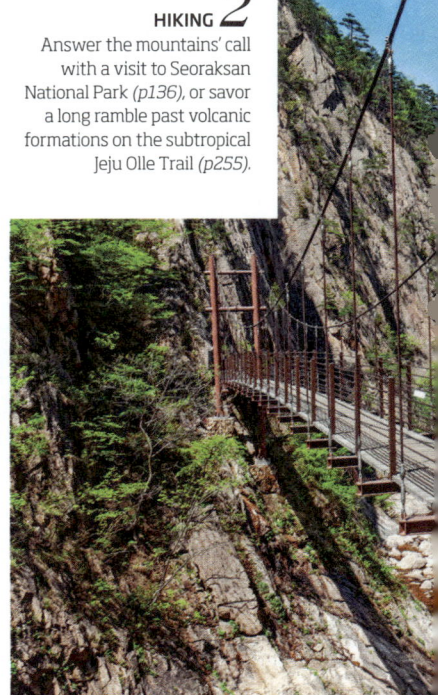

3 TRADITIONAL CULTURE
Korean culture is filled with customs. Discover their history at the Andong Hahoe Folk Village (p232), or learn about them through the Templestay program (p165).

KOREAN BARBECUE 4

Sizzling meat and endless sides: Korean barbecue is a fun way to sample the local cuisine. Dine at Seoul's Majang Meat Market *(mjmm.co.kr)* or in Jeju City *(p256)* for the pork belly.

SHOPPING 5

Fill your bags with the latest fashions in Dongdaemun *(p70)*, traditional crafts in Insa-dong *(p80)*, or delightfully designed home goods in Haeundae *(p208)*.

SELF-CARE 6

Treat yourself to a relaxing spa day at the Cheoksan hot springs in Sokcho *(p134)*. Soak, scrub, and hit the sauna, or simply try one of Korea's coveted beauty treatments.

DISCOVER Reasons to Love South Korea

NIGHTLIFE 7
When the sun goes down, the action in Korean cities is just starting up. Grab a midnight snack in a late-night restaurant or sing your heart out in a karaoke bar *(p46)*.

MARVELOUS MUSEUMS 8
South Korea has a plethora of museums. Uncover Buddhist art at the Gyeongju National Museum *(p226)* and the history of instant noodles at the Seoul Urban Life Museum *(p98)*.

9 CUTTING-EDGE TECH
Korea feels like it's living in the future. Spot robot greeters in the airport, street sensors measuring traffic flow, and e-sports athletes doing digital battle. What's next?

10 ROYAL PALACES
Discover the splendor of the Joseon Dynasty while roaming Gyeongbokgung Palace *(p68)*, Seoul's center of power for centuries, or the beautiful Changdeokgung Palace *(p81)* and its garden.

CRAFT BREWING 11
Korea has excellent craft beer breweries, from Seoul to Jeju, and the same attention is given to traditional alcohols like soju and *makgeolli*, making for some seriously good sipping.

NATURAL WONDERS 12
An abundance of sights – including Manjanggul Lava Tube *(p250)*, Jindo's *(p194)* incredible sea path, and Jirisan National Park *(p234)* – make South Korea a top destination.

EXPLORE SOUTH KOREA

This guide divides South Korea into eight colour-coded sightseeing areas, as shown on this map. Find out more about each area on the following pages.

GYEONGGI-DO PROVINCE p108

SEOUL p58

CHUNGCHEONG-DO PROVINCE p150

JEOLLA-DO PROVINCE p170

JEJU ISLAND p244

GETTING TO KNOW SOUTH KOREA

Around half of South Korea's population lives in the metropolitan area of Seoul. But there's so much more to the country than the urban buzz and tempo. Mountains cover more than two-thirds of its territory, while plains and river valleys host rustic villages and rice fields.

SEOUL
PAGE 58

You'd be excused for thinking that Seoul *is* South Korea, so thoroughly does the capital dominate the country's culture, politics, and economy. Divided by the Hangang River, the city is ideal for quiet exploration of royal palaces and world-class museums, but it also caters to visitors that love all-hours shopping and late-night karaoke.

Best for
Culture, nightlife, shopping

Home to
Gyeongbokgung Palace, Dongdaemun, Bukchon Hanok Village, National Museum of Korea, Hongdae

Experience
A night out in lively Hongdae, Itaewon, or Gangnam

GYEONGGI-DO PROVINCE
PAGE 108

Though often seen as an extension of Seoul, Gyeonggi-do has its own identity. Suwon Hwaseong Fortress is a great historic structure, Incheon has played a major role in modern history, and the scars of the Korean War are more apparent here than anywhere else in the country.

Best for
Korean War history

Home to
Incheon, the DMZ, Suwon Hwaseong Fortress

Experience
A poignant tour of the DMZ's Joint Security Area, where you can peer into North Korea

GANGWON-DO PROVINCE

PAGE 128

Rugged Gangwon-do is Korea's most mountainous and sparsely populated province. Small cities like Gangneung and Chuncheon offer interesting history and travel-worthy regional food, but it's really all about the great outdoors here. Seoraksan National Park has some of the country's best hiking and Yangyang is home to a laid-back surfing scene. There's white-water rafting in Jeongseon, while Pyeongchang's snow-kissed resorts draw skiers all winter long. Gangwon-do also features mainland Korea's top beaches.

Best for
Mountains, hiking

Home to
Gangneung, Sokcho, Seoraksan National Park

Experience
A trek through hidden valleys, past waterfalls, and up to dramatic Ulsanbawi Ridge in Seoraksan National Park.

CHUNGCHEONG-DO PROVINCE

PAGE 150

An urban core centered on Sejong and the lively university city of Daejeon runs down Chungcheong-do's spine, but most of the province is refreshingly rural. To the east, Danyang's scenic surroundings have been a favorite of Korean artists for centuries, and vast lakes offer opportunities for relaxing boat rides. To the west, Gongju and Buyeo preserve remnants of their pasts as royal capitals, while Taeanhaean National Park's beaches provide vantage points for Yellow Sea sunsets.

Best for
Rural relaxation, lakes

Home to
Taeanhaean National Park, Buyeo

Experience
Sinking into the rhythms of rural life during a boat cruise on Chungjuho Lake

JEOLLA-DO PROVINCE

PAGE 170

At the southern tip of the Korean Peninsula, Jeolla-do can feel a long way from the capital, which might explain the province's independent streak. Jeolla-do's two largest cities are both important artistic centers, though of different kinds: Gwangju of the contemporary and boundary-pushing, Jeonju of the culinary and traditional. Beyond its urban spaces, the province possesses a wild beauty. Mountainous national parks dot the interior, while its coast dissolves into the sea in ragged peninsulas and bird-rich islands.

Best for
Traditional cuisine, bird-watching, art

Home to
Jeonju, Byeonsanbando National Park, Gwangju, Juknokwon, Suncheonman Wetland

Experience
Feasting your way through Jeonju, Korea's foodie capital

BUSAN

PAGE 202

Korea's second-biggest city is an easy place to love, with a character entirely its own. Busan extends across narrow strips of land between mountains and the sea, yet somehow manages to coalesce swanky beachside neighborhoods and blue-collar fishing districts into a coherent whole. Busanians are less buttoned-up than their Seoul counterparts, and you'll hear their boisterous accents ring out at Jagalchi fish market and Lotte Giants baseball games. The city is also the center of Korea's film industry and hosts its biggest film festival each fall.

Best for
Film culture, fresh seafood, baseball games

Home to
Jagalchi Market, Haeundae

Experience
People-watching at Gwangalli Beach by day, and seeing the moon rise over the sparkling Gwangan Bridge by night

GYEONGSANG-DO PROVINCE

Past and present collide in Gyeongsang-do. Cities like Ulsan and Daegu are paragons of Korea's modern development, but much else in this province clings tightly to yesterday. Yangdong and Hahoe folk villages look much as they did 200 years ago, filled with traditional *hanok* homes, and Gyeongju preserves the splendor of its ancient past as the capital of the Silla Dynasty. Time stands completely still in the area's remote mountain temples: Buseoksa and Haeinsa.

Best for
Traditional culture, Buddhist temples, cherry blossoms

Home to
Gyeongju, Haeinsa Temple, Andong, Jirisan National Park

Experience
Stay overnight in a traditional village to get a sense of what life was like in Korea two centuries ago

JEJU ISLAND

Subtropical Jeju Island is a world apart from mainland Korea, with its own culture and dialect. Mount Hallasan, the country's tallest peak, rises up from its very center, and dozens of other volcanic features dot the island. This is Korea's best place to road-trip, offering ample opportunities for independent exploration of charming fishing villages and offbeat attractions. Those who prefer two feet to four wheels can set off along the Jeju Olle Trail to discover white-sand beaches, seaside cliffs, and *haenyeo*, Jeju's famed female divers, bobbing just offshore.

Best for
Volcanic formations, beaches, road trips

Home to
Seongsan Ilchulbong, Manjanggul Lava Tube, Hallasan National Park, Jeju Olle Trail

Experience
Jeju's stunning volcanic terrain on the coastal Jeju Olle Trail

1 Cheonggyecheon Stream.
2 Bongeunsa Temple during the Lotus Lantern Festival.
3 KWANGYA, a prime destination for K-pop fans.
4 Painted eaves at Gyeongbokgung Palace.

South Korea's compact size and superb transportation means that visitors can see both bustling cities and peaceful rural areas. These itineraries will help you plan the perfect trip.

3 DAYS
in Seoul

Day 1

Morning Start with Seoul's most important sight: Gyeongbokgung Palace (p68), the seat of Joseon Dynasty power for 500 years. Roam its courtyards and peek inside its halls, making sure you admire the bright *dancheong* paintwork decorating the eaves.

Afternoon Feed your soul with the delicate flavors of Buddhist temple food at Balwoo Gongyang (p82), then your spirit at the National Museum of Modern and Contemporary Art (p82), which always has intriguing shows going on. When you're done, stroll through the heart of the city along the resurrected Cheonggyecheon Stream (p80) to see how Seoul has reinvented itself.

Evening Follow the Cheonggyecheon's current to Dongdaemun (p70), where you can get a bit (OK, a lot) of shopping done in Seoul's fashion hub and check out the spaceship-esque Dongdaemun Design Plaza. Tuck into fried mung bean pancakes and *makgeolli* (unrefined rice wine) at Gwangjang Market (p84) before grabbing a nightcap at one of Euljiro's hip bars (p85).

Day 2

Morning Sample Seoul's incredible coffee scene with an Italian espresso at Leesar or a latte and pastry at Cafe Onion (p76). Then transport yourself to the city's past with a long, slow ramble through Bukchon Hanok Village (p72), admiring its century-old traditional homes.

Afternoon Stay in Bukchon and get hands-on making kimchi at the Kimchi Academy (p73) or a brooch at Bukchon Traditional Crafts Center. Then take the metro to trendy Seongsu (p99) to explore Seoul Forest Park, K-pop-shop at KWANGYA, or just discover a favorite café or boutique.

Evening For an epic night out, grab some friends and head to electric Hongdae (p96). Kick things off with Korean barbecue before going to Sanullim 1992 for traditional tipples or Aura for clubbing (p97). Be sure to swing by the Hongdae Playground to check out buskers, breakdancers, or pop-up markets.

Day 3

Morning Start things slow with a *kkwa-baegi* donut from a local market, and then make for the National Museum of Korea (p94). You won't see it all in a day, so pick a section – ancient history, Buddhist statuary – and take your time admiring its treasures.

Afternoon Grab some quiet time at Bongeunsa Temple (p100) or, for a break from Seoul's historic side, head south of the river to modern Gangnam (p100) and browse the district's high-end shops.

Evening Foodies should book in a meal at Mingles (p101), a Michelin two-star restaurant that takes Korean cuisine to exalted places. For a more modest bill, head back downtown to Woo Lae Ok (p82), known for its *naengmyeon* (cold noodles).

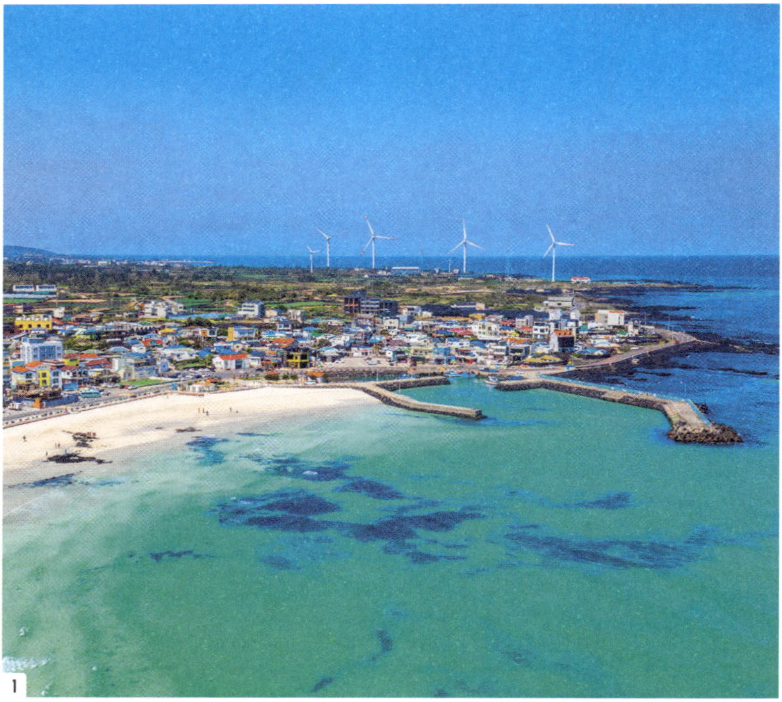

1

2

3

4

←

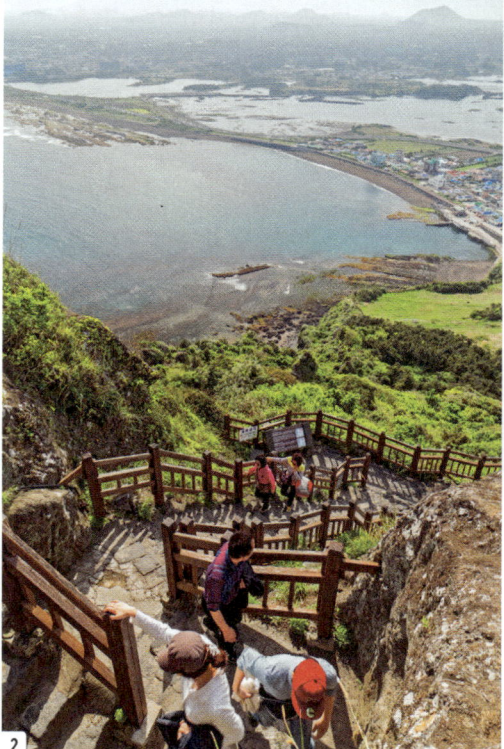

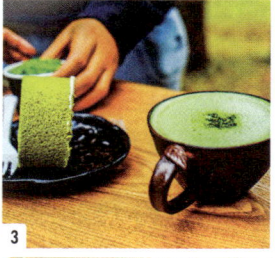

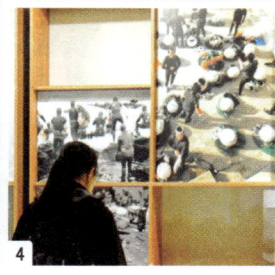

1 Woljeong-ri Beach.

2 Climbing the steps up to Seongsan Ilchulbong peak.

3 Green-tea treats at Osulloc Tea Museum.

4 Haenyeo Museum.

3 DAYS
on Jeju Island

Day 1

Morning After landing at Jeju International Airport and picking up your rental car, spend a bit of time in Jeju City (p256) before you decamp for the island's rural charms. Brush up on Jeju's unique culture at the Jeju National Museum, or peruse the modern art collection at the Arario Museum's three branches, from Nam June Paik to Warhol.

Afternoon Drive to the island's northeast and head underground to explore the 4.6-mile- (7.4-km-) long Manjanggul Lava Tube (p250). Flow lines and a lava column are just some of the incredible features you'll discover. Back above ground, drop by the Haenyeo Museum (p258) to learn about the island's famed female divers.

Evening Wrap up your day with a beach break at Woljeong-ri Beach or Sehwa Beach (p258), both beautiful white-sand expanses dotted with black volcanic stone. Stay at Playce Camp (p256) or another hotel on this side of the island to prepare for an early start tomorrow.

Day 2

Morning Wake up before dawn to ascend Seongsan Ilchulbong (p248) in time for the sunrise. If you're not a morning person, no worries. The coastal volcanic cone is still spectacular after the sun is up. Sleep in and then grab a Nutty Cloud and some breakfast at Dorrell café (p265).

Afternoon Head to Seongeup Folk Village (p262) to see what island settlements looked like centuries ago and wander the lanes between the town's thatch-roofed houses. Restaurants outside the south gate are a good place to grab lunch.

Evening Follow Local Road 1132 to Seogwipo (p263) and the beautiful Jeongbang and Cheonjiyeon waterfalls. If there's time, stop by the Lee Jung-seop Art Gallery before ending the day with some pork belly from Jeju's famed black pigs in the Seogwipo Maeil Olle Market.

Day 3

Morning Dedicate the day to hiking the Jeju Olle Trail system (p255). Route 8 starts near Seogwipo and takes you to the columnar jointing of the Jusangjeolli Cliffs and Jungmun Saekdal Beach. Both are part of the large Jungmun Tourist Complex (p264), where there are plenty of lunch options.

Afternoon Either press on through fishing villages to the end of the 12-mile (20-km) Route 8, or stay at the beach to swim, surf, and soak up the sun. When you're done, catch the bus back to your car.

Evening Swing by the Osulloc Tea Museum (p265) to see rows of green tea bushes and grab some green-tea ice cream. Wrap up your excursion in Aewol, on the northwest coast, watching the sunset from a seaside café such as Haejigae (p265), before returning your car at the airport.

5 DAYS
in the Southern Provinces

Day 1

Start your swing through Jeolla-do and Gyeongsang-do provinces in Jeonju (p174), Korea's foodie capital. Begin with a breakfast of *kongnamul gukbap* (bean sprout and rice soup) at Jeonju Wheng-i Kongnamul Gukbap *(19-10 Myeongdong 10-gil)*, get a bowl of the city's famed bibimbap for lunch, and eat until you can't any more at one of the taverns in Samcheon-dong Makgeolli Alley *(p175)*. Between meals, stroll through Jeonju Hanok Village *(p174)*, an atmospheric neighborhood of traditional homes. Make a point to visit Jeonju Hyanggyo, a centuries-old Confucian school, and the National Intangible Heritage Center, where vivid displays bring Korea's traditional arts and crafts to life. Spend the night in one of the village's *hanok* guesthouses to get a taste of Korean life in a different era.

Day 2

Catch an early train or bus to the rural town of Gurye to spend a few hours exploring Jirisan National Park *(p234)*, the first established in Korea and one of the most beautiful places on the peninsula. Just outside the entrance, a cluster of restaurants serving dishes like stews and green-onion pancakes makes a good place to fuel up. Visit the 6th-century Hwaeomsa Temple to admire its imposing Gakhwangjeon Hall, then set out on the trail that runs from the temple up to Jirisan's main ridgeline, keeping your eyes peeled for the moon bears that live on the mountain. When you've had your fill of hiking, make your way back to Gurye's bus terminal and catch a ride to Busan.

Day 3

Get to know Korea's second city with a visit to the Busan Modern and Contemporary History Museum *(p210)* and a trip up to the Busan Tower observatory *(p210)*, where you can take in the city's sprawling layout from above. Then nose around downtown's Gukje Market and Bupyeong Kkangtong Market *(p211)*, where snack stalls and clothing shops have replaced the black-market goods traded in the postwar years. Next, catch a bus to the hillside Gamcheon Culture Village *(p213)*

1 Jeonju Hanok Village.
2 Buddha statue at Bulguksa Temple, Gyeongju.
3 Bupyeong Kkangtong Market, Busan.
4 The Skywalk at Busan's Haeundae Beach.

to explore the murals, studios, and souvenir shops that have turned this formerly down-on-its-luck neighborhood into a major tourist attraction. In the evening, get a seafood dinner from one of the countless stalls at Jagalchi Market (p206), in the heart of Busan, before joining the crowds around BIFF Square (p210) for shopping and street snacks.

Day 4

On your second day in Busan, take your pick of two islands. Option one is Eulsukdo Island. On the city's west side, it's home to the exciting Busan Museum of Contemporary Art (p212) and a large ecological park filled with marshes and migratory birds. Option two is Yeongdo Island, just south of downtown, where you can view public artworks amid the ship repair yards in Kangkangee Arts Village (p212) and look out to sea from the coastal walking paths of Taejongdae Resort Park (p215). Later in the day, take the metro to the trendy Haeundae (p208) neighborhood. Kick back on Haeundae Beach's wide strip of sand, take in the heady views from the Skywalk, or hit the boutiques in Haeridan-gil before ending the night with pints of locally brewed beer at Galmegi Brewing Co (p208).

Day 5

Take a morning train or bus to Gyeongju (p224), the capital of Korea's ancient Silla Dynasty and one of Korea's richest historic sites. Start in the area that once held Wolseong Fortress, where the highlights include Cheomseongdae, the oldest astrological observatory in Asia, and the gorgeous Wolji Pond, an artificial reservoir with three islands. Spend your afternoon either perusing gold crowns, Buddhist statues, and other Silla treasures in the wonderful Gyeongju National Museum (p226) or visiting Bulguksa Temple and Seokguram Grotto (p225), both among the country's most beautiful and most important Buddhist sites. Wrap up your visit by strolling among the royal burial mounds of the Daereungwon Ancient Tomb Complex (p224) and getting dinner in the nearby Hwangnidan-gil neighborhood.

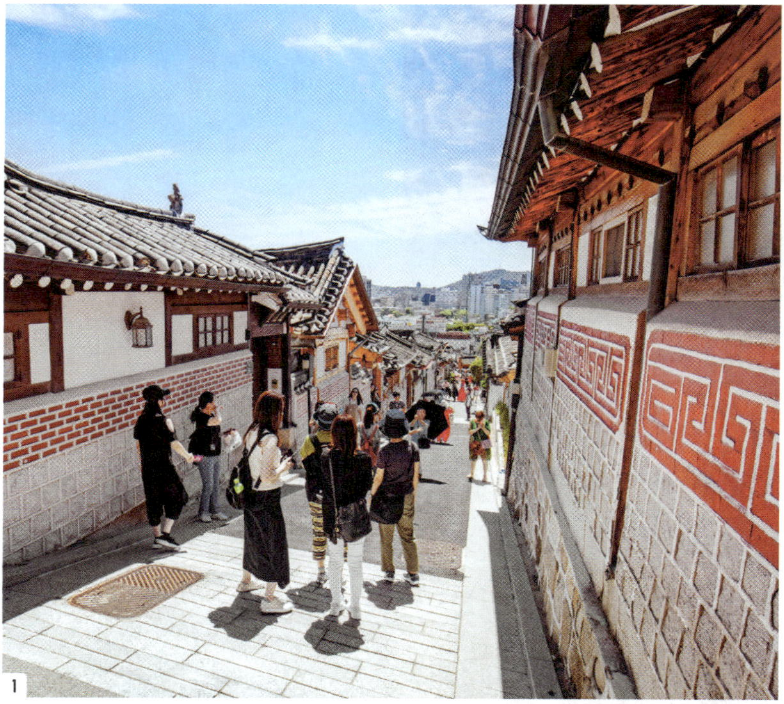

1

2

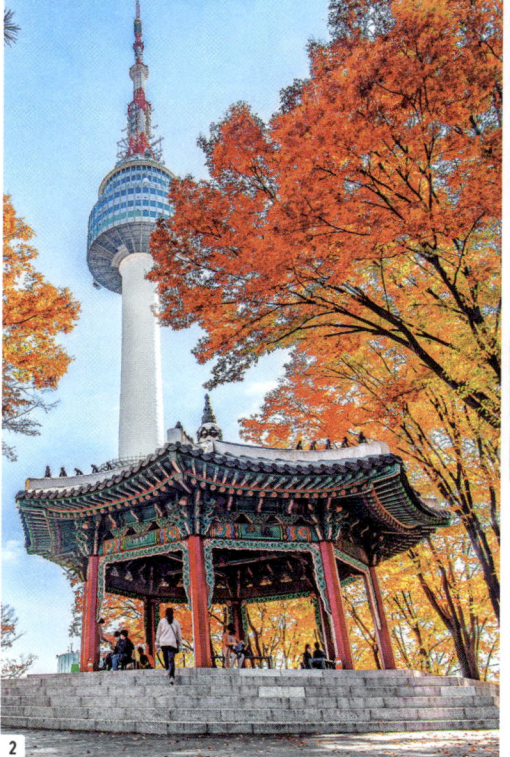

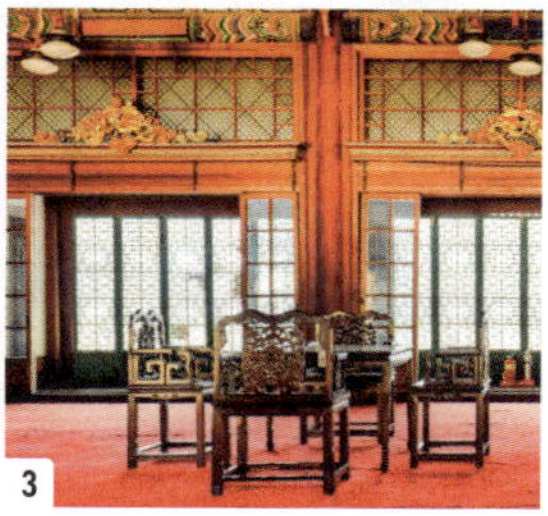

3

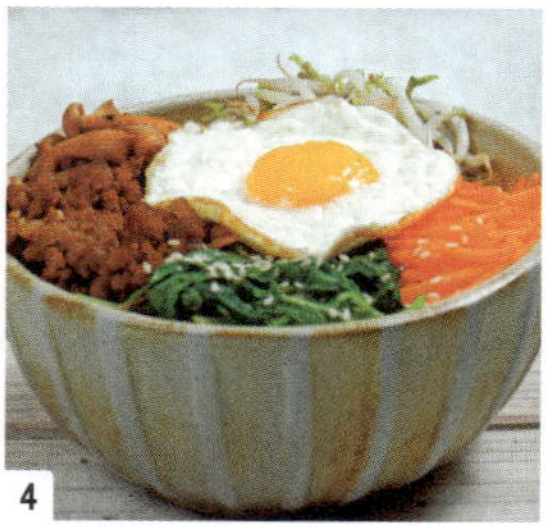

4

←

1 Bukchon Hanok Village.

2 The N Seoul Tower on Namsan Mountain.

3 Huijeongdang Hall at Changdeokgung Palace.

4 Bibimbap in Jeonju.

10 DAYS
in South Korea

Day 1
Start your Korea trip in the capital, focusing on Seoul's historic side. Spend a couple of hours each in Gyeongbokgung (p68), the Joseon Dynasty's main and most impressive palace, and Changdeokgung (p81), its most beautiful. At the latter, reserve a spot on one of the tours that take in the idyllic rear garden. Between the palaces lies Bukchon Hanok Village (p72), the city's best-preserved collection of traditional homes. Explore its quaint alleyways and charming cafés before perusing the traditional craft shops of nearby Insa-dong (p80). In the evening, visit Namdaemun Gate (p84), part of the old city walls, and get lost in the sprawling Namdaemun Market (p85), where people have been doing business for hundreds of years. Restaurants there make a good dinner option.

Day 2
Devote day two to modern Seoul. Once confined to a small area north of the Hangang River, the capital now sprawls across 234 sq miles (605 sq km); head up to the N Seoul Tower observatory at the top of Namsan Mountain (p88) to get a sense of the megacity it's become. Back down on the ground, catch a bus to the Itaewon neighborhood (p89), where Turkish bakeries, Irish pubs, and Nigerian salons show off Seoul's contemporary cosmopolitan character. While you're there, grab a vegan lunch at Monk's Butcher (p101) and visit either the War Memorial of Korea (p88) to learn about the Korean War or the Leeum Museum of Art (p89) to view the Samsung founder's fine private collection. After dark, end your time in Seoul with a bang by diving into Hongdae's exuberant nightlife (p96).

Day 3
It's time for a day trip. If the current geopolitical situation allows it, join one of the guided tours to the Demilitarized Zone (DMZ), separating North and South Korea (p116); you'll need to have booked in advance. Most full-day tours take you to a North Korean infiltration tunnel and the Joint Security Area at the border, where Northern and Southern troops come practically face-to-face. If tours aren't running, take the short train ride to Suwon to spend the day walking the walls of Hwaseong Fortress (p118), a massive late 18th-century fortification that marked the height of Joseon architecture. With hulking gates, secret entrances, a royal palace, a willow-lined pleasure pond, and an absorbing museum, it has more than enough for a day of exploration. In the evening, take a train or express bus to Jeonju (p174).

Day 4
Spend the day eating your way through Jeonju (p174), Korea's magnet for foodies. *Kongnamul gukbap* and Jeonju-style bibimbap at Gogung (*jeonjugogung.modoo.at*) are must-tries, and you shouldn't miss the generous spreads served up with orders of *makgeolli* (unrefined rice wine) at Yongjinjip Makgeolli (p175). Jeonju is also an important center of traditional culture, so make time to delve into this side of the city. Roam the atmospheric streets of Jeonju Hanok Village; visit the stately Gyeonggijeon Shrine, a memorial to the founder of the Joseon Dynasty; and learn about time-honored crafts, rituals, and musical forms at the National Intangible Heritage Center. When you're done exploring, catch a bus down to Gwangju.

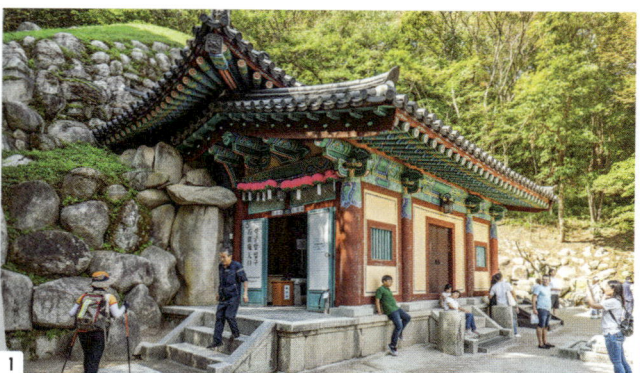

Day 5

In the morning, make your way to Gwangju's May 18 Democracy Square (p182), the center of the 1980 Gwangju Uprising. The popular rebellion against martial law set Korea on the path to democracy and remains central to the city's identity. Today, Gwangju is known equally for its art, so after viewing the square's memorials, head into the Asia Culture Center to check out interactive pieces by Korean creatives, exhibitions on Vietnamese pop music, and live performances on the rooftop. Take a fancy tea break at Teasoha (p191) before heading across town to the Gwangju National Museum (p183), whose collection includes objects recovered from a 14th-century shipwreck.

Day 6

Catch an early flight to Jeju Island, pick up a rental car, and drive to the island's east side to marvel at Seongsan Ilchulbong (p248), a parasitic cone that rises dramatically from the sea. Follow that up with another volcanic wonder, the Manjanggul Lava Tube (p250), which carves through the earth for several miles. Back in the sunshine, treat yourself to some R&R at Woljeong-ri Beach for the rest of the day. On a cozy little north shore bay, the beautiful white sand is studded with volcanic rocks and backed by restaurants.

Day 7

Drive down to Namwon Port on the south coast, the starting point for Route 5 of the Jeju Olle Trail system (p255). Spend your morning hiking this gorgeous 8-mile (13.5-km) path past ocean cliffs and camellias, ending at Soesokkak estuary pool. Catch a bus back to your car and then drive to Seogwipo (p263) to get lunch in the Seogwipo Maeil Olle Market and view the city's two stunning waterfalls: Jeongbang and Cheonjiyeon. Take the long way back to the airport on an afternoon road trip around the island's west coast, following Local Road 1132. There are any number of enticing places to pull over, including the Jusangjeolli Cliffs (p264) and the Sanbangsan lava dome. Return your rental car and board a plane to Busan.

1 Seokguram Grotto.
2 *Dol hareubang* statues in front of Seongsan Ilchulbong.
3 Gamcheon Culture Village.
4 Hahoe Mask Dance.
5 Jeongbang Waterfall.

Day 8

Busan, Korea's second-biggest city, has a very different vibe from Seoul. Start your morning in its fashionable Haeundae neighborhood (p208), getting brunch along Haeridan-gil Street and lounging on Haeundae Beach. Then take the metro downtown and get to know the port town's working-class side. See what its fishing fleets pulled in during a walk through the streets surrounding Jagalchi Market (p206), and then head up to the market's rooftop to look out over the ship repair yards of Yeongdo Island. In the late afternoon, catch a bus to the vibrantly colorful Gamcheon Culture Village (p213); sprinkled with public artworks, it's especially pretty at sunset. When the sun goes down, head to the Gwangalli Beach (p215) area to get dinner at Anmok (tel: 0507 1461 0523) and see the Gwangan Bridge light up.

Day 9

Take a short train ride north to Gyeongju (p224), former capital of the Silla Dynasty. Reminders of its royal era dot the city center, from the scenic Wolji Pond, part of a former palace, to the nearly two dozen grassy tumuli that hold the remains of Silla rulers. Once you've explored downtown, take a local bus to nearby Bulguksa. The 6th-century temple reveals the heights Buddhism reached under the dynasty, while the neighboring Seokguram Grotto (p225) contains one of Korea's most incredible works of Buddhist art.

Day 10

In the morning, catch a bus or high-speed train to the city of Andong (p232), and then take a local bus to Andong Hahoe Folk Village to end your journey with a trip into Korea's past. This beautifully preserved Joseon-era settlement is filled with traditional thatch- and tile-roofed homes by the Nakdonggang River. Walk through its winding alleys, watch a performance of the village's famed Hahoe Mask Dance, and join a traditional craft program to try your hand at something like calligraphy or a tea ceremony. Spend your last night like a Joseon aristocrat with a stay in the luxurious and historic Bukchondaek (p241).

Fit for a King

Royal structures in South Korea are known for their scale and splendor. Seoul is home to five Joseon Dynasty palaces, none as pretty as Changdeokgung (p81), with its brightly painted eaves and tidy garden. Compare that with the austere Jongmyo Shrine (p80), whose lack of decoration signals its purpose as a place for memorial rites. Architectural traces of even older dynasties, like Baekje and Silla, are reasons to visit both Buyeo (p156) and Gyeongju (p224).

→ The striking Changdeokgung Palace, once home to Joseon kings

SOUTH KOREA FOR ARCHITECTURE

Korea's architecture is rich in history. Grand palaces and imposing fortresses hark back to royal dynasties, while humble *hanok* show how lives were traditionally lived. Meanwhile, cities like Seoul and Busan have become the home of jaw-dropping modern structures.

Historic Homes

Built with natural materials and designed for the local climate, traditional *hanok* (p74) are all about living with the land. Many homes were destroyed during the Korean War or the postwar development boom, but they've slowly been restored. For an atmospheric encounter, head to Andong Hahoe Folk Village (p232).

The traditional ↑ Hahoe Folk Village in Andong

Did You Know?

Meaning "Korean home," the word *hanok* wasn't used until after the arrival of Western buildings.

KIM SWOO-GEUN

Korea's contemporary architects all stand on the shoulders of Kim Swoo-geun (1931–1986). Kim was the first Korean architect to earn a global reputation and he paved the way when it came to marrying traditional aesthetics with modern construction. His most recognized design is Seoul's large Olympic Stadium but other structures of note include Kyungdong Presbyterian Church and the Jinju National Museum *(p242)*.

Contemporary Showstoppers

As Korea's population rapidly urbanized in the 1960s and 70s, architecture was about one thing: building fast. Any decorative aesthetics were incidental; architectural ambitions came later. The 1,821-ft (555-m) Lotte World Tower *(p102)* led the way with height, while others dabbled with shape – walk beneath the Tri-Bowl's *(p113)* inverted cones or get lost in Dongdaemun Design Plaza's *(p71)* curved appearance.

← Seoul's impressive Olympic Stadium, with the Lotte World Tower in the background

Fortress Formations

Korean settlements had a nasty habit of getting attacked throughout history. To protect themselves, civilians built fortresses, both high – *sanseong*, or mountain fortresses, such as Namhansanseong *(p127)* – and low – *eupseong*, or walled towns, including Haemieupseong *(p166)*. The hybrid Suwon Hwaseong Fortress *(p118)* is considered the Joseon Dynasty's most impressive achievement.

↑ The Namhansanseong Fortress, a UNESCO World Heritage Site

Fermented Food

Fermentation is key to Korean cuisine. Try kimchi on a trip to a local market like Gwangjang Market (p84) or Jeongseon Arirang Traditional Market (p146), or make your own from scratch. At the Kimchi Academy (p73), you prepare *napa* cabbage kimchi, or sample the hundreds of other varieties, including radish and chive. Just as important to Korean cooking are fermented sauces like *gochujang* and *doenjang* (soybean paste), which inform the complex sweet, savory, and spicy flavors you taste when dining at market stalls, Michelin-starred restaurants like Mingles (p101), and everywhere in between.

→ A vibrant food stall serving kimchi and salads at Gwangjang Market

SOUTH KOREA FOR
FOODIES

Koreans are obsessed with food, and after a few days here you will be, too. Fermented flavors and unique regional dishes make for memorable meals, while the communal eating culture and the DIY fun of Korean barbecue create experiences that are about more than just the food.

Sharing Traditions

In colonial and Korean War times, poverty meant food was often served communally. Today, Koreans still feel meals are better shared. You can experience this at any barbecue joint or at restaurants specializing in stews like kimchi *jjigae* or braised dishes such as *jjimdalk*. The side dishes, *banchan*, which accompany a meal, are there to be shared.

→ Sitting for a traditional barbecue lunch served with *banchan*

Did You Know?

Traditionally, *banchan* (side dishes) are served in odd numbers.

Regional Flavors

For a relatively small country, Korea has a lot of regional diversity when it comes to food. Local dishes to look out for include *chodang sundubu* (soft tofu, made in salt water instead of brine) in Gangneung *(p132)*; *dakgalbi* (stir-fried chicken) in Chuncheon *(p140)*; *dwaeji-gukbap* (pork and rice soup) in Busan *(p202)*; and grilled salted mackerel in Andong *(p232)*. For the ultimate feast, make for Jeonju *(p174)*, known as Korea's foodie capital. Here, bibimbap (a rice bowl with a variety of toppings) is a popular dish, with religious origins. The main ingredients correspond to the colors linked with Buddhism locally: rice for white, egg for yellow, spice for red, vegetables for green, and meat for blue.

← A warming bowl of *dwaeji-gukbap*, best tried in Busan

TEMPLE FOOD

Buddhist monks and nuns have their own approach to food, with ingredients, preparation, and consumption reflecting religious principles like compassion and gratitude. The meals are vegan and avoid the use of the *osinchae*, or "five pungent vegetables" – garlic, green onion, leek, and two types of chives – that are thought to interfere with spiritual practice. Despite these rules, temple food is flavorful. A good place to try it is Balwoo Gongyang *(p82)*, in downtown Seoul (book in advance).

Korean Barbecue

Grilling your own meat, tipping back shots of soju *(p43)*, squeezing a stuffed lettuce wrap into your mouth – no eating experience is as much fun as a night of Korean barbecue. You'll find cuts for every carnivore, whether you want *samgyeopsal* (pork belly), *gopchang* (small intestines), or *galbi* (ribs). Steak-lovers should also try *hanu*, Korea's superb domestic beef, prized for its excellent marbling.

↑ Friends enjoying a meal at a Korean barbecue restaurant

DISCOVER South Korea Your Way

Drama Scenes
If you're a set-jetter and K-drama fan, you've probably already planned a trip to Nami Island (p140), the location for some heartstring-tugging scenes in *Winter Sonata*, one of the first K-dramas to go global. Period drama more your thing? Head to the Korean Folk Village (p125) and Mungyeongsaejae Open Set (p239), where shows like *Dae Jang Geum* and *Kingdom* were filmed. In Seoul, Namsan Mountain (p88) is the backdrop for many TV shows, including *Squid Game*.

→

Namsan Mountain, the popular backdrop for Korean TV shows

SOUTH KOREA FOR
POP CULTURE

If you've found yourself swept up in Hallyu, the global popularity of K-pop, K-drama, and K-beauty, a trip to Korea provides the ultimate chance to ride its pop-culture wave. Visit your favorite drama's filming locations, dance like your beloved K-pop group, or delve into the country's indie music scene.

A family scene from the award-winning film, *Parasite* (2019)

↑

Silver-Screen Success
Korea has made a big impression on the big screen, most notably with *Parasite*, the first foreign-language film to win the Academy Award for Best Picture in 2020. Keen to see more? Visit the site of Asia's biggest film festival, the Busan Cinema Center (p217). It screens free outdoor movies in summer.

Did You Know?
Parasite was the first Korean film to win the Palme d'Or award at Cannes in 2019.

LIVE-MUSIC VENUES

All That Jazz
216 Itaewon-ro, Seoul
allthatjazz.kr
Seoul's top jazz bar, around since 1976.

The Vinyl Underground
32 Suyeong-ro 322-beon-gil, Busan 0507 1487 7758
A Busan stalwart for rock, hip-hop, and jazz.

Jebi Dabang
24 Wausan-ro, Seoul
ctrplus.com/jebi
A cozy basement venue for indie artists.

Beyond K-Pop

Korean music isn't just K-pop. The country has great rock, indie, hip-hop, and electronic scenes, too. In Seoul, neighborhoods like Hongdae (p96) and Itaewon (p89) are home to cavernous nightclubs, jazz bars, and thumping basement venues where underground rappers and punk bands perform. In Busan, the Haeundae (p208) and Gwangalli Beach (p215) neighborhoods are also good places to catch live music.

← Performing live in Haeundae, a lively neighborhood in Busan

Idol Worship

K-pop groups inspire fierce devotion. Idol sightings are rare – you won't spot Blackpink on the metro – but you can pose with their playfully artistic life-sized statues, known as *gangam-dol*, in Gangnam (p100). Alternatively, snap a selfie at the BTS Bus Stop (p148) or test your own dance moves at 1MILLION Dance Studio (p100).

↑ World-famous Korean girl group Blackpink

35

Fresh Fashion

Style is serious business in Korea, where designers create runway-ready haute couture, hip streetwear, and modern takes on traditional styles. Seoul's Dongdaemun neighborhood *(p70)* has hundreds of shops that stay open late, while the Gangnam district *(p100)* is filled with high-end department stores like Galleria and boutiques for shoppers with bigger budgets. In Busan, Gukje Market *(p211)* is also good for vintage finds.

→
Browsing the latest fashion in the popular Gangnam district

SOUTH KOREA FOR
SHOPPERS

When you pack your bags, make sure to travel light. You're going to need the extra space. Korea is a shopper's paradise, and you'll almost inevitably go home with more stuff than you came with. Keep your credit card handy for the latest fashions, traditional crafts, and must-have cosmetics.

Getting Crafty

South Korea has a rich crafting tradition, and a great way to bring home a meaningful souvenir while also supporting local artisans is by purchasing a traditional handmade piece, like a bamboo folding fan, a set of bronze rice bowls, or an intricately embroidered pillow. Seoul's Insa-dong neighborhood *(p80)* is full of craft stores, many of which have been around for decades, while the gift shop at the Gyeonggi Museum of Contemporary Ceramic Art *(p126)* in Icheon sells some lovely vases and tea sets.

←
Pretty bamboo folding fans for sale at a shop in Insa-dong, Seoul

Home Comforts

Koreans don't scrimp on design or detail when it comes to decor. So many products here have a little touch that's clever, whimsical, or just plain cute. Shop for bird-shaped chopstick rests and hourglasses that double as art pieces in KT&G Sangsangmadang's store *(p96)*. In Heyri Art Valley *(p123)*, browse works by artists and designers who create everything from abstract paintings to quirky figurines inspired by *manhwa* (Korean comics). Poke around the shops in Gwangju's Asia Culture Center *(p182)* and you might turn up pretty notebooks, illustrated prints of Korean street scenes, or stickers of Hodori, the 1988 Seoul Summer Olympics mascot, depicted in chunky retro pixels.

←

Patterned cushions on display at Heyri Art Village

Best Face Forward

Korean skin care and cosmetics have earned a zealous following, and rightly so. If you're looking to score all sorts of masks, moisturizers, cleansers, and BB creams, swing by health and beauty shops like Olive Young, Skinfood, and Innisfree. There are clusters of them in Seoul's Myeong-dong neighborhood *(p84)* and the BIFF Square area *(p210)* in Busan, but you'll find at least one in pretty much every commercial area.

→

Shopping for cosmetics at the Innisfree store on Jeju Island

💬 INSIDER TIP
Custom Beauty

In Seongsu *(p99)*, you can get a personalized beauty consultation at Korea's largest Olive Young branch or create custom cosmetics at AMORE Seongsu.

↑ Climbing peaks in Bukhansan National Park

Take a Hike
Some 70 per cent of South Korea is mountainous, so it's little wonder that hiking is a major pastime here. National parks such as Seoraksan *(p136)* and Jirisan *(p234)* give ambitious mountaineers the chance to tackle multiday treks, while urban peaks like Bukhansan *(p98)* and Geumjeongsan *(p217)* let walkers head for the hills without ever leaving town. For coastal walks, try Jeju's popular Olle Trail system *(p255)*, which passes beaches and charming fishing villages.

SOUTH KOREA FOR OUTDOOR ACTIVITIES

With mountains and beaches never more than a short bus ride away, Korea is an excellent destination for active travelers. And you don't need to go to the countryside to enjoy the great outdoors. Bike paths have proliferated in recent years, and many cities have at least one good mountain to climb.

Winter Sports
Snow sports in Korea got a major boost when rural Pyeongchang hosted the 2018 Winter Olympics. There's no shortage of slopes, especially in Gangwon-do Province. Get lift passes to Mona Yongpyong *(p144)* or High1 Resort *(p147)* or head to Muju Deogyusan Resort *(p190)*, which claims Korea's longest and steepest runs.

> **Did You Know?**
>
> Korea won its most Winter Olympic medals at Pyeongchang: 17, including five gold.

↑ Taking to the slopes in mountainous Deogyusan, a region in Jeolla-do Province

↑ Cycling alongside the Hangang River, past the Dongho Bridge

Fun on Two Wheels

Due to its terrain, Korea will probably never be a major cycling destination, but that doesn't mean you can't have fun. Several cities have bike-sharing systems, including Seoul, whose Hangang River paths make for a great ride. More serious cyclists can explore the country's long-distance routes, like the Nakdonggang Bicycle Path, which follows the Nakdonggang River for 242 miles (389 km) from Andong *(p232)* to charming Eulsukdo Island *(p213)* in Busan.

> **INSIDER TIP**
> **Seoul Cycle**
>
> Ttareungi (or Seoul Bike) is Seoul's popular bike-share system. It's cheap to use and has a huge network, with green docking stations dotted all over the capital *(www.bikeseoul.com)*.

On the Water

Believe it or not, South Korea has a solid surf scene and the beaches of Yangyang *(p142)* and Jungmun Tourist Complex *(p264)* are welcoming places for rookies looking to catch a swell for the first time. Plenty of surf shops offer both group and individual lessons, perfect for family holidays and solo trips. Inland, you'll find freshwater adventures in Jeongseon *(p146)*, where outfitters lead white-water rafting trips down the Donggang River.

↑ White-water rafting down the impressive Donggang River, and *(inset)* riding the waves in Yangyang

39

HIKING IN SOUTH KOREA

Korea's mountainous terrain and miles of coastline make the country a walker's paradise. The national passion for hiking means a great deal of effort is put into making and maintaining trails, so routes are well marked, safety features are often added to tricky sections, and shelters can be booked along some multiday treks. The hikes featured here are some of Korea's most iconic routes, whether you want to thru-hike a ridgeline, bag a summit, or spend a week following the shore.

← Hiking along the volcanic Jeju Island coastline

The 27 trail courses that make up the **Jeju Olle Trail** (p255) network circle subtropical Jeju Island and cross a few of its outlying islets. Each can be completed in a day, but terrain and scenery vary significantly.

Did You Know?

The Korea Dulle Trail, which traces the country's coastline, runs for 2,796 miles (4,500 km).

Bagging Korea's tallest peak is doable for most hikers thanks to **Mount Hallasan**'s (p252) gradual slopes. A popular route to the summit follows the Seongpanak Trail up its eastern slope.

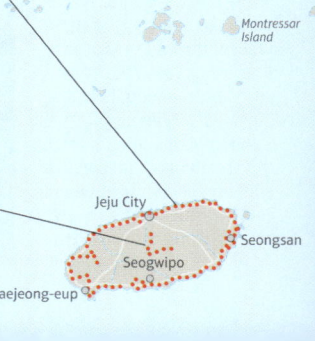

Seoraksan National Park (p136) has arguably Korea's most dramatic terrain. The 15-mile (24-km) **Daechongbong Peak Course** (Baekdam) takes hikers to soaring peaks, lush valleys, and a 7th-century Buddhist temple.

Cheonwangbong 1 Course in Songnisan National Park (p159) is a 10-mile (16-km) lasso-shaped route that takes in scenic mountain peaks, thick forests, and one of Korea's most spectacular Buddhist temples.

The Mount Jirisan Traverse (p234) is a gorgeous three-day epic that follows the east-to-west ridgeline of Jirisan National Park. Lucky hikers might spot a moon bears in the mountain forests.

A solid week-plus hike, yet still just a fraction of this southern trail system, Courses 36–46 of the **Namparang Trail** (p200) run along the coastline of the stunning Namhae region, past ports, bays, and alluring islands.

HIKING SAFETY

Well-maintained trails, the regular presence of other hikers, and largely reliable cell-phone reception mean that hiking in Korea is relatively safe. Still, it's important to take basic precautions. Always pack sufficient food and water, and be sure to wear good hiking shoes and a waterproof jacket. The country's National Disaster and Safety Portal (www.safekorea.go.kr) provides real-time alerts on things like fires and adverse weather conditions.

Cultured Cafés
Coffee culture is huge in Korea and many cafés are exceptionally stylish. Some, occupy reimagined *hanok*, while places like In's Mill *(p265)* have a chic minimalist aesthetic. It's not just a pretty face, either. Places like Champspace Coffee Roasters *(p164)* and Momos Coffee *(p208)* employ award-winning baristas who know their stuff.

Catching up over coffee at a modern Seoul café

SOUTH KOREA
RAISE A GLASS

Korea's drinks list is almost as exciting as its food. The country has a vast menu of traditional alcohols – not least soju and *makgeolli* – and an impressive craft beer scene. An ancient tea culture remains alive and well, too, and you'll find great coffee in effortlessly stylish cafés.

DRINKING ETIQUETTE
Foreigners certainly aren't expected to know Korean drinking etiquette, but you'll impress your hosts by following these simple rules. First, if you see an empty glass on the table, refill it, but never pour your own drink. Second, when pouring or receiving a glass, use two hands if you're younger than the other person. Younger drinkers should also try to keep the rim of their glass below their elders' when toasting to show respect. Want to say cheers with friends in Korean? Easy. It's *geonbae*!

Taste of the Land
A cloudy, unrefined rice wine, *makgeolli* is Korea's most unique alcoholic drink. Long considered a lowly farmer's brew, it's now growing in popularity. Many *makgeolli* bars, like Damotori h and Sanullim 1992 *(p97)* in Seoul, serve sampler flights.

Pouring *makgeolli*, a cloudy, alcoholic rice wine

National Spirit

Soju is something like the national spirit and the familiar green bottle is guaranteed to make an appearance whenever Koreans gather together. As with other alcohols, it's typically consumed with a meal, either straight or mixed into beer. For something a bit regional (and potent) try soju from Andong (p232), the spirit's spiritual home.

Did You Know?

Korea produces some 1.3 million tons of soju annually.

↑ Jinro Chamisul, a leading soju brand in Korea, established in 1924

Tea Time

Southern Korea has an excellent climate for growing high-quality green tea. Savor its delicate notes (or indulge in some green-tea ice cream) while gazing out over lush tea fields at The World of Spreading Green Leaves (p191) in Boseong or spend the afternoon at the Osulloc Tea Museum (p265) in southern Jeju. Feeling fancy? Visit Teasoha in Gwangju (p191), where tea is given the fine-dining treatment.

← Preparing a fresh pot of green tea for visitors

Craft Brewing

Korea's beer scene has undergone a veritable craft revolution. At the forefront was Magpie Brewing Co. (magpiebrewing.com) which has taprooms in Seoul and Jeju City, but even smaller towns are in on the action. Grab a pint at Gunsan Beer Port in Gunsan (p191) or Blue Whale Brew House in Chungju (p164).

→ Blue Whale Brew House, popular for craft beer

↑ The Royal Tomb of King Michu in Gyeongju

Early Kingdoms

The Joseon Dynasty gets most of the attention, but before that, the Goryeo, Silla, and Baekje kingdoms ruled over the peninsula. Learn about Baekje's cultural influence in its former capitals of Buyeo *(p156)* and Gongju *(p164)*, then make your way to Gyeongju *(p224)*, from where the Silla kingdom unified the peninsula for the first time.

SOUTH KOREA FOR HISTORY BUFFS

Korea has seen it all: warring kingdoms, independence struggles, civil war, popular uprisings, and economic booms. Exploring the country through its past is an illuminating way of experiencing its present, and you'll find fascinating historical sites and museums everywhere you go.

Buddhist Temples

Buddhism has shaped Korean culture for well over a millennium, and its remote mountain temples have some of the most beautiful settings in the country. Haeinsa Temple *(p230)* has safeguarded Korea's greatest Buddhist treasure, the Tripitaka Koreana, for over six centuries, while Songgwangsa Temple *(p196)*, one of the "Three Jewels," attracts Zen meditation trainees from around the world. You can experience the monastic life yourself through the popular Templestay program *(p165)*.

←

Colorful lanterns decorating the spacious Songgwangsa Temple grounds

The Modern Age

Korea seemed to squeeze several centuries of history into the second half of the 20th century as it modernized at a rapid rate. Delve into its fight to transform dictatorship into democracy at May 18 Democracy Square *(p182)* in Gwangju, or wander Seoul's Gangnam district *(p100)* to see the fruits of the nation's economic boom. Dotted with boutique shops and towering luxury apartments, it's a far cry from its farmland roots.

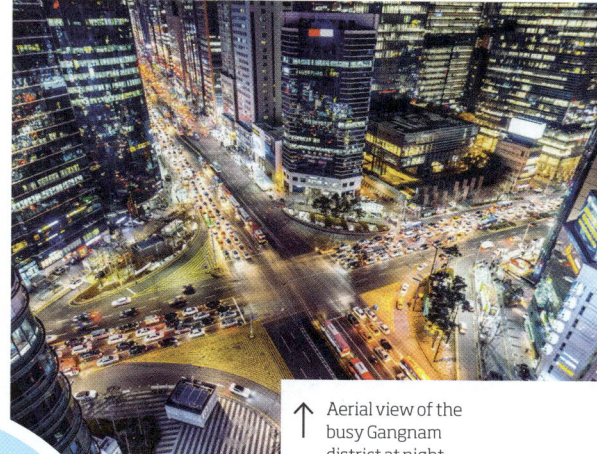

↑ Aerial view of the busy Gangnam district at night

A Nation Divided

The legacy of the Korean War (1950–1953) hardly feels like history, as the peninsula still bears the scar of its most tragic event. Explore the conflict's timeline at the massive War Memorial of Korea *(p88)* before joining a guided tour of the DMZ *(p116)*, which brings you just steps from North Korea. The stories of North Korean refugees continue in places like Sokcho's charming Abai Village *(p134)*.

← Statue of soldiers at the War Memorial of Korea

Joseon Legacy

Traces of the Joseon Dynasty (1392–1910) can be found everywhere you look, with headline attractions like Gyeongbokgung Palace *(p68)* and Hanyangdoseong, the Seoul city wall *(p70)*, good places to start. Its legacy lives on in other ways, too. Learn all about Hangeul, the Korean script, invented by Joseon King Sejong, at the National Hangeul Museum *(p95)*.

> **HIDDEN GEM**
> **Unhyeongung Palace**
>
> This minor Seoul palace was the residence of a powerful prince regent in the mid-19th century. It tends to attract smaller crowds *(unhyeongung.or.kr)*.

↑ Ceremonial guards walking through Gyeongbokgung Palace

DISCOVER South Korea Your Way

Game Time
Koreans have a competitive streak, and sports are a big deal here. Catch a Baseball game at Busan's Sajik baseball Stadium *(p216)* – it'll be a highlight of your trip – or follow the domestic soccer league *(kleague.com)*. If e-sports are more your thing, attend a League of Legends match at LoL Park *(leagueoflegends.com)* in Seoul.

The dramatic e-sports League of Legends semifinals

SOUTH KOREA FOR ENTERTAINMENT

One thing's for sure: you won't be bored in Korea. There are more than enough live shows, sports, and traditional performances to keep even the most jaded traveler entertained. And then there's the nightlife. Seoul comes alive after dark with bars, clubs, and *noraebang* (karaoke rooms).

TOP 3 BARS IN SEOUL

Bar Cham
바참
🏠 34 Jahamun-ro 7-gil
📞 02 6402 4750
Try creative cocktails made with local spirits in a renovated *hanok*.

Namsan Sool Club
남산술클럽
🏠 228-2 Noksapyeong-daero
📞 0507 1326 3921
Choose from a selection of Korean alcohols served by multilingual sommeliers.

Villa Records
빌라레코
🏠 B2 18 Dosan-daero 15-gil
🌐 villarecord.com
One of Seoul's best cocktail bars is run by a furniture company.

Up All Night
Nights out in Seoul are all about endurance. Start things off at a barbecue joint (Hallimdon-ga is a standout; *16-4 Yonsei-ro 7an-gil*) before moving on to a bar or pub for drinks. Seoul has plenty of both but Euljiro Nogari Alley *(p85)* has some of the best. End the night dancing away at a nightclub and belting out tunes at a *noraebang* – it's just what the locals do.

Walking through one of Seoul's neon alleyways at night

↑ Professional Korean dancers from the National Gugak Center

Live Entertainment

Lovers of the performing arts should make plans to visit the Sejong Center for the Performing Arts *(p78)*, Seoul Arts Center *(p103)*, or Gwangju Arts Center *(p183)* for live theater, dance, opera, and classical music. Anyone with an interest in Indigenous art forms will also want to attend one of the weekly performances of *gugak*, or traditional music, that are held at the National Gugak Centers in Seoul and on Jindo Island *(p194)*.

> 💬 INSIDER TIP
> **Subtitle Service**
>
> In the Sejong Center for the Performing Arts' Grand Theater, screens in the seats and on the wall provide subtitles during performances.

LGBTQ+ Venues

Korea's cities are home to welcoming LGBTQ+ spaces, with the largest in Seoul and Busan. In June, Seoul hosts pride celebrations but there are places to visit year-round. In the capital, Itaewon *(p89)* has long been the center of gay nightlife, with whynot? *(tel 02 793 5670)* and other bars clustered around Usadan-ro 12-gil. Most of Busan's gay bars are found around Beomil-ro 89-beon-gil, near Beomil Station.

↑ Gay rights march in Seoul, and *(inset)* bikers leading the city's Pride Parade

Sacred Creations

Buddhism has the deepest roots of any organized religion in Korea, and it accounts for most of the country's religious art. Both the National Museum of Korea *(p94)*, in Seoul, and the Gyeongju National Museum *(p226)* have extensive collections of Buddhist statues, paintings, and more. Also in Gyeongju, Bulguksa Temple *(p225)* holds several National Treasures, including two of the country's most impressive stone pagodas, while the neighboring Seokguram Grotto is an astonishing display of both artistic skill and religious devotion.

→ The vibrant interiors of the Bulguksa Buddhist Temple

SOUTH KOREA FOR
ART LOVERS

Korea's place on the international art scene has grown with its economic rise, and you'll find plenty to provoke, challenge, and charm you in the country's galleries. Museums and Buddhist temples, meanwhile, preserve traditional art forms, and public art projects bring beauty to the streets.

Joseon Beauty

The arts flourished under the Joseon Dynasty with *buncheong* ceramics and *baekja* porcelain casting a spell throughout Asia. Today, you can view examples at the National Museum of Korea *(p94)* and the Leeum Museum of Art *(p89)*. Both also have large collections of Joseon paintings with mysterious landscapes, everyday scenes, and herons in flight.

 HIDDEN GEM
Seoul's Secret Museum

The Kansong Art Museum *(kansong.org)* has one of Korea's best private collections of Joseon and Goryeo art. The catch? It's only open a few weeks a year, in spring and fall.

↑ Sin Yun-bok's *Dance with Two Swords*, a Joseon-era painting

Contemporary Work

Korea has emerged as a major destination for modern art in the 21st century, showcasing homegrown talent and bringing in works by top international artists. See both at the Asia Culture Center in Gwangju *(p182)*, and don't miss the city's biennale if you're in town at the right time. Seoul's National Museum of Modern and Contemporary Art *(p82)* always has several thrilling shows going on, while the Nam June Paik Art Center *(p124)* in Yongin stays tuned to the legacy of the video artist.

← The modern Nam June Paik Art Center, Gyeonggi-do

TOP 5 CONTEMPORARY KOREAN ARTISTS

Hun Kyu Kim
Produces paintings that review the modern world.

Lee Bul
Creates art that explores gender and dystopia.

Heejoon Lee
Layers photos and paint to examine urban spaces.

Lee Jinju
This artist is known for Joseon-style paintings of the female body.

Sungsil Ryu
Their interdisciplinary art captures consumerism.

↑ Playful street art in Gamcheon Culture Village

Public Art

Sometimes art is right under your nose. Many cities have embarked on public art projects, like Gwangju Folly *(p184)* in downtown Gwangju, and Busan's Kangkangee Arts Village *(p212)*, in a dockside neighborhood. Busan is also home to Gamcheon Culture Village *(p213)*, the most well-known example of Korea's mural village trend, where typically low-income neighborhoods have been enlivened by public murals and sculptures.

A YEAR IN SOUTH KOREA

JANUARY

△ **Hwacheon Sancheoneo Ice Festival** *(mid-Jan to early Feb)*. A family-oriented ice-fishing festival in Hwacheon-gun County – with lots of sledding.
Seollal *(late Jan to mid-Feb)*. Korea celebrates the Lunar New Year with family gatherings, ancestral rites, and folk games.

FEBRUARY

Seoul Fashion Week F/W *(early Feb)*. Designers reveal their latest collections at Dongdaemun Design Plaza during Korea's biggest fashion event.
△ **Daeboreum** *(mid-Feb to early Mar)*. The first full moon of the lunar year is marked with rituals like bonfires and cracking nuts with one's teeth.

MAY

Children's Day *(May 5)*. Families celebrate their little ones with new toys, picnics, and trips to the amusement park on this public holiday.
△ **Gangneung Danoje** *(mid–late May)*. Gangneung's celebration of the traditional Dano festival features games, mask dramas, and shamanistic rituals.

JUNE

△ **Busan One Asia Festival** *(mid-Jun)*. The southeastern city of Busan hosts this K-culture festival, featuring concerts by idol groups and solo musicians.

SEPTEMBER

Seoul Fashion Week S/S *(early to mid-Sep)*. Models return to the catwalks to show off the new spring/summer collections.
Chuseok *(mid-Sep to early Oct)*. The fall harvest festival is one of Korea's most important holidays.
△ **Andong Mask Dance Festival** *(late Sep to early Oct)*. Andong is famous for its mask dance, and this festival features performers from around the world.

OCTOBER

△ **Busan International Film Festival** *(early to late Oct)*. Stars, screenings, and a whole lot of red carpet at Korea's biggest film festival.
Jarasum Jazz Festival *(mid-Oct)*. Three days of top international jazz on an island in the Bukhangang River east of Seoul.
Gwangju Kimchi Festival *(late Oct to early Nov)*. Korea's biggest kimchi festival lets attendees try making kimchi or watch demonstrations by chefs and kimchi masters.

MARCH

Independence Movement Day *(Mar 1)*. Commemorates the reading of an independence proclamation and protests against Japanese colonial authorities in 1919.

△ **Cherry blossom festivals** *(late Mar to late Apr)*. Municipalities throughout Korea hold celebrations to welcome the fleeting arrival of everyone's favorite flower. The most famous is Jinhae Gunhangjae Festival.

APRIL

Black Day *(Apr 14)* To counter Valentine's Day, single Koreans celebrate their "freedom" by eating black-themed foods such as *jjajangmyeon* noodles.

△ **Yeondeunghoe (Lotus Lantern Festival)** *(late Apr to mid-May)*. Temples and city streets are strung with brightly colored lanterns to celebrate the birth of the Buddha.

JULY

Daegu Chimac Festival *(early to mid-Jul)*. Daegu celebrates Korea's favorite combination, chicken and beer, turning a city park into a giant restaurant and concert venue.

△ **Boryeong Mud Festival** *(mid-Jul to early Aug)*. Daecheon Beach becomes the setting for one of Korea's biggest parties, with mud pits, mud obstacle courses, and concerts in the mud.

AUGUST

Seoul Fringe Festival *(early to late Aug)*. Independent and experimental art is in the spotlight across venues in Hongdae and Sinchon.

△ **Gwangbokjeol** *(Aug 15)*. National Liberation Day commemorates the end of Japanese colonial rule on this date in 1945. Offices and many businesses are closed.

NOVEMBER

△ **Kimjang** Families and neighbors gather for the traditional activity to celebrate cabbages and prepare large batches of kimchi before the winter, a cultural practice recognized by UNESCO.

DECEMBER

Chilgapsan Ice Fountain Festival *(mid-Dec to mid-Feb)*. Frozen fountains and sculptures carved from snow create a fairy-tale landscape in Cheongyang-gun County.

△ **Christmas** *(Dec 25)*. Christians attend Mass; for other Koreans, Christmas is less a family holiday than a chance to spend time with friends.

New Year's Eve *(Dec 31)*. Seoul marks the new year by tolling the bell in downtown's Bosingak bell pavilion, the only time it's rung all year.

A BRIEF HISTORY

A small country with a strategic location, Korea has spent much of its 4,000-year history squeezed between larger powers, struggling to maintain its independence. Today, Korea is a flourishing country that punches above its weight both economically and culturally.

The First Koreans

The first clan societies on the Korean Peninsula formed some 10,000 years ago, but the birth of the Korean people as such is commonly dated to 2333 BCE, when Dangun, mythologized as a descendant of Heaven, founded the kingdom of Gojoseon. Occupying what's now Manchuria (northeast China) and the northern reaches of the peninsula, it survived until 108 BCE, when it was overtaken by China's Han Dynasty, establishing commanderies to control parts of Gojoseon's former territory.

Did You Know?

In Korean myth, Dangun was the son of a bear that transformed into a woman.

Timeline of events

c 8000 BCE
The first clan societies form on the Korean Peninsula.

2333 BCE
Dangun founds the kingdom of Gojoseon, establishing the Korean people.

17 BCE
Goguryeo's King Yuri writes the first Korean song.

42 CE
The Gaya confederacy is founded and develops a sophisticated iron-working culture.

367
Baekje establishes relations with Japan, introducing Buddhism to the islands.

Power Struggles

A trio of kingdoms – Goguryeo, Baekje, and Silla – was formed in the wake of Gojoseon's collapse, ushering in an era of conflict and alliances known as the Three Kingdoms Period. Goguryeo grew into a powerful military state, expanding into Manchuria. Baekje established itself in what's now Seoul, occupied the Hangang River Valley, and made ties with Tang China. Established in what's now Gyeongju, the Silla kingdom emerged relatively late, taking until the 4th century to secure the southeast.

A Unified Peninsula

The Three Kingdoms' jockeying for power came to a head in the 6th and 7th centuries. Silla turned on Baekje, conquering it in the mid-600s. It then aligned with Tang China to defeat Goguryeo in 668, thereby uniting the peninsula. This initiated an era marked by the remarkable construction of palaces and temples like Bulguksa (p225), Buddhist art, and strong economic trade, with merchants exchanging precious metals, ceramics, and silks.

1 An ancient political map of South Korea.

2 Royal treasure from the Silla kingdom, preserved in Gyeongju.

3 A 7th-century painting depicting envoys from the Three Kingdoms.

4 The grand Bulguksa Temple, surrounded by fall foliage.

391
Gwangaeto becomes Goguryeo's king and expands Korean territory to its greatest extent.

372
Buddhism becomes the state religion in Goguryeo; Korea's first Confucian academy is founded.

520
Silla codifies its bone-rank system to signal social status.

892
Gyeon Hwan founds Later Baekje, initiating the Later Three Kingdoms era.

668
Silla defeats Goguryeo, bringing the peninsula fully under its control.

DISCOVER A Brief History

Splintering and Reunion

By the late 700s, Silla was riven by internal power struggles. After overthrowing the leader of a breakaway fiefdom, General Wang Geon established the Goryeo kingdom in 918 in what's now Kaesong. He incorporated Silla in 935 and soon brought smaller kingdoms to heel, unifying the peninsula once again. Buddhism and Confucianism thrived, trade routes stretched from Japan to the Middle East, and culture reached new heights, epitomized by Goryeo celadon (pottery) and the world's first movable metal printing type. Mongol invasions in the mid-13th century weakened the kingdom and turned it into a vassal state of China's Yuan Dynasty.

The Capital Comes to Seoul

In 1392, the Goryeo general Yi Seong-gye took advantage of the kingdom's diminished state to overthrow its rulers and found a new dynasty: Joseon. Two years later, as King Taejo, he moved the capital to what's now Seoul, building Gyeongbokgung Palace (*p68*), among other structures. The new kingdom was guided by Confucian principles, and Buddhism fell out of favor. Hangeul,

1 A 12th-century artwork, portraying Goryeo nobility.

2 Photograph of Gyeongbokgung Palace, where royals lived until the Japanese annexation of Korea.

3 A painting of Chinese and Korean forces attacking a Japanese-held fortress in Korea in 1598.

4 The Japan-Korea Annexation Treaty, signed in August 1910.

Timeline of events

1145
Kim Bu-sik publishes *Samguk Sagi*, a history of the Three Kingdoms.

1251
The last of the 81,258 Tripitaka Koreana woodblocks is completed.

1394
King Taejo moves the Joseon capital to what is now Seoul.

1443
King Sejong invents Hangeul, bringing literacy to the masses.

1450
King Sejong the Great dies.

the Korean script, was created; science and technology advanced; and the arts flourished. The Imjin War, a series of Japanese invasions between 1592 and 1598, decimated the country, but it recovered, only for internal strife to take hold in the 19th century. Japan again threatened, and Joseon's closed-door policy saw it fall behind rising industrial powers. In 1897, King Gojong introduced reforms and rechristened the dynasty the Korean Empire, but his efforts proved too little, too late.

Loss of Independence

Flush with power after military victories over China and Russia, Japan again set its sights on Korea, annexing the peninsula in 1910. Industrialized Japan spurred a period of modernization, building ports and railways, but the decades up to the end of World War II were primarily a time of hardship for Koreans. Japan extracted the country's resources, forced citizens to take Japanese names, and conscripted Koreans to provide forced labor and sex work for its military. While some Koreans took up arms against the occupiers, it wasn't until Japan's surrender to Allied forces that Korea would regain its independence.

KING SEJONG THE GREAT

King Sejong, the beloved Joseon Dynasty's fourth monarch (r. 1418-50), is best known for creating Hangeul, which vastly improved literacy across Korea. He also commissioned literary works, oversaw the development of a musical notation system, and sponsored scientific inventions including rain gauges and astronomical maps.

1597
Admiral Yi Sun-sin defeats the Japanese in the battle of Myeongnyang.

1895
Japanese agents assassinate Empress Myeongseong in Gyeongbokgung Palace.

1905
Korea becomes a protectorate of Imperial Japan.

1910
Japan annexes Korea, beginning a 35-year period of colonial rule.

1938
Samsung is founded as a grocery trading company in Daegu.

Korea's Greatest Tragedy

Independence came with a major asterisk, however, as Korea once again found itself at the mercy of outside powers. At the end of World War II, the US and USSR divided the peninsula at a latitude line, known as the 38th Parallel. What was meant to be a temporary arrangement solidified in the Cold War's chill, and the two powers set up loyal regimes in Seoul and Pyongyang, each claiming to be the legitimate government. On June 25, 1950, North Koreans crossed the border, starting the Korean War. After three years of fighting, the border remained almost exactly where it was first drawn up. An armistice signed on July 27, 1953, fixed the border in place, where it remains today.

Dictatorship, Development, Democracy

The next decades would be a struggle for democracy and economic growth. After the war, South Korea was among the world's poorest countries, and its president, Syngman Rhee, was growing increasingly authoritarian. Demonstrations pushed him out in 1960, only for General Park Chung-hee to seize power in a coup the following year. Park's 18-year rule

1 Investigating the assassination of leader Park Chung-hee.
2 War Memorial of Korea.
3 Refugees checked at the 38th parallel.
4 Queuing for street food in Seoul.

Did You Know?
After North Korea invaded in 1950, Seoul fell to its forces in just three days.

Timeline of events

1950
North Korea invades the South, starting the Korean War.

1953
An armistice halts fighting but does not officially end the Korean War.

1970
The Saemaul Undong campaign to modernize rural areas starts.

1979
President Park Chung-hee is assassinated by Kim Jae Kyu, his intelligence chief.

1980
Deaths follow the Gwangju Uprising, a protest against the military government.

was marked by rigged elections and the torture of political dissidents but also by unprecedented economic growth that came to be known as the "Miracle on the Han." In 1979, Park was assassinated by his head of intelligence, but any hope for democratic reform was quashed when General Chun Doo-hwan launched his own coup and declared martial law. As the economy continued its rapid ascent, political repression persisted, until pro-democracy protests in 1987 forced the junta to bow to public will. Finally, democracy arrived in Korea.

South Korea Today

After a 20th century of colonialism, civil war, and military dictatorship, Korea has emerged as a vibrant democracy, a pop-culture powerhouse, and a leading economy, with the world's 14th-highest GDP. Despite this success, the country faces major challenges. President Yoon Suk-yeol's brief declaration of martial law on December 3, 2024, raised the specter of past dictatorships, and the world's lowest fertility rate is posing serious questions about whether Korea can carry its current vibrant society into the future.

> **MARTIAL LAW**
>
> President Yoon Suk-yeol ended Korea's four-decade-old democracy by declaring martial law on December 3, 2024. With protestors slowing the military's arrival, National Assembly members voted to overturn this, forcing Yoon to lift martial law after six hours. On December 14, the Assembly impeached Yoon for his actions. In April 2025, he was removed from office.

1988 — Seoul hosts the Summer Olympics, marking Korea's arrival on the world stage.

2016 — President Park Geun-hye is impeached for abuse of power.

2018 — BTS becomes the first Korean group to hit No 1 on Billboard's Artist 100 chart.

2024 — President Yoon Suk-yeol declares martial law; hours later, the National Assembly overrules him.

EXPERIENCE SEOUL

Lantern Festival at Bongeunsa Temple

| Central Seoul | 64 |
| Beyond the Center | 90 |

EXPLORE
SEOUL

This guide divides Seoul into two sightseeing areas, as shown on this map. Find out more about each area on the following pages.

- JEONGNEUNG-DONG
- YEOKCHON-DONG
- Seodaemun Prison History Hall
- SEODAEMUN-GU
- War and Women's Human Rights Museum
- YEJANG-DONG
- NAEBALSAN-DONG
- Seonyudo Park
- National Museum of Korea
- Noryangjin Fisheries Wholesale Market
- Hangang
- DAERIM-DONG

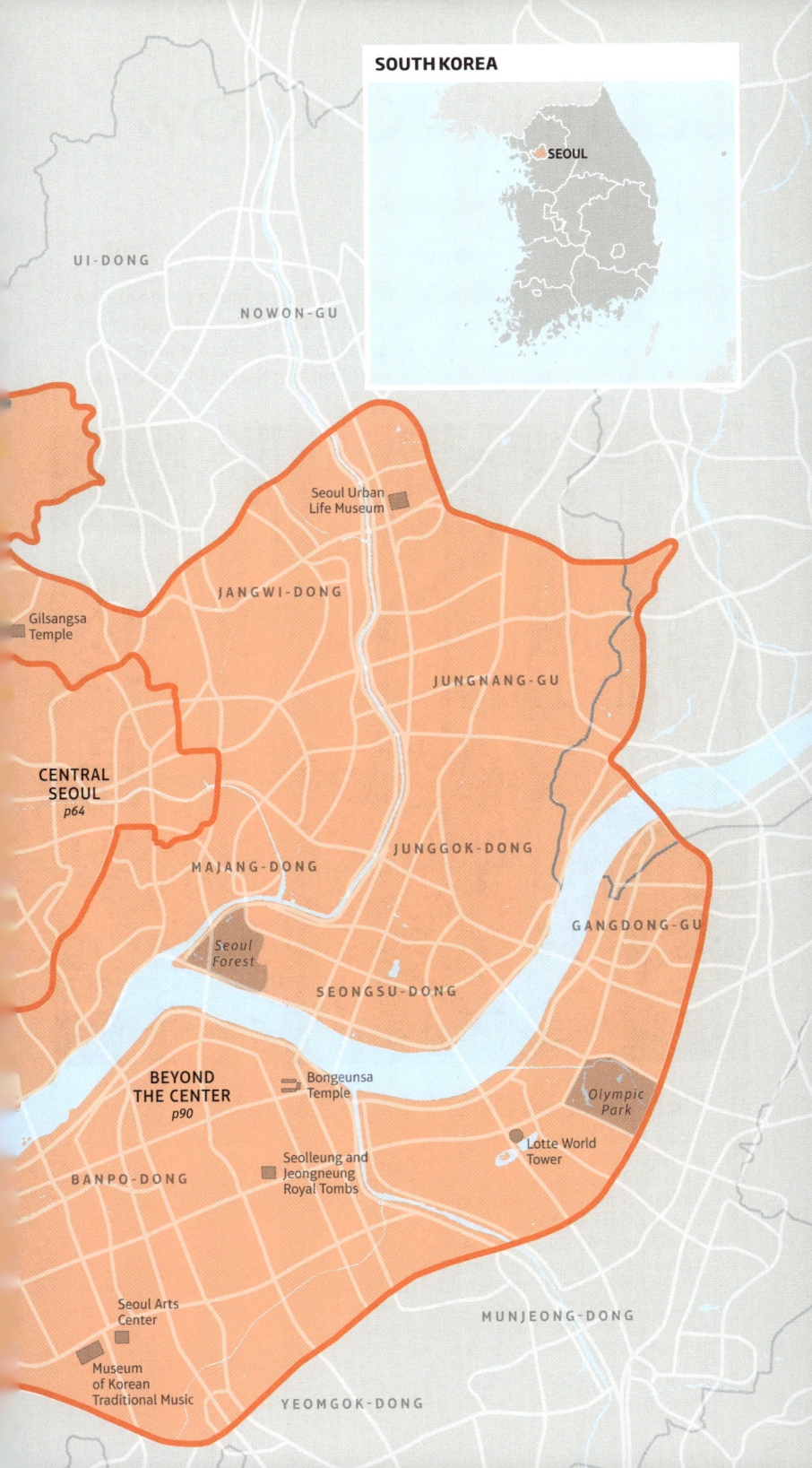

GETTING TO KNOW SEOUL

Epitomizing the modern Asian megacity, Seoul has so much to see and do that it would take a lifetime to tackle it all. Its historic center is filled with royal palaces, top museums, and traditional homes. Surrounding areas show off the city's contemporary side with trendsetting neighborhoods.

CENTRAL SEOUL

PAGE 64

Seoul was founded between Bukhansan Mountain and Namsan Mountain, and that area remains the center of the modern city. This is where you'll find almost all of the capital's historic sites, including its royal palaces, the Joseon royal shrine, and neighborhoods filled with 100-year-old homes. The city's biggest markets, Dongdaemun and Namdaemun, are here, and so are many of its best museums. Take a deep dive into the city's past at the Seoul Museum of History or check out what's new and now at the National Museum of Modern and Contemporary Art.

Best for
Royal palaces, traditional hanok buildings, museums

Home to
Gyeongbokgung Palace, Dongdaemun, Bukchon Hanok Village

Experience
A tour of the Joseon royal palaces and a shopping trip in Bukchon Hanok Village

BEYOND THE CENTER

Within the city limits but outside the historic core, Seoul sprawls across both banks of the Hangang River. Interspersed with the capital's countless apartment towers are important business districts, peaceful urban temples, and even a national park on the slopes of Bukhansan Mountain. There's more great green space in Olympic Park and Seoul Forest, two of the best parks in the city, while the concrete and glass canyons of the wealthy Gangnam district are a shopper's paradise. When the sun goes down, follow the young and artsy crowd to Hongdae for its pulsing nightlife.

Best for
Nightlife, shopping, parks

Home to
National Museum of Korea, Hongdae

Experience
Boutique-hopping in Gangnam's posh Apgujeong neighborhood

Shop signs on busy Dongdaemun Market Street

CENTRAL SEOUL

Seoul has been at the center of the Korean story since the dawn of the Three Kingdoms Period in 57 BCE, but it was when King Taejo moved the Joseon dynasty's capital here in 1394 that the city began to take on the royal palaces and city walls it retains today. The opening of Korean ports in 1876 marked a turning point, setting Seoul on the path to becoming a modern, international city. Development accelerated during the Japanese colonial era, but the city largely had to start from scratch after the Korean War, which destroyed countless buildings and turned nearly three-quarters of its residents into internal refugees.

Taejo may have been onto something when he chose Seoul for his capital, though: its location, shadowed by Bugaksan Mountain and with Namsan Mountain and Cheonggyecheon Stream to its front, was said to be the most auspicious on the peninsula. Since the Korean War, the city has risen from the ashes and historic treasures like Gyeongbokgung Palace have been restored to their former glory. Today, Seoul is home to one in every five Koreans and, with a globally influential economy and culture, can claim a place among the world's greatest cities.

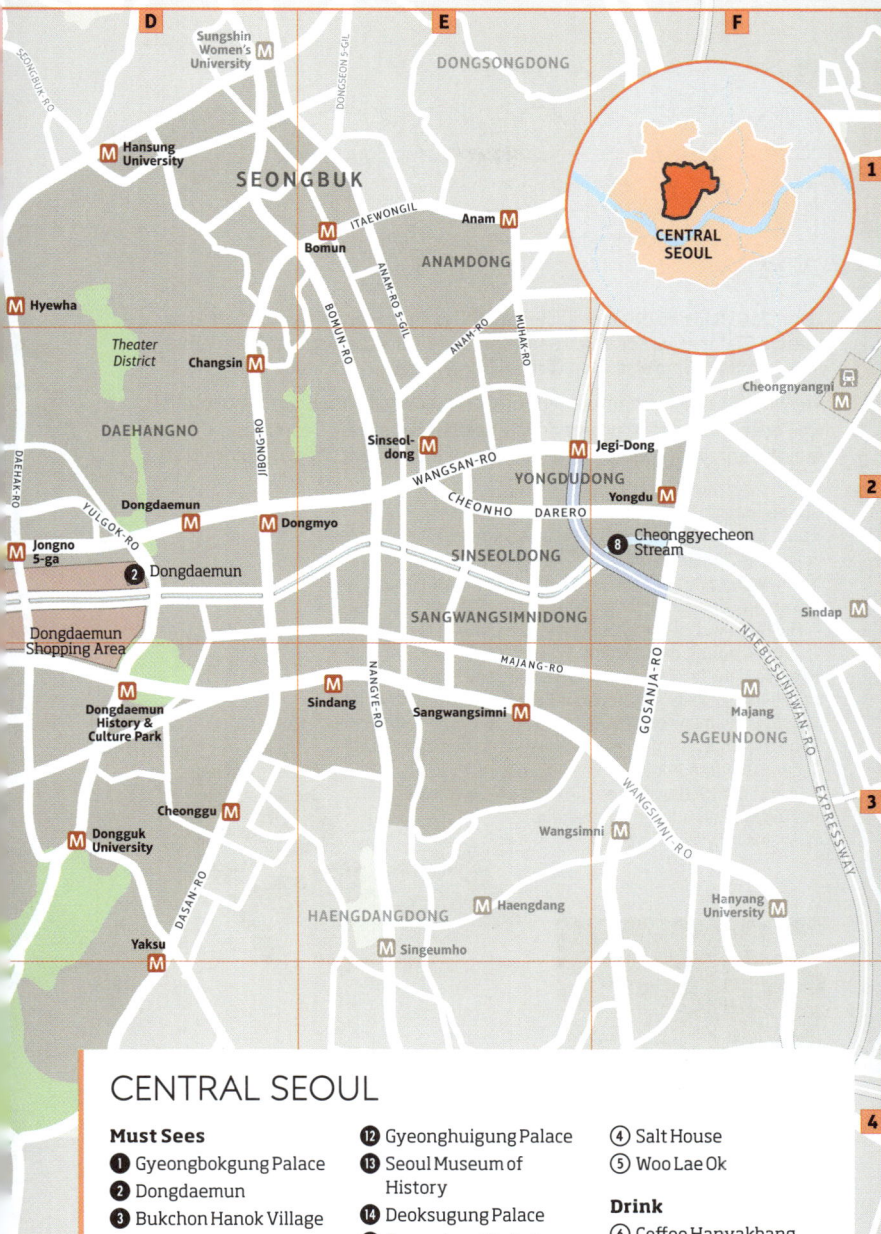

CENTRAL SEOUL

Must Sees
1. Gyeongbokgung Palace
2. Dongdaemun
3. Bukchon Hanok Village

Experience More
4. Gwanghwamun Square
5. Jogyesa Temple
6. Insa-dong
7. Jongmyo Shrine
8. Cheonggyecheon Stream
9. Changgyeonggung Palace
10. Changdeokgung Palace
11. National Museum of Modern and Contemporary Art
12. Gyeonghuigung Palace
13. Seoul Museum of History
14. Deoksugung Palace
15. Gwangjang Market
16. Myeong-dong
17. Namdaemun
18. Euljiro
19. Namsan Mountain
20. War Memorial of Korea
21. Itaewon
22. Leeum Museum of Art

Eat
1. Balwoo Gongyang
2. Cafe Layered
3. Hadongkwan
4. Salt House
5. Woo Lae Ok

Drink
6. Coffee Hanyakbang
7. Demue
8. Seendosi

Stay
9. Nostalgia
10. Rakkojae
11. Songhyundami

Shop
12. Kukje Embroidery

GYEONGBOKGUNG PALACE

경복궁

B2 161 Sajik-ro ⓜGyeongbokgung Gyeongbokgung, Gyeongbokgung Station ⓘMar-May, Sep & Oct: 9am-6pm daily; Jun-Aug: 9am-6:30pm daily; Nov-Feb: 9am-5pm Wed-Mon ⓦroyal.khs.go.kr/gbg

The largest and most important of the Joseon palaces, Gyeongbokgung was once the locus of power on the Korean Peninsula. Despite the dynasty's fall, the sprawling compound remains an impressive site to explore today.

Gyeongbokgung was originally built in 1395, at the foot of Mount Bugaksan, shortly after King Taejo moved the Joseon Dynasty to Seoul. The palace was given a name meaning "the new dynasty shall prosper," and for the most part, it was accurate – it would reign for the next 500 years.

The history of Gyeongbokgung itself is rockier. It was destroyed during the Japanese invasion of 1592 and remained a ruin until 1867, when it was restored and expanded, but it faced large-scale destruction during the Japanese colonial period, when many of its buildings were torn down and Gwanghwamun, its main gate, was replaced by the Japanese General Government Building. A massive restoration project begun in the 1990s returned the palace to its former glory, and today it has a pair of interesting museums for visitors to enjoy.

1 The majestic Geunjeongjeon Hall, a former throne hall.

2 Pink skies over Gyeongbokgung Palace.

3 Costumed guards in the Changing of the Guard Ceremony.

Gwanghwamun Gate is the palace's main gate, restored to its original form in 2010.

Must See

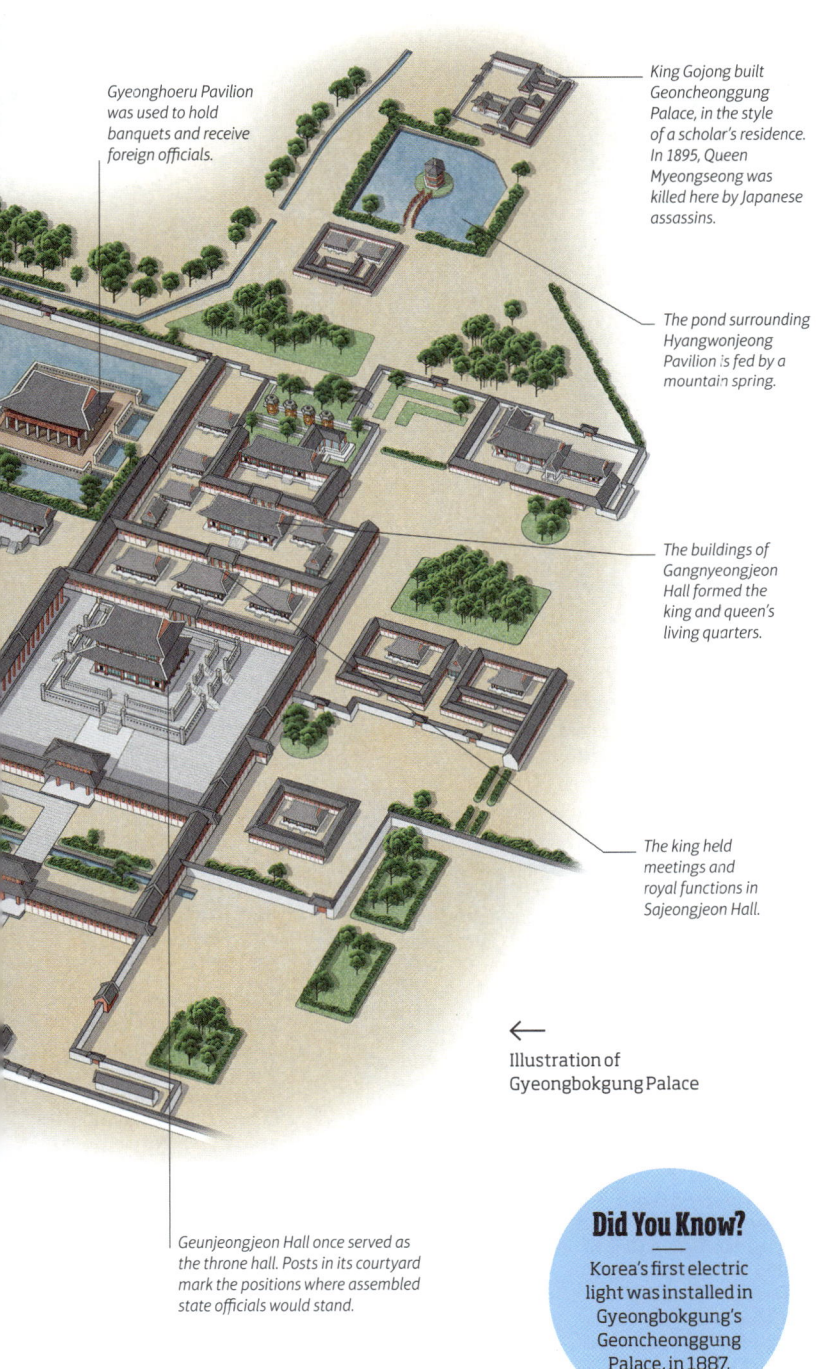

Gyeonghoeru Pavilion was used to hold banquets and receive foreign officials.

King Gojong built Geoncheonggung Palace, in the style of a scholar's residence. In 1895, Queen Myeongseong was killed here by Japanese assassins.

The pond surrounding Hyangwonjeong Pavilion is fed by a mountain spring.

The buildings of Gangnyeongjeon Hall formed the king and queen's living quarters.

The king held meetings and royal functions in Sajeongjeon Hall.

← Illustration of Gyeongbokgung Palace

Geunjeongjeon Hall once served as the throne hall. Posts in its courtyard mark the positions where assembled state officials would stand.

Did You Know?

Korea's first electric light was installed in Gyeongbokgung's Geoncheonggung Palace, in 1887.

The futuristic Dongdaemun Design Plaza, designed by architect Zaha Hadid

❷ DONGDAEMUN
동대문

🔲 D2 Ⓜ Dongdaemun, Dongdaemun History & Culture Park (DDP)

Dongdaemun is where old Seoul and new Seoul collide. Centuries-old structures bump up against modern architecture, and secondhand goods sit side by side with cutting-edge design. The neighborhood is also the center of the Korean fashion industry, attracting shoppers with its many stores and markets, which stay open until the early hours.

Heunginjimun Gate
흥인지문

🏛 288 Jong-ro
Ⓜ Dongdaemun
🚌 Dongdaemun, Dongdaemun Station, Heunginjimun

The imposing Heunginjimun Gate, also referred to as Dongdaemun, is one of the ancient city wall's two surviving main gates (the other, Namdaemun, is also known as Sungnyemun Gate; p84). Built in 1396, it underwent renovation after a fire in 1453 and a major rebuild in 1869. Original design features can still be seen today, including a hipped roof decorated with figures that ward off evil spirits. Heunginjimun's most distinctive feature is its *ongseong*, or protective wall. It was the only city gate to have one, as the flat terrain required additional defenses. While Heunginjimun hasn't been damaged, walls on either side were torn down by Japanese colonial authorities in the early 1900s, leaving the gate somewhat stranded.

> **Did You Know?**
>
> Seoul is the native Korean word for *doseong*, a walled city where a ruler resides.

Seoul City Wall Museum
한양도성박물관

🏛 283 Yulgok-ro
Ⓜ Dongdaemun 🚌 Dongdaemun, Dongdaemun Station, Heunginjimun
🕘 9am-6pm Tue-Sun
🚫 Jan 1 🌐 museum.seoul.go.kr/scwm/NR_index.do

Just north of Heunginjimun, a stretch of Hanyangdoseong, the Seoul city wall, climbs up Naksan Mountain. Built in 1396, the 18.6-km (11.6-mile) wall encircled the historic city, marking its boundaries and protecting it from attacks. Set just inside the wall, the absorbing Seoul City Wall Museum covers topics like

70

Must See

the evolution of construction techniques, the functions of each gate, how the wall shaped life in the capital, and modern restoration efforts. Visitors can learn about the poetry clubs that gathered at scenic spots on the wall and the military pass system used to open gates after curfew.

③
Dongdaemun Shops and Markets

 Dongdaemun, Dongdaemun History & Culture Park (DDP) Dongdaemun History & Culture Park, Cheonggye 6-ga, Ogansugyo Bridge

If you can put it on, you can pick it up in Dongdaemun. The district is the epicenter of Korea's fashion industry, home to numerous malls, tens of thousands of shops, and countless independent manufacturers.

Just west of Dongdaemun Design Plaza (DDP), Doota Mall, The Migliore, and Hyundai City Outlets are popular retail outlets that carry both international brands and local labels. East of the Dongdaemun Design Plaza are two other large shopping centers: Nuzzon Mall, with its 1,200 shops, and DDP Fashion Mall, a must-visit for the latest in womenswear. Filling several long buildings south of the Cheonggyecheon Stream (p80) is Pyounghwa Market, which was founded in 1953 by North Korean refugees selling secondhand army uniforms. It's primarily a wholesale market that attracts shop owners as well as an older crowd hunting for a bargain.

Just across the stream lies Dongdaemun Shopping Complex, which draws in designers looking for fabric, thread, clasps, and other raw materials. If a button exists, you'll find it here.

④
Dongdaemun Design Plaza
동대문디자인플라자

281 Eulji-ro Dongdaemun History & Culture Park (DDP) Dongdaemun History & Culture Park 10am-8pm daily; check website for hours for specific spaces and events Jan 1, Seollal, Chuseok ddp.or.kr

It's hard to upstage Heunginjimun, but Dongdaemun Design Plaza (DDP) does. Designed by the late Pritzker Prize-winning architect and artist Zaha Hadid, the sinuous silver structure dominates its surroundings and is especially mesmerizing at night, when lights play across the 45,133 aluminum panels that make up its facade. More than a decade after opening, it still looks like it was sent from the future. The DDP is one of Seoul's major cultural complexes, and anyone with even a passing interest in style and design should set aside time to explore it.

> ### SEOUL FASHION WEEK
>
> Seoul held its first ever fashion week (p50) in 2000, in an effort to promote Korean fashion on a global level. In 2014 the event moved to to Dongdaemun Design Plaza and has since become known as a celebration of both Korean culture and Seoul's creative street style.

In addition to housing galleries, performance spaces, and a design shop, the DDP hosts concerts, film screenings, pop-ups, and major events like Seoul Fashion Week. There are also two small museums. The Dongdaemun Stadium Memorial is dedicated to the old athletics stadium that once stood here, while the Dongdaemun History Museum displays relics that were excavated during the building's construction.

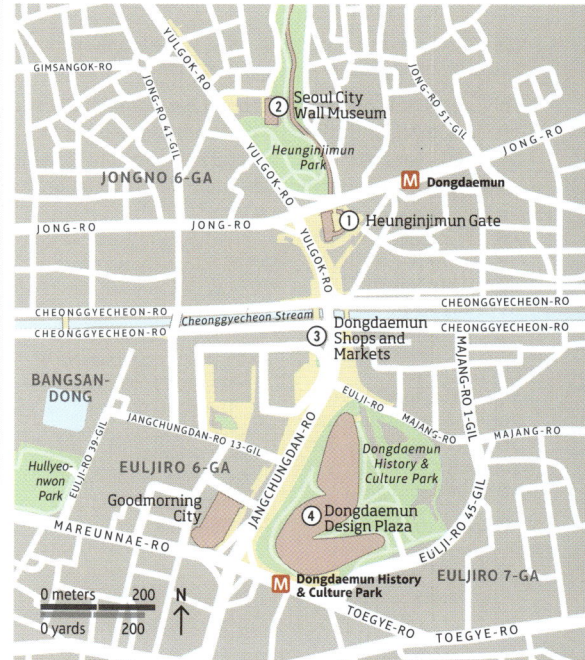

BUKCHON HANOK VILLAGE
북촌한옥마을

B2　Anguk　Anguk Station & Seoul Museum of Craft Art, Anguk Station Exit 2, Duksung Girls' Middle and High School

The pretty Bukchon neighborhood has Seoul's largest concentration of *hanok* (p74), or traditional Korean homes, many of which are more than 100 years old. Today, several have been turned into cafés, shops, restaurants, and guesthouses, while others function as cultural centers.

① Seoul Museum of Craft Art
서울공예박물관

4 Yulgok-ro 3-gil Anguk Anguk Station & Seoul Museum of Craft Art 10am-6pm Tue-Sun　Jan 1　craftmuseum.seoul.go.kr

Occupying the former site of a residence for Joseon princes, the Seoul Museum of Craft Art's expansive remit stretches from pottery and furniture to embroidery and *bojagi*, the do-it-all, patterned, square-shaped wrapping cloths that Koreans use for everything from presenting gifts to carrying groceries.

The museum does an admirable job of giving equal weight to crafts high, like *hwagak*, decorative work utilizing sheets of ox horn, and low, like *ongjang*, earthenware pots for storing food, such as grains and sauces.

② Bukchon Traditional Culture Center
북촌문화센터

37 Gyedong-gil Anguk 9am-6pm Tue-Fri, 9am-5pm Sat & Sun hanok.seoul.go.kr

This "modern" *hanok* was built in 1921. A small exhibition hall explores local history, from how Bukchon was laid out according to feng shui principles to the

↑ Traditional Bukchon Hanok Village and the modern Seoul skyline

> **INSIDER TIP**
> **Traditional Experiences**
>
> Make kimchi at the Kimchi Academy (*kimchischool.net*) or try a traditional craft like knot tying at the Bukchon Traditional Crafts Experience Center (*02 741 2148*).

late 20th-century drive to develop. It also hosts workshops on traditional culture, including calligraphy.

③ The Sool Gallery
전통주갤러리

🏠 18 Bukchon-ro
Ⓜ Anguk ⏱ 10am–7pm Tue–Sun 🗓 Jan 1, Seollal, Chuseok 🌐 thesool.comr

Learn about Korean alcohols (*sool*) like soju and *yakju*, clear refined rice wine, at this small exhibition space inside E:eum. The gallery hosts tastings in English at 3pm and 4pm.

④
Kukje Gallery
국제갤러리

🏠 54 Samcheong-ro
Ⓜ Anguk ⏱ 10am–6pm daily (Sun: to 5pm) 🗓 Jan 1, Seollal, Chuseok
🌐 kukjegallery.com

This major contemporary art gallery has showcased works by the likes of Robert Mapplethorpe but it is best known for having been a leading advocate of Dansaekhwa, a 20th-century Korean art movement characterized by monochrome paintings. Today, the gallery showcases contemporary artists and details Korean art history.

⑤
Arario Museum
아라리오뮤지엄

🏠 83 Yulgok-ro
Ⓜ Anguk ⏱ 10am–7pm Tue–Sun 🌐 arariomuseum.org

The Arario Museum displays works from the personal collection of billionaire Ci Kim. The assemblage includes pieces by Andy Warhol and Keith Haring but also work by exciting young Korean artists such as Yoon Hyangro.

Must See

STAY

Nostalgia
노스텔지어

Operates luxury *hanok* in some of Bukchon Hanok Village's most charming areas.
🏠 1 Bukchon-ro 8-gil
🌐 nostalgiaseoul.com

₩₩₩

Rakkojae
해밀톤호텔

This 140-year-old building was renovated by a master carpenter.
🏠 218 Gahoe-dong
🌐 rkj.co.kr

₩₩₩

Songhyundami
송현다미

This simple yet utterly winsome *hanok* has a courtyard and an open-air bath.
🏠 40-21 Yulgok-ro 1-gil
📞 0507 1419 8704

₩₩₩

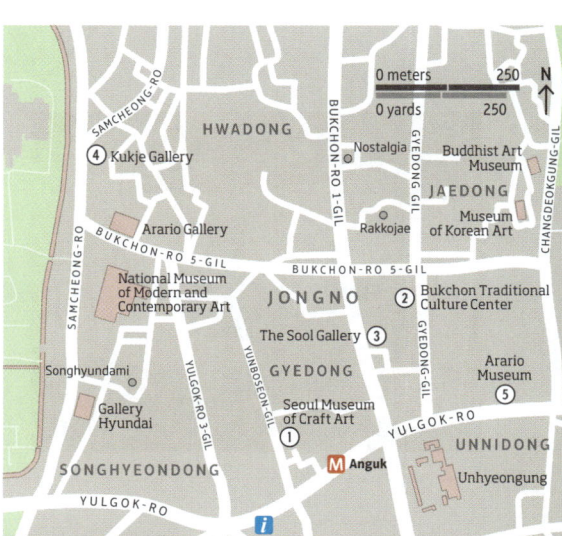

HANOK

Hanok, traditional Korean homes, have historically been built from three natural materials – wood, stone, and earth – oriented toward the south, to best take advantage of the sun's warmth, and positioned according to principles of feng shui. Within these commonalities, however, *hanok* exhibit variations to suit local climates, aiming to keep out cold winds or maximize airflow in warmer climes. In the 20th century, as the population urbanized, people built *hanok* adapted for city living, of the type seen in Bukchon Hanok Village *(p72)*, using materials like glass and bricks.

Did You Know?

The word "*hanok*" didn't appear in Korean dictionaries until around 1975.

Walls are filled in with a mixture of straw and packed earth, often a moisture-absorbing red clay called hwangto.

At the back of the home was a detached outhouse called the dwitgan.

→ Illustration of a typical *hanok*

The *buok*, or kitchen, centered on a fireplace that also provided heat for the home. The *ondol* system directed warm air from here through a series of flues running beneath the floors.

← The interior of a traditional *hanok* in Bukchon Hanok Village

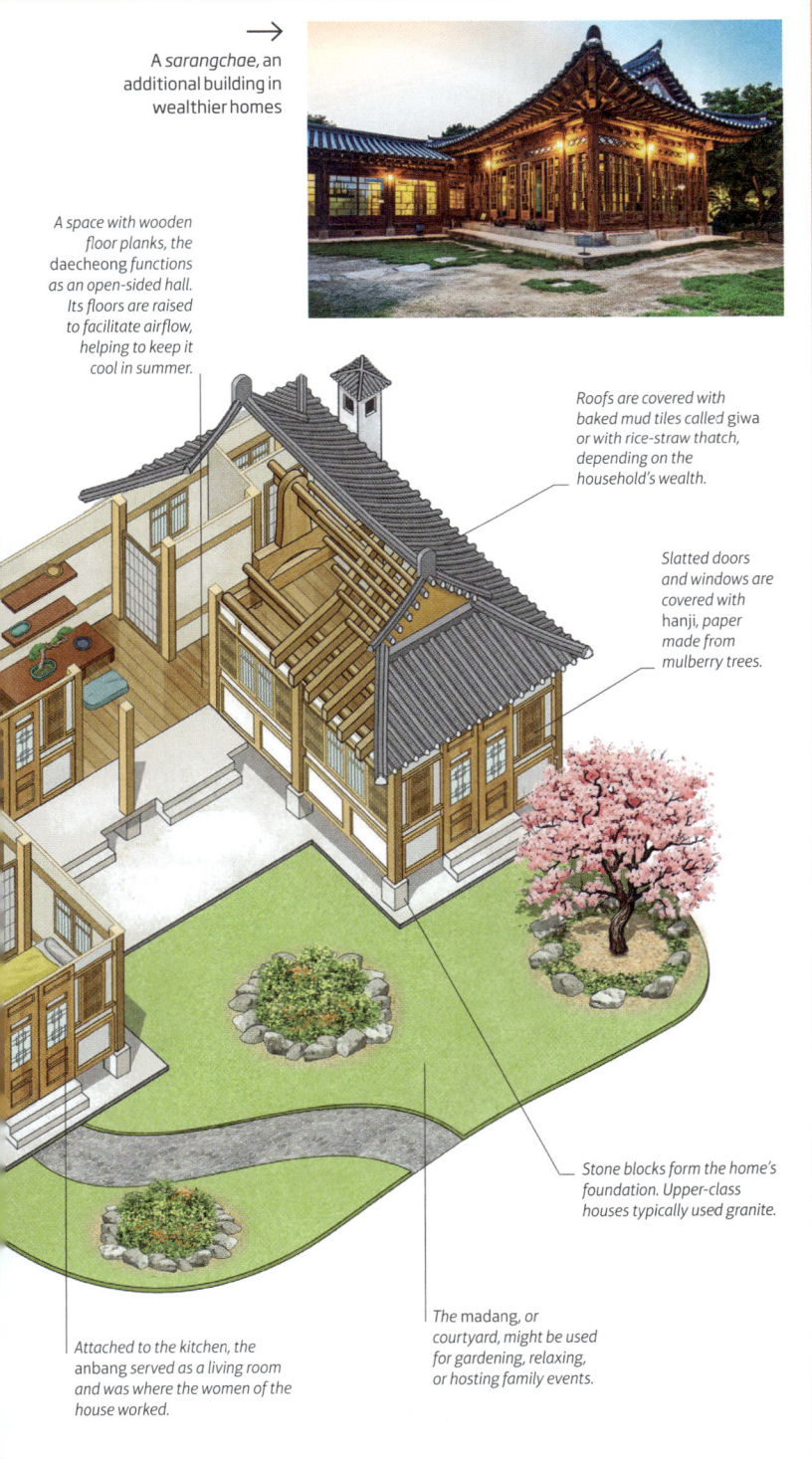

→ A *sarangchae*, an additional building in wealthier homes

A space with wooden floor planks, the daecheong functions as an open-sided hall. Its floors are raised to facilitate airflow, helping to keep it cool in summer.

Roofs are covered with baked mud tiles called giwa or with rice-straw thatch, depending on the household's wealth.

Slatted doors and windows are covered with hanji, *paper made from mulberry trees.*

Stone blocks form the home's foundation. Upper-class houses typically used granite.

Attached to the kitchen, the anbang *served as a living room and was where the women of the house worked.*

The madang, or courtyard, might be used for gardening, relaxing, or hosting family events.

A SHORT WALK
BUKCHON HANOK VILLAGE

Distance 1.3 miles (2.1 km) **Time** 40 minutes
Nearest metro Anguk

Seoul's historic character is best experienced on a wander around Bukchon Hanok Village, where you can admire its handsome hundred-year-old homes and pop into the many *hanok* that have been thoughtfully remodeled into modern cafés, restaurants, and boutiques. This walk takes you down both narrow alleyways where tiled *hanok* roofs practically touch and lively commercial arteries where the past and present coexist. Want to really get in Bukchon's historic spirit? Join the crowds wearing traditional *hanbok* outfits, available for rent at many local shops.

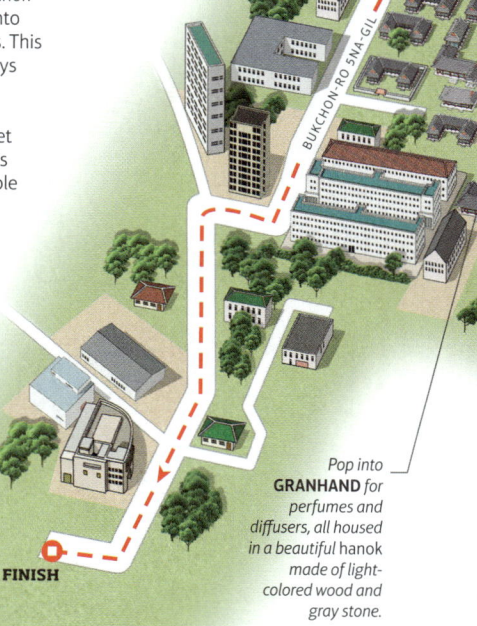

Pop into **GRANHAND** for perfumes and diffusers, all housed in a beautiful *hanok* made of light-colored wood and gray stone.

Embodying modern Bukchon, **Cafe Onion** serves terrific coffee and pastries from a large renovated *hanok* that dates to the 1930s.

↑ Exploring the well-preserved Bukchon Hanok Village

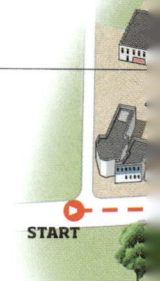

Bukchon-ro 11-gil *is the prettiest street in Bukchon. The narrow residential road is lined entirely by* hanok, *providing a glimpse of what Seoul looked like a century ago.*

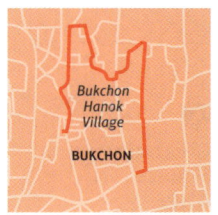

Locator Map
For more detail see p66

Try your hands at crafts at the **Bukchon Traditional Crafts Experience Center** *(p73). No reservation is required.*

The **Kimchi Academy** *(p73) runs classes on how to make kimchi (Wed–Sun). The school will even vacuum-pack your finished product so you can take it home with you.*

Learn about local history at the **Bukchon Traditional Culture Center** *(p72), which also hosts lectures on topics like traditional flower arrangement and folk painting.*

↑ Walking through Bukchon Traditional Culture Center

EXPERIENCE MORE

❹

Gwanghwamun Square
광화문광장

📍 B2 Ⓜ Gwanghwamun 🌐 gwanghwamun.seoul.go.kre

Historically, the land from Jong-ro to Gwanghwamun Gate has been Seoul's pathway to power. It leads straight to Gyeongbokgung Palace (p68) and, in the Joseon era, was lined with government ministries. Much of it was turned into Gwanghwamun Square in 2009, while 2022 renovations gave the space its current look. The plaza is often the site of protests but it also hosts things like concerts and Christmas markets. Statues here commemorate Korea's two most celebrated figures: Yi Sun-sin (p55) and the Joseon king Sejong the Great, who developed Hanguel (p55), the Korean script, among many other accomplishments.

Within the plaza is the **National Museum of Korean Contemporary History** (대한민국역사박물관), which whisks you through the country's independence movement, the Korean War, and democratization to the present day. Interactive spaces let you experience history through the lens of different generations and listen to pop songs across the decades. English tours run on Thursdays at 3pm. On the plaza's west side is the **Sejong Center for the Performing Arts** (세종문화회관), Korea's premier venue for opera, ballet, dance, and traditional music (tickets can be purchased in person or by phone).

National Museum of Korean Contemporary History

♿ 📍 198 Sejong-daero 🕐 10am–6pm Sun-Tue, Thu; 10am–9pm Wed, Sat ❌ Jan 1, Seollal, Chuseok Ⓜ Gwanghwamun 🌐 much.go.kr

Did You Know?

Admiral Yi Sun-sin never lost a battle throughout the Imjin War (1592–98).

Sejong Center for the Performing Arts

♿ 📍 175 Sejong-daero Ⓜ Gwanghwamun 🕐 Hours vary, check website 🌐 sejongpac.or.kr

---

❺

Jogyesa Temple
조계사

📍 B2 📍 55 Ujeongguk-ro Ⓜ Anguk, Jonggak 🌐 jogyesa.kre

Jogyesa is the head temple of the Jogye order, Korean Buddhism's largest sect, which emphasizes meditation and takes the Diamond Sutra as its guiding text. This city temple may lack the otherworldly atmosphere of its mountain counterparts, but it remains an oasis amid Seoul's frenzy. It's especially lovely during the Buddha's birthday celebrations in spring, when colorful glowing lanterns decorate the courtyard. On the temple grounds you'll also find the **Central Buddhist Museum** (불교중앙박물관), which opened in 2007. Here, visitors can learn about the faith and view historic statues, tapestries, and other artifacts.

Central Buddhist Museum

📍 55 Ujeongguk-ro Ⓜ Anguk, Jonggak 🕐 10am–5pm Tue-Sun ❌ Jan 1, public holidays 🌐 museum.buddhism.or.kr

↑ The statue of beloved Admiral Yi Sun-sin in Gwanghwamun Square

RELIGION IN KOREA

Although most Koreans profess not to follow any faith, religion has long played a significant role in Korean society. Ancient shamanistic beliefs fostered spiritual connections with the country's mountains; Buddhism has influenced Korean thought and art for over 1,500 years; and Christianity shapes contemporary politics. Perhaps the best measure of religion's impact are the many practices that at first glance seem less spiritual than simply part of everyday culture, from Templestay retreats to consultations with fortune tellers.

BUDDHISM

Historically, Buddhism has been Korea's dominant faith, influencing the Korean view and producing most of the country's important religious artworks. It arrived on the peninsula via China in the 4th century CE and grew in influence until the establishment of the Confucian Joseon Dynasty, which forced its temples into the mountains. Today, 17 per cent of Koreans identify as Buddhists, with the majority belonging to the Jogye order.

↑ The sermon hall of Jogyesa, the main temple of the Jogye order

CHRISTIANITY

Christianity made its first appearance in Korea during the late 1600s. Later, the Joseon government saw it as a threat and over 8,000 Catholics were executed. Christianity boomed after the Korean War, and it now represents Korea's largest religion. Though less than a third of Koreans identify as Christian, those who do tend to be enthusiastic in their beliefs and churches play an influential role in politics; interestingly, Korea sends more missionaries abroad than any country except the U.S. and Brazil.

↑ Myeong-dong Cathedral, a prominent Catholic church

OTHER RELIGIONS

Korea's original beliefs were shamanist and centered on connecting with the spirits of natural features and the deceased. *Mudang* (shamans) facilitate this communion through divination and rituals called *goot*. Though few Koreans identify as shamanist today, many dabble in its practices.

Combining aspects of Buddhism, Christianity, and Shamanism, plus Taoism and Confucianism, is Cheondogyo. Founded in 1860, the faith has just 65,000 practitioners, but it played a huge role in Korea's independence movement. Half of the 33 signatories of the March 1, 1919 Declaration of Independence were followers.

↑ Shamanistic ritual at the Gangneung Danoje Festival

EXPERIENCE Central Seoul

 A ceremony honoring the spirits of ancient kings and queens at Jongmyo Shrine

⑥
Insa-dong
인사동

📍 C2 Ⓜ Anguk, Jongno 3-ga
🌐 hiinsa.com

Insa-dong's artsy roots go back to the Joseon Dynasty, when it was home to a government office in charge of painting. Today, this well-touristed neighborhood's main road, the semi-pedestrianized Insa-dong-gil (also known as Insa-dong Culture Street), is one of Seoul's best places to hunt for souvenirs, antiques, and traditional crafts. Many stores selling things like wooden masks and calligraphy brushes have been around for decades, but you'll also find shops stocking work by young artisans giving new spins to old art forms. A good place to browse those is **Ssamziegil** (쌈지길), a multi-floor shopping space with dozens of fun boutiques. Off the main road, Insa-dong's side streets and alleys hide many excellent restaurants and tea rooms.

At Insa-dong-gil's south end is Tapgol Park (탑골공원). Designed in 1897, it was Seoul's first modern park. It was here, on March 1, 1919, that activists read the Korean Declaration of Independence, inspiring nationwide protests against the Japanese colonial authorities. On the park's north side is a ten-story stone pagoda, the only remnant of a Buddhist temple that once stood here.

Ssamziegil
🏠 44 Insa-dong-gil
Ⓜ Anguk 🕐 10:30am–8:30pm daily

⑦
Jongmyo Shrine
종묘

📍 C2 🏠 157 Jong-ro
Ⓜ Jongno 3-ga 🕐 General admission: hours vary, check website; English-language tours: Mon–Fri 10am, noon, 2pm & 4pm
🌐 royal.khs.go.kr

This dignified complex was the Joseon Dynasty's most spiritually important site. Built to house the memorial tablets of deceased kings and queens, it was one of the first structures the dynasty constructed after moving the capital to Seoul. The original shrine, completed in 1395, burned down in the Japanese invasions of the 1590s, but the current version has stood since 1601. The buildings are a paragon of Joseon architecture but exhibit none of the exuberantly colorful painting found in the era's palaces, befitting their solemn purpose. Jongmyo can be visited freely on weekends, holidays, and the last Wednesday of each month; on weekdays, you must join a scheduled tour.

⑧
Cheonggyecheon Stream
청계천

📍 F2 Ⓜ Gwanghwamun, Jonggak

This waterway runs for 7 miles (11 km) through central Seoul, from Gwanghwamun to Seongsu. A popular green space and haven for waterfowl, it represents the capital's modern history in microcosm, having gone from the site of a post-Korean War low-income neighborhood to a paved-over elevated highway in the 1970s to a restored urban oasis today. The downtown headwaters feature fountains and regularly host festivals, but the farther east you go, the greener things get. Learn all about this fascinating waterway at the **Cheonggyecheon Museum** (청계천박물관). Guided tours are conducted in Korean.

→ The extensive Changgyeonggung Palace complex

SHOP

Kukje Embroidery
You'll find beautiful bags, jewelry boxes, pillows, and table runners perfect for brightening up the home at this Insa-dong craft store that's been open since 1979.

📍 C2 🏠 12 Insadong-7-gil 🌐 kjasuwon.com

Cheonggyecheon Museum

530 Cheonggyecheon-ro Yongdu 9am-6pm Tue-Sun Jan 1 museum.seoul.go.kr/cgcm/index.do

9 Changgyeonggung Palace
창경궁

C2 185 Changgyeonggung-ro Hyehwa Changgyeonggung & Seoul University Hospital 9am-9pm Tue-Sun royal.khs.go.kr

King Seongjong commissioned Changgyeonggung in 1483. It was destroyed in the Japanese invasion of 1592 and rebuilt in 1616, though many of its current structures were part of an 1830 renovation following a fire. One building that survived the conflagration was the main throne hall; dating to the 1616 rebuild, it's the oldest of the throne halls in Seoul's palaces. During the colonial period, the Japanese turned Changgyeonggung into a public park with a zoo and botanical garden, complete with a Victorian-style greenhouse. It was only in 1983 that it was restored to palace status.

10 Changdeokgung Palace
창덕궁

C2 99 Yulgok-ro Anguk Changdeokgung 9am-6.30pm Tue-Sun (Feb-May, Sep & Oct: to 6pm; Nov-Jan: to 5:30pm) royal.khs.go.kr

Gyeongbokgung (p68) may be Korea's largest and oldest palace, but Changdeokgung is its most beautiful. A UNESCO World Heritage Site, it represents the peak of traditional Korean architecture, its buildings in perfect harmony with the landscape. Changdeokgung was constructed in the 15th century, but was destroyed by Japanese invaders in 1592 along with Seoul's other palaces. It was the first to be rebuilt, and for 270 years was the king's primary residence, until Gyeongbokgung's reconstruction was completed.

Notable parts of the palace include Donhwamun, the main gate and oldest palace gate in Seoul, and Injeongjeon, the throne hall. The palace's marquee feature, however, is its rear garden, often referred to as the Secret Garden. Laid out in 1406 and expanded over the ensuing centuries, it's an impeccable example of design that utilizes natural features and complements the landscape. The garden encompasses valleys, ponds, a stream, and pavilions where Joseon kings and their guests would write poetry, discuss state affairs, and hold parties. While the palace buildings can be visited independently, you must join a guided tour to view the garden. English-language tours are conducted at 10:30am, 11:30am, and 2:30pm (with an additional 3:30pm tour from March to November). Tickets can be reserved online or purchased in person.

Did You Know?

Changdeokgung's Geumcheongyo Bridge is adorned with mythical guardian animals.

EXPERIENCE Central Seoul

EAT

Balwoo Gongyang
Tasting menus take a refined approach to the delicate flavors and meditative eating practices of Buddhist temple food.

📍B2 🏠56 Ujeongguk-ro 🌐balwoo.or.kr

Cafe Layered
Scrumptious scones and cakes to satisfy even the sweetest of tooths.

📍C2 🏠2-3 Bukchon-ro 2-gil

Hadongkwan
Open since 1939, this *gomtang* (beef and rice soup) joint is clearly doing something right.

📍B3 🏠12 Myeongdong-9-gil 🌐hadongkwan.co.kr

Salt House
House-made mortadella, salami, and other cured meats go into this deli's drool-inducing sandwiches and charcuterie boards.

📍C2 🏠19 Bukchon-ro 4-gil 🌐salthousekorea.com

Woo Lae Ok
A renowned restaurant most famous for its Pyongyang *naengmyeon*, buckwheat noodles in chilled broth.

📍C2 🏠62-29 Changgyeonggung-ro 📞02 2265 0151

11

National Museum of Modern and Contemporary Art
국립현대미술관 서울

📍B3 🏠30 Samcheong-ro Ⓜ Anguk 🕐10am-6pm daily (Wed & Sat: to 9pm) 🚫Jan 1, Seollal, Chuseok 🌐mmca.go.kr

The main branch of Korea's national modern-art museum serves up consistently thrilling exhibitions of work by both Korean and international artists. A typical month might feature screenings of avant-garde cinema and an exhibition on ceramics or boundary-pushing digital art. If you're an art lover or just want to tap into Korea's creative spirit, this is a must-visit. Don't skip the excellent gift shop, which stocks imaginative products related to the current exhibitions.

12

Gyeonghuigung Palace
경희궁

📍A2 🏠45 Saemunan-ro Ⓜ Gwanghwamun, Seodaemun 🕐9am-6pm Tue-Sun 🚫Jan 1 🌐museum.seoul.go.kr

This minor Joseon palace was built in 1623 on a site supposedly chosen for the royal energy it emanated. It briefly served as a royal residence after rebels set fire to Changdeokgung (*p81*) in 1624, but at the beginning of the colonial period, it was dismantled and a middle school was built in its place. The city government began excavations and reconstruction work in 1987, and in 2002 it reopened as a palace site. While Gyeonghuigung lacks the size and splendor of other Seoul palaces, it's a good place to experience royal architecture without the crowds.

13

Seoul Museum of History
서울역사박물관

📍B2 🏠55 Saemunan-ro Ⓜ Gwanghwamun, Seodaemun 🕐9am-6pm Tue-Sun (Fri: to 9pm) 🚫Jan 1 🌐museum.seoul.go.kr

The stage for royal dynasties, liberation struggles, civil war, dictatorships, democracy movements, and globe-conquering pop culture, Seoul has a fair claim to being the most interesting city in the world. This museum on the Gyeonghuigung grounds dives deep into its story, beginning with the establishment of the Joseon capital, when the city was known as

↑ Rank stones in Gyeonghuigung Palace courtyard, indicating where officials would line up

Hanseong, and culminating in the present day. Exhibits cover everything from the city's layout to how early firefighters trained, the development of Gangnam, and 1990s teen magazines. The museum is particularly good at elucidating how Seoulites experienced, and drove, the breakneck changes of late 20th-century Korea.

Deoksugung Palace
서울역사박물관

📍 B3 🏛 99 Sejong-daero 🚇 City Hall 🕘 9am-9pm Tue-Sun 🌐 royal.khs.go.kr

Completed in 1593, Deoksugung served as a secondary Joseon palace. It rose to prominence during the short-lived Korean (or Daehan) Empire (1897–1910), when it was expanded by Emperor Gojong and made the site of his imperial court. Though a number of its buildings were destroyed in a 1904 fire and more were demolished by the Japanese colonial authorities, Gojong lived there until his death in 1919.

Deoksugung is by far the most eclectic of Seoul's palaces. Besides traditional Korean buildings, it includes four Western or Western-influenced structures. Jeonggwanheon Pavilion mixes Korean and Romanesque elements and was built partly to serve as a coffeehouse for Gojong. Dondeokjeon and Jungmyeongjeon are both brick buildings originally built around the turn of the 20th century. Dondeokjeon was used as a banquet hall

> HIDDEN GEM
> **Seoul Museum of Art (SEMA)**
> Just south of Deoksugung is the superb Seoul Museum of Art (sema.seoul.go.kr). Exhibitions run the gamut from Korean webtoons to renowned contemporary artist Lee Bul.

↑ A traditional pavilion at Deoksugung Palace and *(inset)* Seokjojeon Hall

and guesthouse but it was later torn down in the 1920s. The current hall is a 2023 reconstruction. Jungmyeongjeon is infamous for being where the 1905 treaty that made Korea a Japanese protectorate was signed. Most striking is Seokjojeon Hall, a colonnaded Neo-Classical beauty from 1910 that wouldn't look out of place in London. Once Gojong's royal residence, it now houses the Daehan Empire History Museum, which can be visited on a guided tour (English tours held at 11:50am and 2:50pm daily).

15

Gwangjang Market
광장시장

📍 B3 🚇 88 Changgyeonggung-ro Ⓜ Jongno 5-ga
🕐 Shops: 9am–6pm Mon-Sat; restaurants: 9am–11pm daily
🌐 kwangjangmarket.co.kr

Consisting of two interlinking covered arcades with innumerable side alleys, Gwangjang is Korea's oldest permanent market, founded in 1905. While it sells the usual market staples, it's particularly known for its textiles. Numerous shops sell fabric for traditional *hanbok* that tailors turn into custom pieces. Gwangjang's other claim to fame is its food, and while in recent years the market's street food outlets have gone from locals' favorites to popular tourist draws, squeezing in at a rickety old bench and chowing down on spicy rice cakes and blood sausage amid the din remains one of Seoul's best eating experiences. Don't skip the market's specialty: *bindaetteok* (fried mung bean pancakes) served with *makgeolli* rice wine.

16

Myeong-dong
명동

📍 B3 Ⓜ Euljiro 1-ga, Myeong-dong

Myeong-dong has been one of Seoul's main commercial districts for decades. Today, it's especially popular with international visitors, and you'll hear smatterings of Chinese, Japanese, Vietnamese, English, and other languages mixed in with the K-pop blaring from shop speakers. Most stores here belong to major Korean and international brands, and you'll also find a couple of posh department stores. Alongside its embrace of mammon, the area is also home to Myeong-dong Cathedral, the main church of the Archdiocese of Seoul. Completed in 1898, the Gothic structure was an important sanctuary for democracy activists in the 1970s and 80s.

Did You Know?
Myeong-dong has the ninth-most expensive commercial real estate in the world.

17

Namdaemun
남대문

📍 B3 Ⓜ Hoehyeon, Seoul Station

Sungnyemun Gate, like Heunginjimun Gate (p70), is one of Seoul's most recognizable landmarks, a majestic structure with an imposing stone base and a beautifully painted two-story superstructure. It was the main southern gate in Seoul's old city walls, a status that gave it the colloquial name Namdaemun, or Great South Gate. Completed in

1398 and partially rebuilt in the 15th century, it was the city's oldest wooden building until it was burned down in a 2008 arson attack by a 69-year-old upset over an entirely unrelated land deal. Following five years of painstaking restorations, the gate reopened in 2013.

Sprawling over several blocks east of the gate is **Namdaemun Market** (남대문시장). Seoul's best-known outdoor market, its roots go back some 500 years. Among the thousands of shops here you'll find clothing, eyeglasses, souvenirs, and medical supplies. It's an especially good place to score Korean kitchen tools like stone bowls and metal chopsticks. Some mild haggling is acceptable, but don't expect a huge drop in the listed price. Food options are also in surplus here. Make for the alley in the market filled with restaurants specializing in *galchi jorim*, a spicy concoction of braised hairtail fish and radishes.

Namdaemun Market
M Hoehyeon ⊙ Hours vary, check website
w namdaemunmarket.co.kr

Euljiro
을지로

C3 M Euljiro 3-ga

Just blocks from glitzy Myeong-dong, the neighborhood around Eulji-ro Street has long been a blue-collar collection of machine shops and printers, where motorcycle couriers whizz through alleys and the screech of power sanders echoes off the walls. Over the past decade, however, young artists and entrepreneurs in search of cheap rent have moved in, opening studios, bars, and cafés, making Euljiro one of Seoul's trendiest enclaves. Many of these places are tucked down tiny alleyways or on upper floors, so patient exploration or a bit of advance research is required.

DRINK

Coffee Hanyakbang
커피한약방
Sip on hand-drip coffee in this opulent old-school venue.

C3 ⌂ 16-6 Samil-daero 12-gil

Demue
드므
Cozy wine bar whose terrace has views of downtown towers.

C3 ⌂ 24 Chungmu-ro 5-gil, 4F

Seendosi
을지로 노가리골목
There's funky decor and lots of neon at this bar-cum-art-space.

C3 ⌂ 31 Eulji-ro 11-gil, 5F

← Gwangjang Market, a hub of market stalls and haggling

Nightfall at Sungnyemun Gate

> **Did You Know?**
>
> N Seoul Tower's lights indicate air pollution levels, from blue (clear) to green, yellow, and red (hazardous).

19

Namsan Mountain
남산

 C4 Myeong-dong, Hoehyeon, Dongguk University, Hangangjin Namsan Seoul Tower

Located in the center of the city, Namsan Mountain is a perfectly positioned bit of greenery. Its slopes are criss-crossed with walking and biking trails, and at only 886 ft (270 m), its summit makes for an invigorating but not strenuous hike. In spring, its many cherry trees burst into bouquets of white and pink.

Atop the peak and visible from across the city is **N Seoul Tower** (남산서울타워). Unveiled as Korea's first general radio wave tower in 1971, it's now mainly a tourist attraction. Lower levels are filled with restaurants and cafés, but the main draw is, of course, the observatory. Combining the mountain and tower, it provides unimpeded views of the metropolis from 1,663 ft (507 m). Try to visit at dusk to watch the city slowly light up. The tower can be reached on foot, by bus, or via the scenic **Namsan Cable Car** (남산케이블카), which was Korea's first and has been in operation for six decades.

At the foot of the mountain is **Namsangol Hanok Village** (남산골한옥마을), a collection of five late-Joseon *hanok* that were reconstructed or relocated here from elsewhere in the city. Together, they provide an intimate look at how the era's middle and upper classes lived.

N Seoul Tower

105 Namsangongwon-gil N Seoul Tower 10am-10:30pm Mon-Fri, 10am-11pm Sat & Sun nseoultower.co.kr

Namsan Cable Car

83 Sopa-ro Myeong-dong Shuttle bus from Myeong-dong Station, Exit 1 10am-11pm daily cablecar.co.kr

Namsangol Hanok Village

28 Toegye-ro 34-gil Chungmuro Apr-Oct: 9am-9pm Tue-Sun; Nov-Mar: 9am-8pm Tue-Sun hanokmaeul.or.kr

20

War Memorial of Korea
전쟁기념관

B5 29 Itaewon-ro Samgakji 9:30am-6pm Tue-Sun warmemo.or.kr

The massive War Memorial of Korea functions as both a place of tribute to Korea's war dead and a fascinating museum about the history of Korean warfare. Outside, the grounds are dotted with commemorative statues and some seriously impressive military hardware, including a hulking B-52 bomber and a North Korean semi-submersible. Inside, exhibitions begin with the tangle of confrontations between Baekje, Goguryeo, and Silla dynasties during the Three Kingdoms period (57 BCE–668 CE) before moving on to later conflicts with the Mongols and Japanese marauders. Military advancements on display include the *hwacha*, essentially a mobile rocket launcher for 100 arrows, and the famed turtle ships Admiral Yi Sun-sin used to such devastating effect in the 1597 Battle of Myeongnyang *(p55)*.

Naturally, much space is given over to the Korean War. Visitors can learn about the South Korean military's fateful decision to lift an emergency alert the day before the North invaded, see samples of propaganda leaflets, and experience the tide-turning Incheon Landing *(p112)* in a 4D theater. Displays occasionally omit some of Korea's more controversial

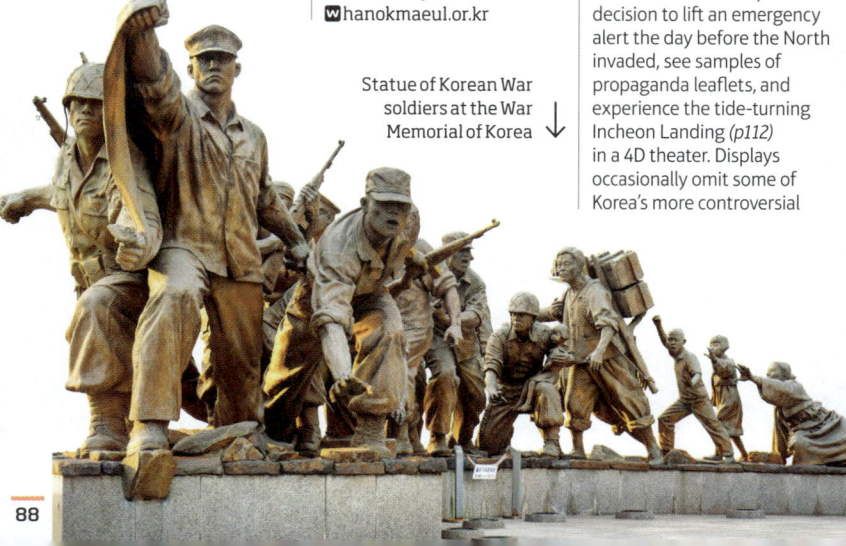

← Statue of Korean War soldiers at the War Memorial of Korea

↑ Striking architecture at the esteemed Leeum Museum of Art

episodes – the military atrocities committed during the Jeju Uprising (p257), for example – but on the whole, the museum provides an engrossing overview of the country's martial history.

Itaewon
이태원

◉ C5 Ⓜ Itaewon

Itaewon is Seoul's most multicultural neighborhood and a major nightlife destination. Once primarily a playground for expats and US soldiers at the now-vacated Yongsan Garrison, it's become a popular destination for young people who enjoy its international feel and the sense that traditional Korean social strictures don't apply here. Streets are a melange of Irish pubs, Turkish bakeries, Islamic bookstores, French restaurants, Korean nightclubs, and everything else that makes up the global village. Itaewon's come-as-you-are attitude also means that it's a center of Seoul's LGBTQ+ culture and there are numerous gay bars clustered on and around lively Usadan-ro 12-gil.

Leeum Museum of Art
리움미술관

◉ C5 ⌂ 60-16 Itaewon-ro 55-gil Ⓜ Hangangjin ⓒ 10am-6pm Tue-Sun ⊘ Jan 1, Seollal, Chuseok ⊕ leeumhoam.org

Part of the Samsung conglomerate's charitable arm, the Leeum (as it's universally known) was started with works from Samsung founder Lee Byung-chul's personal collection. Since it opened in 2004, it has grown into one of Korea's premier art museums and a cornerstone of Seoul's upscale Hannam-dong neighborhood.

A beautiful symphony of architectural styles, the museum is split into several halls, each with its own distinctive design. The traditional Korean art collection includes several designated National Treasures, among them a gold crown from the Gaya confederacy (42–562 CE) and works by the famed Joseon painter Jeong Seon. The modern and contemporary collection is a veritable who's who of 20th- and 21st-century art, with pieces by Cindy Sherman, Mark Rothko, Takashi Murakami, and the pioneering Korean painter Kim Whanki.

CHAEBOL

Koreans sometimes joke that they live in the Republic of Samsung. The company is the largest of Korea's *chaebol*, family-run conglomerates that include, among others, Hyundai, SK, and LG. They were birthed in the wake of the Korean War, when a few well-connected families were supported financially in order to help rebuild the shattered economy. Today, *chaebol* – still under family control – dominate virtually every corner of the economy, with the five biggest accounting for roughly half of Korea's GDP.

Trading at Noryangjin Fisheries Wholesale Market

BEYOND THE CENTER

In 18 BCE, the Baekje kingdom founded the first important settlement in the surrounding Seoul area, establishing its capital near what's now the Olympic Park, where traces of the fortress can still be seen today. The strategic Hangang River Valley location was a coveted prize, and in the Three Kingdoms Period (57 BCE–668 CE), the Baekje, Goguryeo, and Silla forces all laid claim to it at various points. During the Joseon Dynasty (1392–1910), the areas beyond the center were the realm of commoners, and for much of the era, the people who lived there were only permitted to enter the walled city of central Seoul to take government examinations or provide services to the elite.

In the latter decades of the 20th century, however, Seoul's outskirts became just as important as its historic center. As the city's population ballooned, from 1 million in 1950 to 8.2 million in 1980, the government annexed parts of surrounding counties, doubling the city's size. A period of intense development saw Yeouido Island transformed from little more than a sandbar to a center of finance and government, while Gangnam went from rice fields to Seoul's most moneyed district. What were once outlying areas have become some of Seoul's most desirable real estate, the site of top universities, prized parks, and many of the capital's trendiest neighborhoods, such as Hongdae and Seongsu.

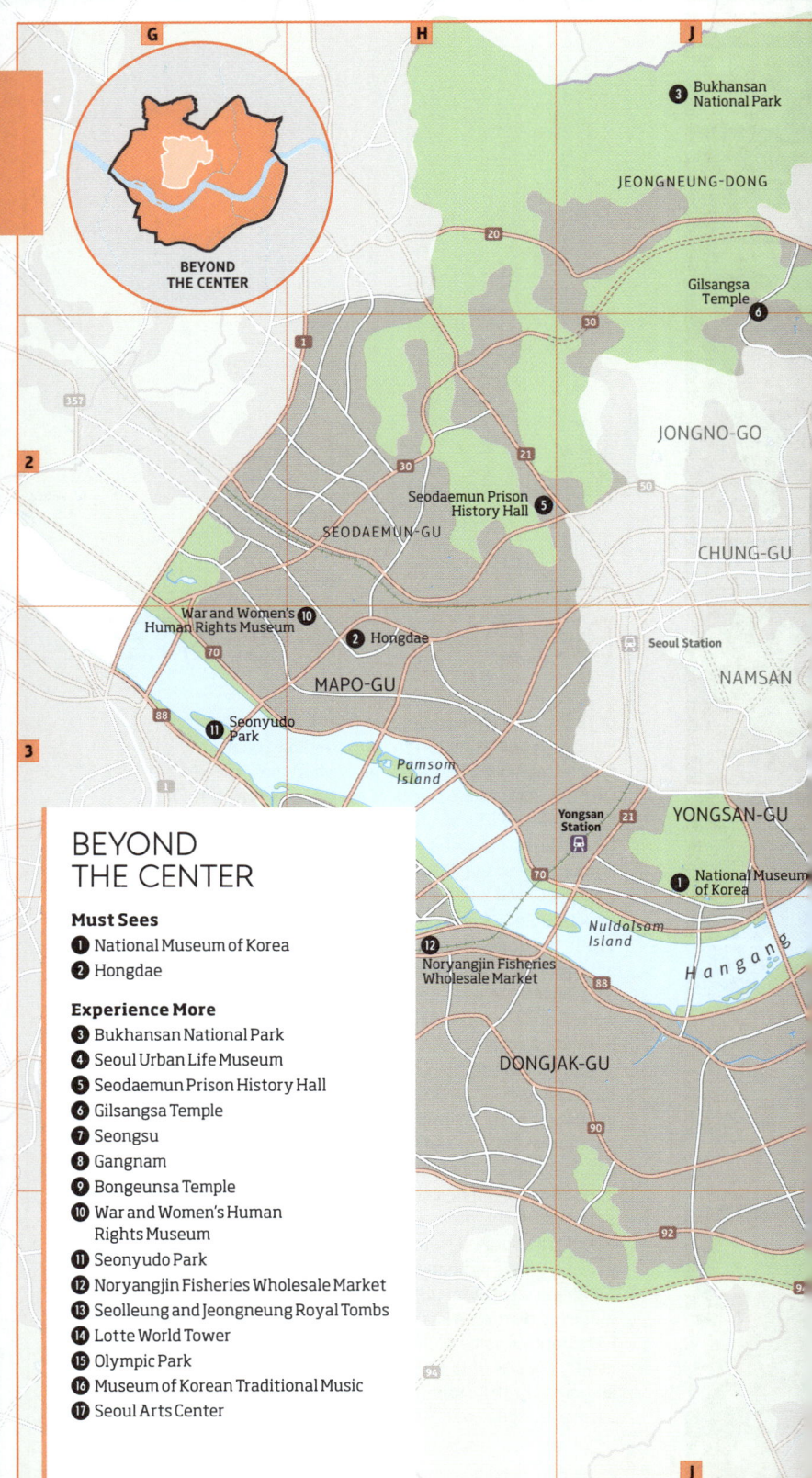

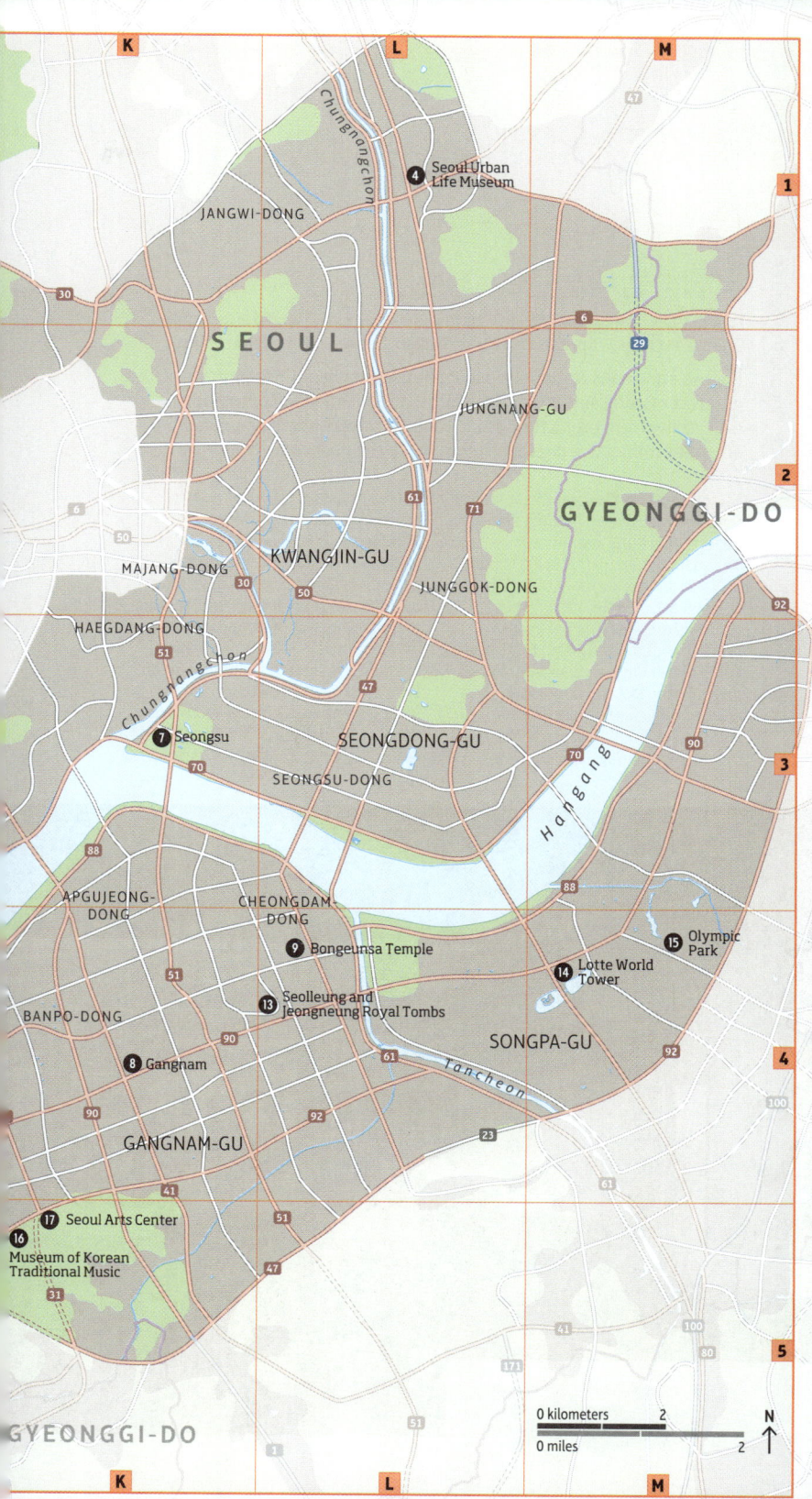

NATIONAL MUSEUM OF KOREA

국립중앙박물관

J3 137 Seobinggo-ro Ichon 10am–6pm daily (Wed & Sun: to 9pm) Jan 1, 1st Mon in Apr & 1st Mon Nov, Seollal, Chuseok museum.go.kr

Korea's enormous National Museum houses many of the country's greatest historic and artistic treasures. Its collection encompasses everything from prehistoric stone tools to transcendent Buddhist art, while immersive digital displays make the past come alive.

Established shortly after independence, the National Museum is Korea's most important cultural institution. It safeguards more than 310,000 historic artifacts and artworks, 12,000 of which are on display. First-floor galleries guide visitors from the peninsula's prehistory to the early 20th century via paleolithic handaxes, Baekje inkstones, Joseon compasses, and far more. There are also rooms devoted to lesser-known kingdoms, like the northern Balhae and the Gaya Confederacy.

Galleries upstairs focus on the arts, exhibiting white porcelain moon jars, Buddhist paintings, and lacquerware with mesmerizingly intricate mother-of-pearl inlay. Another addition is a room devoted to a set of Joseon royal records that the French army looted in 1866 and were returned in 2011. Many of the records were created exclusively for the king, but a digital exhibition – one of several in the museum – gives visitors equal access, letting them flip pages and review important royal events.

Admiring displays in the museum's Silla Art Exhibition Hall

Must See

HANGEUL

Within the museum's grounds is the National Hangeul Museum *(hangeul.go.kr)*, which is dedicated to the Korean script, created by King Sejong the Great in 1443. Previously, Korean was written with Chinese characters, an arrangement that left the vast majority of people illiterate. In seeking to create a writing system accessible to the masses, Sejong took a scientific approach, modeling the shapes of consonants on the shapes the mouth and tongue make when pronouncing them. Vowels, for their part, were given forms representing heaven, earth, and humans. The result was an elegant alphabet.

Museum Highlights

Gold Crown from Hwangnamdaechong Tomb

▷ This extravagant crown from the 4th or 5th century CE belonged to a Silla queen - though who, exactly, remains a mystery. The solid gold headpiece features a trio of upright branches decorated with carved jade and six dangling pendants, which would have framed the monarch's face.

Pensive Bodhisattvas

These two late-6th- and early-7th-century CE statues depict bodhisattvas lost in thought, their right hands pressed gently to their cheeks. They're displayed together in a darkened room, where visitors are invited to join them in contemplation.

Celadon Incense Burner with Openwork Geometric Design

Atop a base supported by three tiny rabbits are sculpted leaves with carefully incised veins and a smoke vent of symmetrical interlocking rings. It's hard to look at this 12th-century burner's precision and believe it was handmade.

Ten-Story Stone Pagoda of Gyeongcheonsa Temple

◁ The museum's signature piece, this 44-ft (13.5-m) marble pagoda was made in 1348 and once stood at a temple in Gyeonggi-do Province. It's a representation of the Pure Land, featuring detailed carvings of arhats, bodhisattvas, and scenes from the Buddhist canon.

Clearing After Rain on Mount Inwang by Jeong Seon

▷ Jeong was one of Korea's most important painters, and *Clearing After Rain on Mount Inwang* is widely considered his masterpiece. Painted in 1751, when Jeong was 76 years old, it uses only ink to create a moody landscape of Seoul's western mountain, with mist lingering in the valley, below towering dark peaks.

HONGDAE
홍대

 H3 Hongik University, Sangsu

For Seoul's best nightlife, head to Hongdae, the maze of streets outside Hongik University – Hongik Daehakyo in Korean, or "Hongdae" for short. A white-hot ball of energy on weekends, the area is home to slick nightclubs, after-dark shopping, and all-night eats. It's long been the cradle of Korea's alternative culture, and visitors will find vibrant hip-hop and punk scenes, plus one of the country's most LGBTQ+-friendly areas.

① Eoulmadang-ro

Hongdae, the university, has one of Korea's top arts programs, and in the 1980s and 90s, its graduates and other artistic souls began laying the foundations for Hongdae, the neighborhood, opening art studios and freewheeling basement clubs. The area has seen a good deal of gentrification in recent years, but it retains much of its outsider spirit. Eoulmadang-ro, sometimes just referred to as Hongdae Street, curves the length of the neighborhood from a block southeast of Hongik University Station and serves as a great introduction to this ethos. The plazas and sidewalks at its northeastern end are a magnet for buskers, while southwest of Hongik-ro, the street is lined with clothing boutiques, fortune tellers, and all sorts of funky little shops. It's a terrific place to just stroll and people-watch, especially after dark, when it's thronged with a stylish crowd out shopping and clubbing.

② KT&G Sangsangmadang
KT&G상상마당

 65 Eoulmadang-ro
sangsangmadang.com

On the corner of Eoulmadang-ro and Jandari-ro, this striking building has a concert hall, art-house cinema, galleries, and a shop selling fun stuff by Korean creatives.

③ Gyeongui Line Forest Park
경의선숲길

Created along a century-old railway line that once linked Seoul with Sinuiju, a North Korean city on the Chinese border, this park on Hongdae's

> It's a terrific place to just stroll and people-watch, especially after dark, when it's thronged with a stylish crowd out shopping.

Crowds thronging Hongdae's streets and *(inset)* a neighborhood street-food seller

④ Hongdae Playground
홍익문화공원

📍 406 Mapo-gu

Near the university's main gate is Hongdae Playground, where most nights out in Hongdae seem to end up at some point. The popular open space serves as a stage for breakdancers and musicians, and provides an easy meeting point for groups of friends to plot their next move or meet new acquaintances.

northern edge is lined with stylish bars, cafés, and brunch spots, and acts as a gateway to the trendy Yeonnam-dong neighborhood.

Also known as Yeontral Park (a cute portmanteau of Yeonnam-dong and New York's Central Park), the area offers a similar but much more laid-back scene to the livelier Hongdae Playground.

> **1-CHA, 2-CHA, 3-CHA**
>
> The classic Korean night out is a play in three acts. The first act, *il-cha*, is dinner, often barbecue accompanied by beer and soju. Act two, *i-cha*, is set at a bar, where, in a bit of a role reversal, drinks are often accompanied by *anju* (bar snacks). Then it's off for *sam-cha* at a *noraebang*, a karaoke bar with private rooms. After the closing number, anyone in need of a curtain call might head to a street-food stall or nearby convenience store for more drinks and food.

Must See

DRINK

Aura
클럽아우라

This club is always packed and raucous.

📍 H3 📍 37 Wausan-ro 21-gil 📞 010 6667 6460

Damotori h
다모토리 ㅎ

Try *makgeolli* from craft brewers across Korea.

📍 J3 📍 31 Sinheung-ro

Sanullim 1992
산울림1992

Country tavern vibes and traditional spirits.

📍 H3 📍 60 Seogang-ro 9-gil

Zest
제스트

Named one of the world's best bars in 2024.

📍 K3 📍 26 Dosan-daero 55-gil

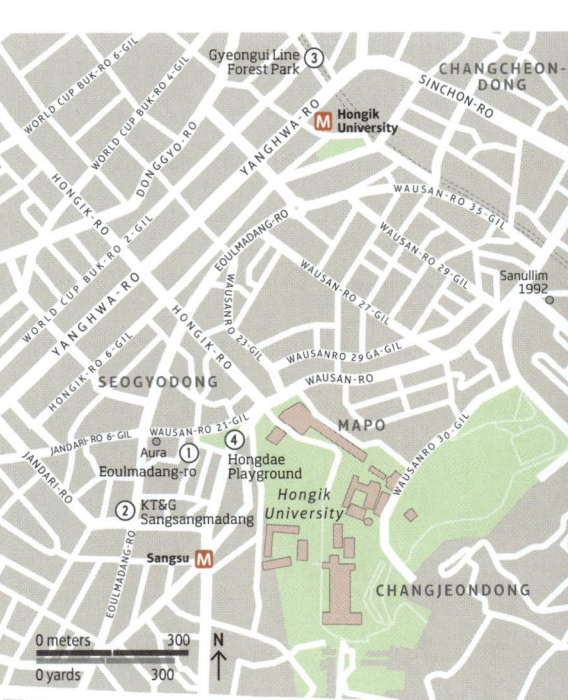

EXPERIENCE MORE

3
Bukhansan National Park
북한산국립공원

◐ J1 ◐ 262 Bogungmun-ro Ⓜ Bukhansan Bogungmun, Bulgwang, April 19th National Cemetery, Dobongsan, Bukhansan Ui Ⓦ knps.or.kr

Not many cities have a national park you can reach by metro, but Seoul does. Bukhansan covers 30 sq miles (77 sq km), split between the capital and Gyeonggi-do Province, and several points along its southern and eastern edges are a short walk from a metro station. The preserve is a lovely escape, filled with temples, streams, and granite massifs that rise out of the greenery like icebergs poking out of a leafy ocean.

The park can generally be divided into the Bukhansan Mountain region in the south and the Dobongsan Mountain region in the north. The former contains Baegundae, Bukhansan's highest peak at 2,743 ft (836 m). A popular if strenuous trek begins at Doseonsa Temple and traces a ridgeline to the summit, where views of the city are truly majestic. If you like your ascents more vertical, head to Insubong Peak; its multi-pitch routes attract climbers from all over Korea.

Bukhansan's location has long made it an important military site. As you explore the mountain, note the well-preserved walls and gates of Bukhansanseong Fortress – construction of which began in 1711.

> **INSIDER TIP**
> **Seoul Hiking Tourism Center**
>
> The Seoul Hiking Tourism Center at 52 Samyang-ro 173-gil 5F *(seoulhiking.or.kr)* rents boots, poles, and other supplies to visitors. You can even reserve gear online.

4
Seoul Urban Life Museum
서울생활사박물관

◐ L1 ◐ 27 Dongil-ro 174-gil Ⓜ Taereung ⊙ 9am-6pm Tue-Sun ⊗ Jan 1 Ⓦ museum.seoul.go.kr/sulm

Learning about kings and historic battles is all well and good, but what if you want to know which instant noodles Seoulites ate in the 1980s or what Kia's first car looked like? The Seoul Urban Life Museum eschews so-called "historical figures" to explore the lives of everyday folk in the Korean capital from the 1950s onwards. Exhibitions cover everything from toys and school uniforms to wedding culture, and there's a reproduction of an old alleyway that you can walk through. The museum is a fun, fascinating, and totally relatable experience. Notably, all items on display here were purchased from or donated by Seoul citizens.

→ The huge temple bell at historic Gilsangsa Temple

⑤
Seodaemun Prison History Hall
서대문형무소역사관

📍 H2 🏛 251 Tongil-ro
Ⓜ Dongnimmun 🕐 9:30am-6pm daily (Nov-Feb: to 5pm)
🚫 Jan 1, Seollal, Chuseok
🌐 sphh.sscmc.or.kr

The peaceful appearance of this complex of red-brick buildings belies its terrible history. It was built as a prison by the Japanese in the early stages of the colonial period, and though the original design was meant to hold just 500 inmates, by 1919 there were 3,000 crammed between its walls.

Today the site functions as a museum and memorial to political prisoners held here during the occupation. Displays provide information on resistance movements and some of Korea's most famous independence activists, among them the schoolgirl Yu Gwan-sun, who, after organizing protests in her hometown of Cheonan, was imprisoned and tortured to death here in 1920. Visitors can step into the cramped cells prisoners lived in, see where they were forced to produce goods for the Japanese war effort during World War II, and view the harrowing building used for executions. Sadly, the prison's story did not finish with the end of colonial rule. After liberation, Korea's military regimes locked up pro-democracy activists here. The prison was finally shuttered in 1987.

←

A steep ascent in Bukhansan National Park, amid a riot of fall colors

⑥
Gilsangsa Temple
길상사

📍 J2 🏛 68 Seonjam-ro 5gil
Ⓜ Hansung University
📧 🌐 gilsangsa.or.kr

Nestled in the foothills of Seongbuk-dong, Gilsangsa has perhaps the most interesting backstory of any Korean temple. It was originally a restaurant and *gisaeng* house, where women trained in poetry and music entertained guests. In 1987, the restaurant's owner, Kim Young-han, sought to donate the complex to the revered Buddhist monk Beopjeong, moved by his writings on non-possession. It took her years to convince him to accept the property, which was valued at 100 billion won, or $130 million in today's currency, but eventually he relented and, in 1995, reopened it as a temple.

⑦
Seongsu
성수

📍 K3 Ⓜ Seongsu, Ttukseom, Seoul Forest

Once an industrial area of factories and shoemakers, Seongsu is now one of Seoul's trendiest neighborhoods, with stylish restaurants and shops occupying its warehouses. **SM Entertainment** moved its headquarters here a few years ago, and K-pop fans of aespa, Girls' Generation, and EXO will want to make a pilgrimage to the label's KWANGYA shop.

Seongsu's western corner is taken up by Seoul Forest (서울숲), actually one of the city's biggest and best parks.

SM Entertainment

🏛 83-21 Wangsimni-ro
Ⓜ Seoul Forest
🕐 10:30am-8pm daily
🌐 smentertainment.com

THE K-POP ECONOMY

K-pop's cultural impact is matched only by its economic one. Boy band BTS alone contributes around $3.5 billion to Korea's economy annually, putting the group nearly on a par with Korean Air. As more young people chase K-pop dreams, private academies have sprung up to offer singing, dancing, and acting lessons. The tourism industry has been reshaped by the genre, too, with popular Seoul neighborhoods like Seongsu and Gangnam (p100) now home to dance studios and idol makeover services that let fans get a taste of the K-pop lifestyle.

EXPERIENCE Beyond the Center

8
Gangnam
강남

📍 K4 Ⓜ Gangnam

It's hard to imagine now, but until the 1970s, the land that makes up Gangnam was mostly farmland. Today, this moneyed neighborhood of sweeping boulevards and gleaming skyscrapers is a hub of businesses, luxury shopping, and ultra-posh apartments. Although Gangnam, meaning "south of the river," can describe everything on that side of the Hangang, it typically refers to Seoul's southeastern districts, especially the neighborhood surrounding the eponymous station. You'll find a bevy of bars, brunch spots, and chain stores on and around Gangnam-daero between Gangnam and Sinnonhyeon stations, while farther north, the Sinsa and Apgujeong neighborhoods are home to luxury brands and K-pop-related sites like K-Star Road.

TOP 3 POP CULTURE EXPERIENCES

Stroll K-Star Road
Statues representing famous K-pop groups on Apgujeong-ro make a great photo-op.

Take a K-pop Dance Class
📍 33 Ttukseom-ro 13-gil 🌐 1milliondance.com
Learn the moves from a professional choreographer at 1MILLION Dance Studio.

Pick up Idols' Beauty Secrets
🌐 seoulhallyu.com
Sign up for a makeup class through the Seoul Hallyu program.

9
Bongeunsa Temple
봉은사

📍 L4 📍 531 Bongeunsa-ro Ⓜ Bongeunsa 🕐 5am–10pm daily 🌐 bongeunsa.org

Just across the street from the enormous Starfield Coex Mall, Bongeunsa Temple is an island of tranquility amid Gangnam's currents of consumerism. The complex was built slightly to the southwest in 794 CE and moved to its present location in the mid-16th century. Much of it had to be reconstructed after the Korean War. The temple is most well known for its 75-ft- (23-m-) high statue of the Maitreya Buddha and its collection of woodblock carvings of the Avatamsaka Sutra. Thanks to its handy central location, Bongeunsa is also a popular Templestay venue (p165).

Bongeunsa Temple and (inset) details from the temple's exterior

10

War and Women's Human Rights Museum
전쟁과여성인권박물관

📍 H3 📍 12 World Cup Buk-ro 11-gil Ⓜ Mangwon, Hongik University 🕐 10am–6pm Tue–Sat 🚫 Jan 1, Seollal, Buddha's Birthday, Chuseok, Christmas 🌐 womenandwar.net

This affecting museum is dedicated to the so-called "comfort women," young women and girls who were forced into sexual slavery by the Japanese military between the early 1930s and the end of World War II. Of the estimated 200,000 victims across Asia, Koreans made up the largest cohort, and the museum does a superb job of not only documenting the historical record, but also telling their personal stories. Tickets are printed with an introduction to an individual *halmoni*, or "grandmother," as the survivors are affectionately known, and interactive installations throughout let you hear their stories in their own words.

Seonyudo Park
선유도공원

G3 343 Seonyu-ro Seonyu 6am-midnight parks.seoul.go.kr/seonyudo

From 1978 to 2000, this island in the middle of the Hangang River was the site of a large water purification plant, but in 2002 it was turned into a public park. Instead of removing all the industrial infrastructure, though, the city incorporated much of it into the park's design. Hulking concentration tanks have been turned into an amphitheater and playground, and a former chemical settling basin is now a multilevel garden where ladders and catwalks let you move between bamboo groves and elevated concrete water channels populated by lily pads and water striders. There's also a greenhouse and an exhibition space.

Noryangjin Fisheries Wholesale Market
노량진수산물도매시장

H4 674 Nodeul-ro Noryangjin Daily susansijang.co.kr

This market handles upward of some 250 tons of marine products every day, or roughly half of all the seafood that gets sold in Seoul. It's a watery marvel of mackerel, crabs, clams, sea cucumbers, seaweed, and anything else you can pull out of the sea, all overseen by a small army of rubber-gloved fishmongers. Foodies can buy what they want to eat on the first floor and then take it up to one of the restaurants on the second floor to have it turned into sashimi or *haemultang*, a spicy seafood soup. Lively wholesale auctions are held from midnight to around 4am.

EAT

Gangchon Ssambap
강촌쌈밥

It's all about comfort food here. Try the *ssambap* - rice and side dishes - wrapped in leaves and served with boiled pork and stew.

J1 9 Pyeongchang-30-gil 02 395 6467

Hanokjib
한옥집

This old-school joint specializes in *kimchi-jjim* (savory braised pork and aged kimchi).

J2 12 Tongil-ro 9-gil 0507 1391 8653

Mingles
밍글스

The two-Michelin-star Mingles takes Korean food to elevated places.

K3 19 Dosan-daero 67-gil restaurant-mingles.com

Mongsil Korean Beef
몽실이네 토종한우

Fresh cuts of *hanwoo*, high-quality Korean beef, straight from the market next door.

K2 70 Majang-ro 35-gil 02 2299 3365

Monk's Butcher
몽크스부처

Upscale vegan and vegetarian dining, with curries, pastas, and seasonal offerings.

K3 228-1 Itaewon-ro 02 790 1108

↑ Seonyudo Park, an island in the middle of the Hangang River

⑬
Seolleung and Jeongneung Royal Tombs
선릉과 정릉

📍L4 🏠1 Seolleung-ro 100-gil Ⓜ Seolleung ⏰6am-9pm Tue-Sun (Nov-Feb: from 6:30am) 🌐royal.khs.go.kr

Seolleung and Jeongneung are the most accessible of the Joseon royal tombs, occupying several square blocks in Gangnam. Seolleung, on the west side of the complex, is the burial site of King Seongjong (r. 1469–94) and Queen Jeonghyeon. Jeongneung, on the east side, is the tomb of their son, King Jungjong (r. 1506–44). The tombs are flanked by stone statues of military and civil officials. The actual burial sites take up only a small portion of the grounds, the rest of which

Did You Know?
Elevated sections of paths at royal tombs are called *sindo* and are reserved for spirits.

is occupied by forested hills and walking paths perfect for a contemplative stroll.

---

⑭
Lotte World Tower
롯데월드타워

📍M4 🏠300 Olympic-ro Ⓜ Jamsil ⏰Hours vary, check website 🌐lwt.co.kr

Korea's tallest building and the sixth-tallest in the world, reaching 1,821 ft (555 m), Lotte World Tower and the attached Lotte World Mall hold several notable sites. The **Lotte World Aquarium** (롯데월드 아쿠아리움) is Seoul's largest and home to 650 marine species. The **Lotte Museum of Art** (롯데뮤지엄) hosts exhibitions that range from historic jewelry to the work of the French street artist JR. And **Seoul Sky** (서울스카이) encompasses a cafe, restaurant, and indoor and outdoor observation decks, spanning the tower's 118th to 123rd floors. Views are accordingly epic.

Lotte Museum of Art
 🏠Lotte World Tower, 7F ⏰10:30am-7pm daily 🌐lottemuseum.com

Lotte World Aquarium
🏠Lotte World Mall, B1F ⏰10am-8pm (Fri-Sun & holidays until 10pm) 🌐lotteworld.com

Seoul Sky
🏠Lotte World Tower, B1F ⏰10:30am-10pm (Fri & Sat: to 11pm) 🌐lotteworld.com

---

⑮
Olympic Park
올림픽공원

📍M4 🏠424 Olympic-ro Ⓜ Mongchontoseong, Hanseong Baekje, Olympic Park ⏰5am-10pm daily 🌐ksponco.or.kr/olympicpark

This sprawling park on Seoul's southeastern edge is one of its nicest green spaces. Built for the 1988 Olympics, the athletic facilities continue to host sporting events, while Olympic Hall is a major concert venue. At the park's main entrance, visitors are greeted by the winged World Peace Gate, past which are

---

STAY

Owall Hotel
오월호텔

Austere lines and minimalism are taken to the max in this zen escape amid Gangnam's hubbub. Rooms come with privtae terraces.

📍K4 🏠27 Eonju-ro 85-gil 🌐owallhotel.com

Ryse
라이즈

A magazine library, skate shop, hip-hop cocktail lounge, and creative rooms capture Hongdae's free-wheeling spirit.

📍H3 🏠130 Yanghwa-ro 🌐rysehotel.com

expansive lawns, an artificial lake, a rose garden, and a wildflower hill painted with red poppies in spring and yellow cosmos in fall.

The northern portion of the park is dominated by the remains of Mongchontoseong (몽촌토성), an earthen fortress built by the Baekje kingdom, whose capital was located in the area for several centuries until 475. Walking paths run along the fortification, which is surrounded by a moat. On the park's south side, the **Seoul Baekje Museum** (한성백제박물관) illuminates the kingdom's history and how its people worked, prayed, played, and fought. Nearby is the **Seoul Olympic Museum of Art** (SOMA) (소마미술관), which is best known for its large sculpture park. Visitors interested in the 1988 Summer Games should check out the **Seoul Olympic Museum** (서울올림픽기념관) when it reopens after renovations in 2026.

Seoul Baekje Museum

71 Wiryeseong-daero Hanseong Baekje Hours vary, check website Mon, Jan 1 baekje-museum.seoul.go.kr

Seoul Olympic Museum

424 Olympic-ro Mongchontoseong 10am-6pm Tue-Sun Jan 1, Seollal, Chuseok 88olympic.kspo.or.kr

Seoul Olympic Museum of Art

 51 Wiryeseong-daero Hanseong Baekje 10am-6pm Tue-Sun Jan 1, Seollal, Chuseok soma.kspo.or.kr

---

16

Museum of Korean Traditional Music
국악박물관

K5 2364 Nambusunhwan-ro 10am-6pm Tue-Sun Jan 1 gugak.go.kr

This engrossing museum delves into the world of *gugak*, or traditional music. You can listen to a wide range of instruments and learn about how they were performed in different contexts,

↓ Lotte World Tower, rising above the other buildings in central Seoul

↑ A *janggu*, on display at the Museum of Korean Traditional Music

from festivals to formal ceremonies. Other displays explore the traditional notation methods and the lives of master musicians. Interactive areas allow visitors to play percussion instruments and create their own digital ensemble. If you like what you hear, the National Gugak Center *(2364 Nambusunhwan-ro)* holds *gugak* concerts at 3pm every Saturday.

17

Seoul Arts Center
예술의전당

K5 2406 Nambusunhwan-ro Nambu Bus Terminal Hours vary, check website sac.or.kr

A major visual and performing arts venue, the Seoul Arts Center (SAC) contains a 2,505-seat concert hall, an opera house, an intimate theater, and four other performance spaces. Tickets for plays and concerts can be purchased in person or online *(global interpark.com)*. The venue's Hangaram Design Museum (한가람디자인미술관) and the multi-gallery Hangaram Art Museum (한가람미술관) both host rotating exhibitions. Also in the SAC is the Seoul Calligraphy Art Museum (서울서예박물관), the world's first museum dedicated to calligraphy. Today, it has around 1,300 pieces of contemporary calligraphy pieces from East Asia.

A LONG WALK
HANYANGDOSEONGP

Distance 11.6 miles (18.6 km) **Terrain** Mountain paths, city streets **Stopping-off points** Namdaemun Market and the cafés along the Seongbukcheon Stream **Nearest metro station** Dongdaemun **Nearest bus stop** Yoon Dong-ju Literature Museum

Hanyangdoseong, the Seoul fortress wall, divides the capital's historic center from its more modern additions. Although parts of the wall have been lost since it was completed in 1396, most of it remains, either in its original or reconstructed form. Its path runs across mountain ridges and through bustling urban neighborhoods, and walking its circumference is a fascinating way to experience Seoul in all its complexity. With an early enough start, you can hike the wall in a day, or you can tackle its six sections individually, all of which take between one and three hours to walk.

The **January 21 Incident Pine Tree** *is pocked with bullet holes from a 1968 gun battle between South Korean soldiers and North Korean commandos attempting to assassinate President Park Chung-hee.*

Guksadang *is Seoul's most important shamanist shrine. Female shamans called* mudang *regularly carry out rituals that seek to connect with the spirits of the deceased here.*

↑ Culture Station Seoul 284, occupying Seoul's former train station

Seoul's former train station is now **Culture Station Seoul 284** *(seoul284.org), a fine setting for art exhibitions.*

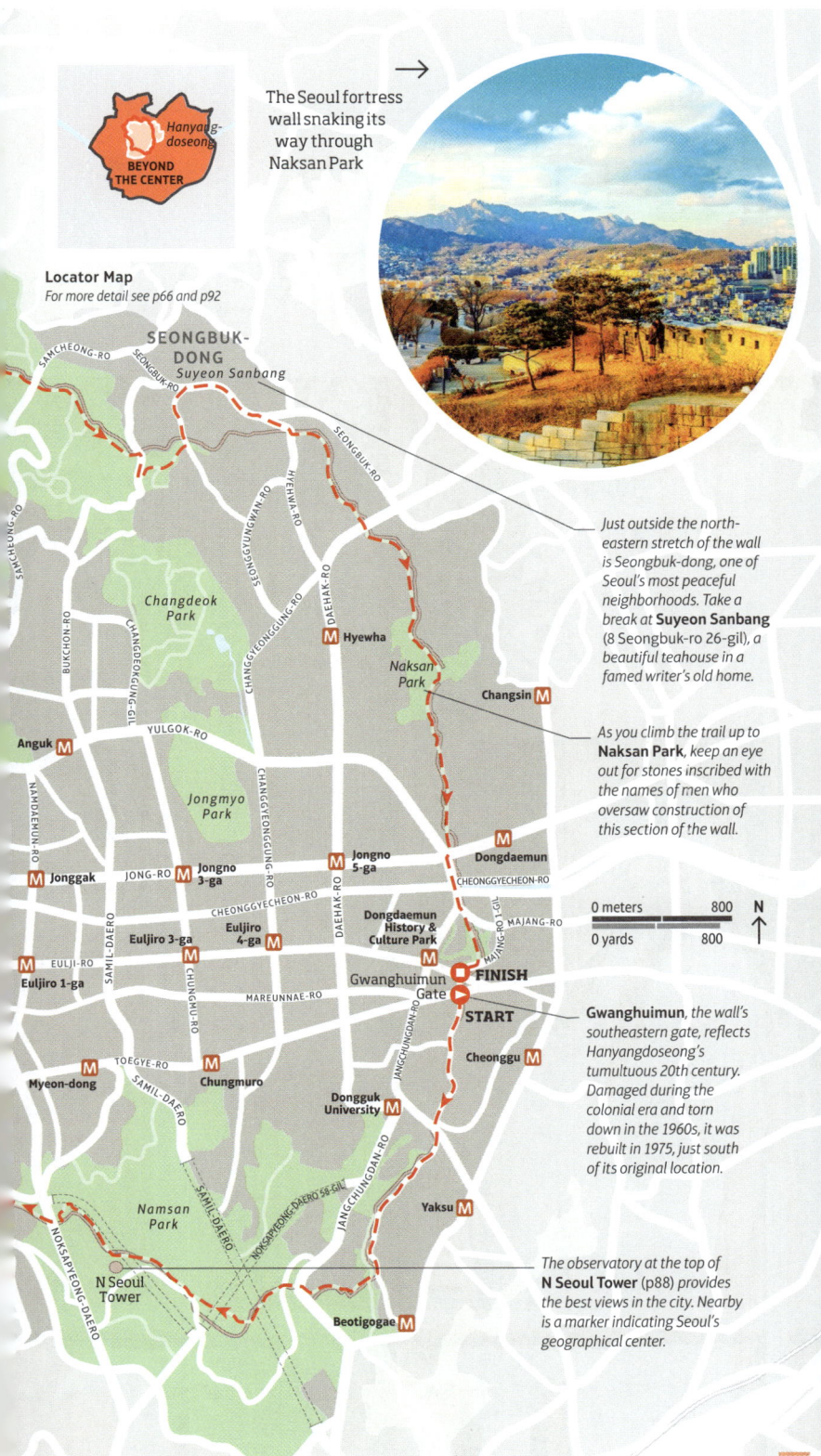

The Seoul fortress wall snaking its way through Naksan Park

Locator Map
For more detail see p66 and p92

Just outside the north-eastern stretch of the wall is Seongbuk-dong, one of Seoul's most peaceful neighborhoods. Take a break at **Suyeon Sanbang** (8 Seongbuk-ro 26-gil), a beautiful teahouse in a famed writer's old home.

As you climb the trail up to **Naksan Park**, keep an eye out for stones inscribed with the names of men who oversaw construction of this section of the wall.

Gwanghuimun, the wall's southeastern gate, reflects Hanyangdoseong's tumultuous 20th century. Damaged during the colonial era and torn down in the 1960s, it was rebuilt in 1975, just south of its original location.

The observatory at the top of **N Seoul Tower** (p88) provides the best views in the city. Nearby is a marker indicating Seoul's geographical center.

105

EXPERIENCE SOUTH KOREA

Ssanggyesa Buddhist temple, Gyeongsang-do

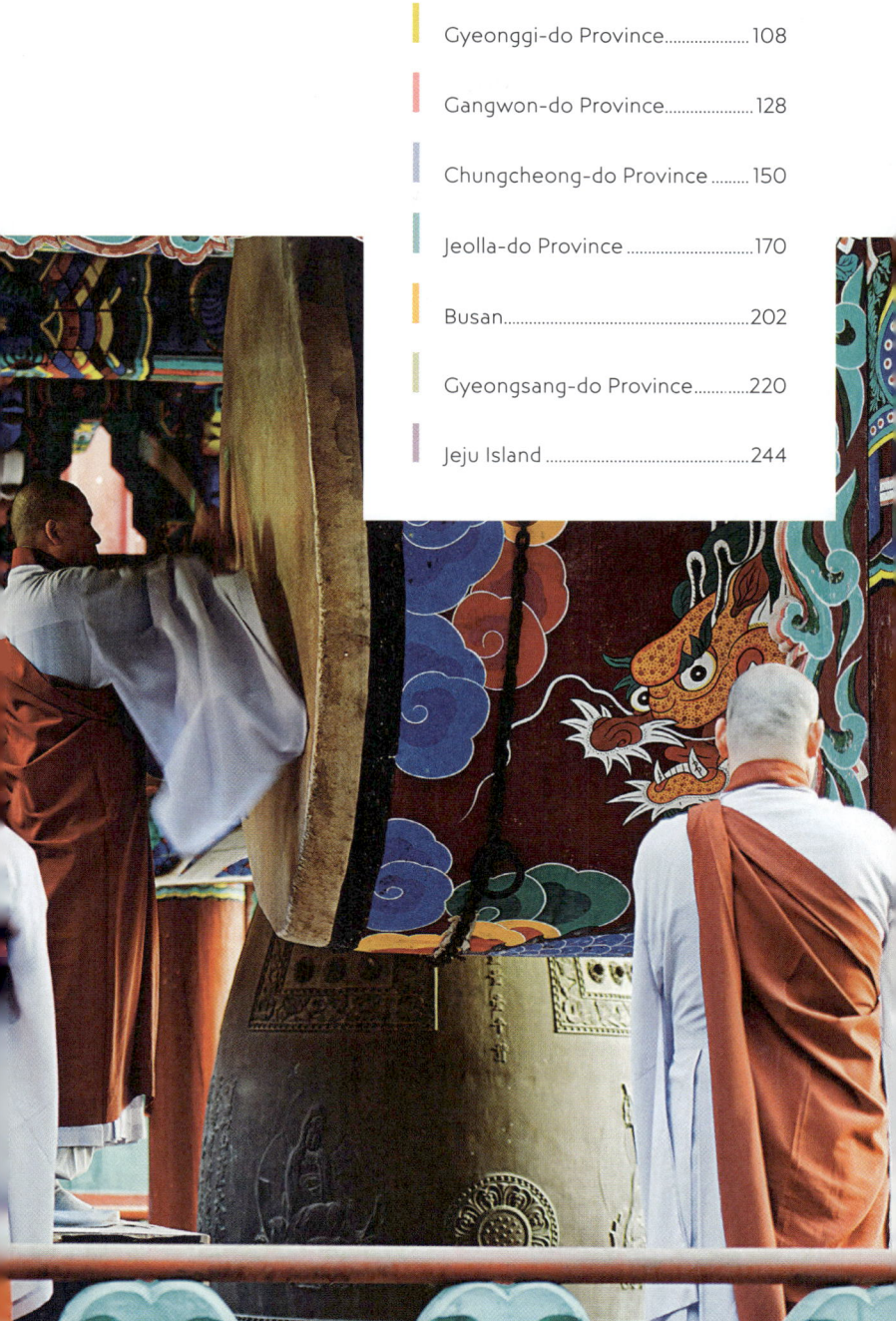

Gyeonggi-do Province	108
Gangwon-do Province	128
Chungcheong-do Province	150
Jeolla-do Province	170
Busan	202
Gyeongsang-do Province	220
Jeju Island	244

Overlooking Songdo Central Park, Incheon

GYEONGGI-DO PROVINCE

Excavated relics show that people have been living in what's now Gyeonggi-do Province since the Paleolithic Age. In the 1st and 2nd centuries BCE, the region was home to a collection of small tribes known as the Mahan Confederacy, one of which, Baekje, would emerge to establish a kingdom here in 18 BCE.

The name Gyeonggi means, roughly, "the land around the capital." The designation emerged not from the province's relation to Seoul, but to Kaesong, which was the primary seat of the Goryeo kingdom from 918 to 1392. When Goryeo collapsed and the newly established Joseon kingdom moved the palace to Seoul in 1394, Gyeonggi found that – despite the change in dynasties – its name remained as apt as ever.

Naturally, Gyeonggi-do's geographic relationship to Seoul has shaped its history. In the Joseon era, the province was both the capital's granary – its fertile plains producing rice, wheat, and barley – and the site of important military installations. As Seoul grew in the 20th century, Gyeonggi-do developed important transportation links and was filled with factories producing textiles, glass, and steel. Today, the province functions less like the land around the capital than like an extension of it, as cities such as Suwon, Paju, Bucheon, and Seongnam are seamlessly integrated with Seoul's transportation network, and thousands of commuters make the journey to the capital and back each day. Despite Incheon splintering off and being designated a self-governing city in 1981, Gyeonggi-do remains by far Korea's most populous province, home to 13 million residents.

GYEONGGI-DO PROVINCE

Must Sees
1. Incheon
2. The DMZ
3. Suwon Hwaseong Fortress

Experience More
4. Ganghwado Island
5. Heyri Art Valley
6. Paju Book City
7. Nam June Paik Art Center
8. Everland
9. Korean Folk Village
10. Yangsu-ri
11. Garden of Morning Calm
12. Seoul Grand Park
13. Gyeonggi Museum of Contemporary Ceramic Art
14. Namhansanseong Fortress
15. Donggureung

↑ Colorful entrance gate to Incheon's historic Chinatown

① INCHEON
인천

🅲2 🚌 21 miles (34 km) SW of Seoul 🚆 From Seoul 🚌 From Seoul ℹ️ 234 Incheon Tower-daero/271 Jemullyang-ro; itour.incheon.go.kr

Incheon has been the gateway to Korea ever since it opened as one of the country's first ports, back in 1883. Today, the city balances traces of the first Chinese, Japanese, and Western peoples who came ashore here with glittering testaments to its future ambitions.

① Chinatown
차이나타운

Ⓜ Incheon Station

Its entrance marked by a beautiful *pai-lou* gate, Incheon's Chinatown is the oldest and largest in Korea. Soon after the city's port opened, the area became a concession of the Qing Dynasty, and Chinese merchants began settling here. Some of their row houses still line the streets. One notable structure is the bright red **Uiseondang Temple** (의선당), founded by immigrants in 1883. Dragons curl along the roof, and statues of Chinese folk gods are enshrined inside. Korean tourists mainly come to Chinatown to eat, and you'll find restaurants everywhere serving their own take on *jjajangmyeon* (noodles in black bean sauce). The dish was invented at the (now closed) Gonghwachun restaurant, which occupied a handsome gray brick building that is now the **Jjajangmyeon Museum** (짜장면박물관). There's minimal English, but you don't need much to enjoy displays on instant *jjajangmyeon* packaging and the evolution of carriers used to deliver take-out orders. There's also a reproduction of the Gonghwachun's kitchen.

Uiseondang Temple
📍 34 Chinatown-ro

Jjajangmyeon Museum
📍 56-14 Chinatown-ro
🕘 9am–6pm Tue–Sun
🚫 Jan 1, Seollal, Chuseok

② Incheon Open Port
인천개항장

Ⓜ Incheon Station 🕘 9am–6pm Tue–Sun 🚫 Jan 1, Seollal, Chuseok

This area, which includes Chinatown, was where foreign traders, missionaries, adventurers, and sundry others settled when Incheon's port opened. Housed in a former Japanese bank, the **Incheon Open Port Modern**

BATTLE OF INCHEON

Caught off-guard by the North's invasion in June 1950, Korean and US forces had to do something drastic to avoid losing the Korean War. Their bold response was an amphibious landing behind enemy lines at Incheon. It worked, and within days of capturing the port, UN forces retook Seoul, turning the tide of the war.

Must See

Architecture Museum
(인천개항장 근대건축전시관) has scale models of local historic buildings and covers the port's transformation from a minor fishing village into a boom-town. Almost next door is the beautiful **Incheon Open Port Museum** (인천개항박물관). Erected in 1899, the one-story Renaissance-style structure has a small dome and an interior with chandeliers and arched windows. On the same street, the **Daebul Hotel Exhibition Hall** (대불호텔전시관) occupies what was Korea's first Western-style hotel, opened in 1888. On display are re-creations of its old rooms, complete with gramophones. Connected to the hall is the Jung-gu Life History Museum (중구생활사전시관), which has reconstructions of a family home, barber shop, and the like from the 1960s and 70s. A block south, on Jemullyang-ro, Incheon Art Platform (인천아트플랫폼) houses a theater, and a number of galleries and studios in former warehouses.

Incheon Open Port Modern Architecture Museum
77 Sinpo-ro 23-beon-gil 9am–6pm Tue–Sun Jan 1, Seollal, Chuseok

Incheon Open Port Museum
89 Sinpo-ro 23-beon-gil 9am–6pm Tue–Sun Jan 1, Seollal, Chuseok

↑ The observation tower at Wolmi Park, offering spectacular views

Daebul Hotel Exhibition Hall
101 Sinpo-ro 23-beon-gil 9am–6pm Tue–Sun Jan 1, Seollal, Chuseok

Wolmido Island
월미도

Now united with the mainland, this former island in Incheon's harbor has long been a center of recreation. Most of it is taken up by Wolmi Park (월미공원), which has gardens, walking paths, and an observation tower. On the park's southern edge, the interesting **Museum of Korea Emigration History** (한국이민사박물관) is devoted to the stories of those who left the country from the 1800s onward: to Hawaii to work on sugar plantations; to Germany to work as miners and nurses; and to many other places. Another section focuses on the increasing number of immigrants now coming to Korea in search of a better life.

Running along Wolmido's western shore is Wolmido Culture Street (월미문화의거리), a seaside promenade lined with cafés, restaurants, and arcades.

Museum of Korea Emigration History
329 Wolmi-ro 9am–6pm Tue–Sun Jan 1

Songdo
송도

Ⓜ Central Park

Built on land reclaimed from the Yellow Sea, Songdo didn't exist a few decades ago. The aim was to turn it into an international business hub and Korea's city of the future with glittering skyscrapers and traffic-flow sensors embedded in the streets, but it hasn't attracted as many residents as hoped, and it can feel soulless. Still, the large Songdo Central Park (송도 센트럴파크), with its seawater canal and futuristic Tri-Bowl performance space, is deserving of a few hours.

A SHORT WALK
HISTORIC INCHEON

Distance 1 mile (1.6 km) **Time** 35 minutes
Nearest metro Incheon Station

When Japan's gunboat diplomacy forced Joseon Korea to open to trade in the late 19th century, Chinese, Japanese, and Western peoples poured into the newly established port at Incheon. These newcomers quickly put their stamp on the city, setting up concessions with their own laws and consulates and erecting buildings in their native styles. A walk through Incheon's historic Open Port district reveals their lasting influence, turning up historic structures, culinary legacies, and a time-capsule feel you won't find anywhere else in the country.

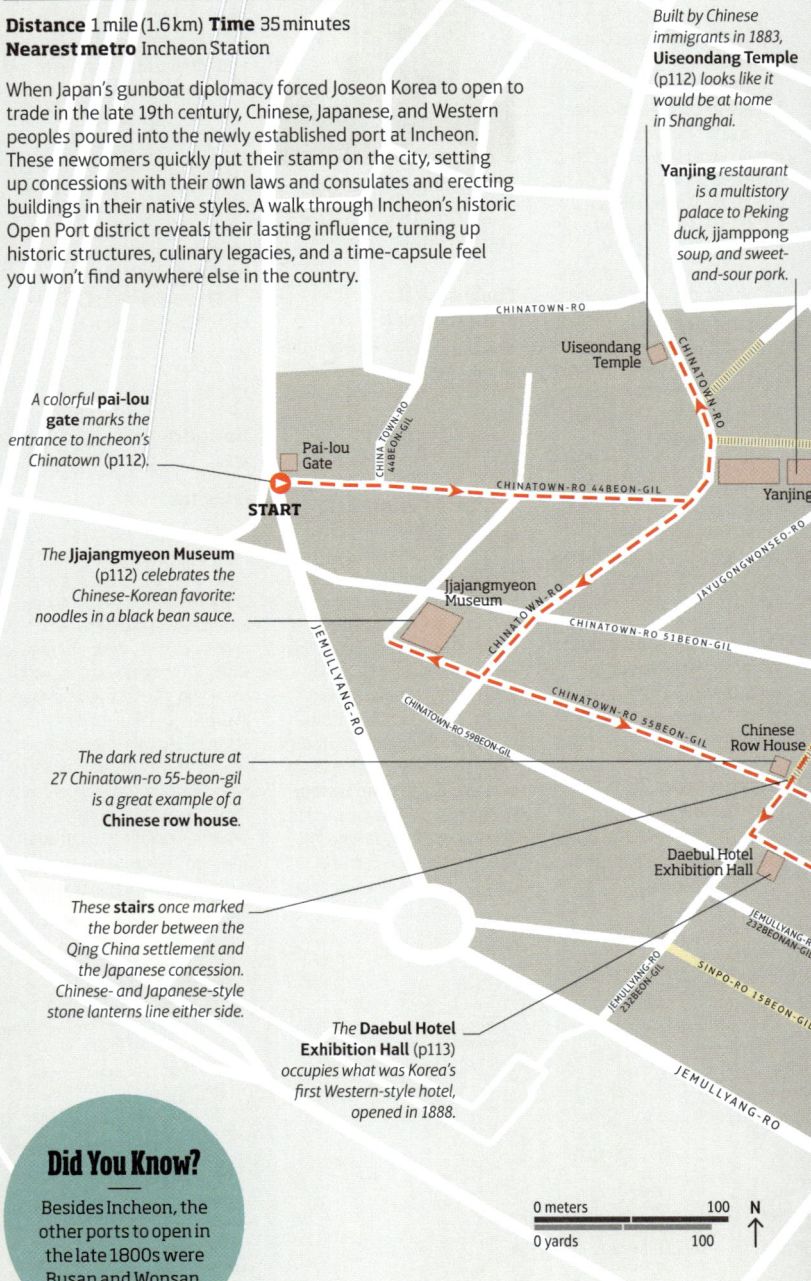

Built by Chinese immigrants in 1883, **Uiseondang Temple** (p112) looks like it would be at home in Shanghai.

Yanjing restaurant is a multistory palace to Peking duck, jjamppong soup, and sweet-and-sour pork.

A colorful **pai-lou gate** marks the entrance to Incheon's Chinatown (p112).

The **Jjajangmyeon Museum** (p112) celebrates the Chinese-Korean favorite: noodles in a black bean sauce.

The dark red structure at 27 Chinatown-ro 55-beon-gil is a great example of a **Chinese row house**.

These **stairs** once marked the border between the Qing China settlement and the Japanese concession. Chinese- and Japanese-style stone lanterns line either side.

The **Daebul Hotel Exhibition Hall** (p113) occupies what was Korea's first Western-style hotel, opened in 1888.

Did You Know?

Besides Incheon, the other ports to open in the late 1800s were Busan and Wonsan.

↑ Decorative stairs leading from Chinatown to Freedom Park

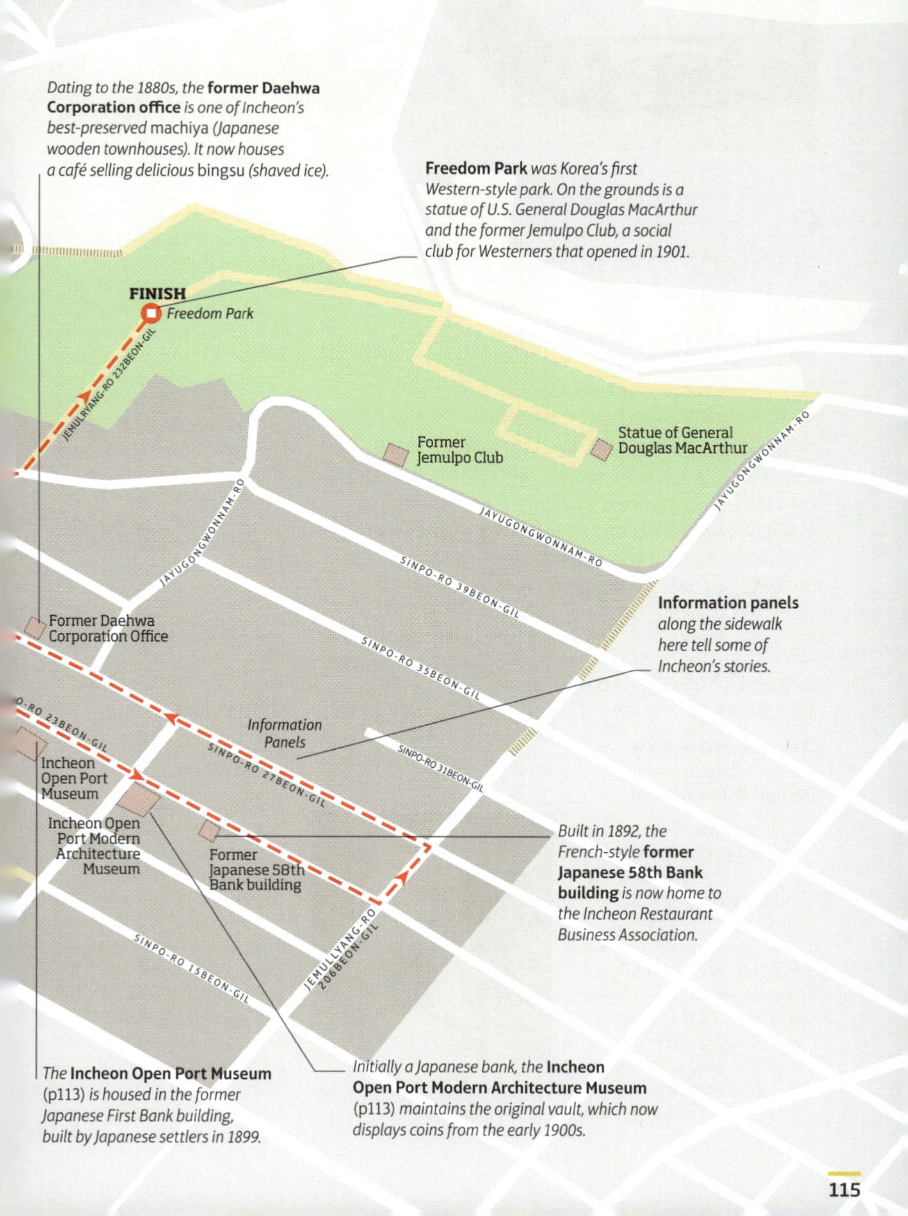

Locator Map
For more detail see p113

Dating to the 1880s, the **former Daehwa Corporation office** is one of Incheon's best-preserved machiya (Japanese wooden townhouses). It now houses a café selling delicious bingsu (shaved ice).

Freedom Park was Korea's first Western-style park. On the grounds is a statue of U.S. General Douglas MacArthur and the former Jemulpo Club, a social club for Westerners that opened in 1901.

Information panels along the sidewalk here tell some of Incheon's stories.

Built in 1892, the French-style **former Japanese 58th Bank building** is now home to the Incheon Restaurant Business Association.

The **Incheon Open Port Museum** (p113) is housed in the former Japanese First Bank building, built by Japanese settlers in 1899.

Initially a Japanese bank, the **Incheon Open Port Modern Architecture Museum** (p113) maintains the original vault, which now displays coins from the early 1900s.

THE DMZ
비무장지대

C1 **32 miles (51 km) NW of Seoul**
148-40 Imjingak-ro, Paju; www.panmuntour.go.kr

Dividing North and South Korea is the Demilitarized Zone (DMZ), a 2.5-mile- (4-km-) wide, 155-mile- (250-km-) long strip studded with guard posts and land mines. A visit here is both a fascinating and sobering look at the Korean War's painful legacy. Sites within the DMZ can only be visited on an organized tour.

①
Imjingak Tourist Area
임진각 관광단지

31 miles (50 km) NW of Seoul **Imjingang Station** **From Seoul**

Just outside the DMZ, this park on the banks of the Imjingang River is as far as you can travel without a guided tour. Its grounds feature a collection of memorials and Korean War remnants. The Imjingak Peace Bridge (임진각 자유의다리), the rebuilt half of a railway span that was destroyed in the war, crosses the river, while alongside it the concrete remnants of its other half poke up out of the water. The best views of the bridge are to be had from the Paju Imjingak Peace Gondola (파주임진각평화곤돌라), which you can ride across the river and back. Not far from the gondola's southern terminus

is a locomotive that came under attack as it was carrying supplies to UN troops in Pyongyang, now rusted out and riddled with over 1,000 bullet holes. Near that is Mangbaedan, a memorial altar used by North Korean refugees and their descendants for ancestral rites, as division makes visiting their relatives' tombs impossible. Also within the complex is Imjingak Pyeonghwa Nuri Park (임진각 평화누리), a peaceful expanse of grass lawns and art installations.

↑ The "30 Years Lost" memorial, one of several at Imjingak

Dorasan Peace Park
도라산 평화공원

32 miles (52 km) NW of Seoul

Dorasan Peace Park focuses largely on the DMZ's ecological value. Left mostly untouched by humans for 70 years, the buffer zone has turned into a haven for wildlife, a small silver lining in the strip's otherwise tragic story. Visitors will find exhibits on the DMZ's ecology and a pond shaped like the Korean peninsula. There's also an observation deck with telescopes that let you peer at the North Korean city of Kaesong and statues of former DPRK

Conference Row in the JSA, where talks between the two Koreas take place

④ Joint Security Area
공동경비구역

📍 **37 miles (60 km) NW of Seoul**

Commonly referred to as Panmunjom (판문점), for the former village where the armistice ending Korean War hostilities was signed, the Joint Security Area (JSA) is where North and South Korean leaders have historically met for negotiations. It's also the only place in the DMZ where DPRK and ROK (South Korea) troops come face to face.

The JSA can only be visited on an organized tour. The first stop is usually Camp Bonifas, where you'll be briefed on the JSA's history and tour regulations. Visitors can also check out the world's most infamous golf course, a one-hole par-three surrounded by land mines. At the actual border, you can view DPRK soldiers at the steps of Panmungak, a hulking Stalinist structure, and spot the North Korean flag flying above the village of Kijong-dong. Within one of the negotiation buildings, you can even, for just a moment, step across the border.

Must See

DMZ TOURS

Sites in the DMZ can only be visited on half- or full-day guided tours. Recommended operators include VIP Travel *(vviptravel.com)*, KORIDOOR Tours *(koridoor.co.kr)*, and Panmunjom Tour *(panmuntour.go.kr)*, which is run by the Ministry of Unification. Note that any rise in political tensions can see tours canceled at short notice. You must bring your passport.

Did You Know?

It's estimated that 30,000 soldiers could have passed through the Third Tunnel within one hour.

(North Korea) leader Kim Il Sung. The park can only be visited on a guided tour.

③ The Third Tunnel
제3땅굴

📍 **34 miles (55 km) NW of Seoul**

When the DPRK engineer Kim Bu-seong defected in the mid-1970s, he brought with him intel on a 6.5-ft- (2-m-) high, 6.5-ft- (2-m-) wide tunnel under construction by the North. It took South Korean authorities four years, but they finally uncovered it on October 17, 1978. As its name implies, it wasn't the only tunnel dug by the North for the purposes of espionage or, potentially, invasion. Visitors on tours can don hard hats and descend to explore a portion of the tunnel.

↑ The mighty perimeter walls of Suwon Hwaseong at sunset

SUWON HWASEONG FORTRESS
수원화성

Did You Know?
More than 700,000 people and 600 oxen were employed to build Hwaseong Fortress.

🅐 C2 📍 320-2 Yeongwha-dong, Suwon Ⓜ Maegyo Station 🚌 From Seoul 🕐 24 hr ℹ 138-5 Paldal-ro 1-ga, Suwon; swcf.or.kr

Completed in 1796, this magnificent fortress is the crowning achievement of Joseon Korea, a grand summation of the dynasty's scientific and bureaucratic accomplishments. It also happens to be one of history's great gestures of filial piety. Spend a day on its walls exploring Joseon heritage and taking in the views over Suwon.

① The Fortress Walls
요새의 성벽

In 1779, the Joseon king Jeongjo decided to move the tomb of his father, Crown Prince Sado, from Seoul to a more auspicious spot here on Hwasan Mountain. To complement the move, he commissioned this fortress, to both provide him with a place to stay when visiting his father's tomb and bolster national defenses.

Incorporating watchtowers, archery platforms, secret entrances, and other military structures, the fortress's walls run for 3.6 miles (5.7 km) over Paldalsan Mountain in the west and flatlands in the east. Though parts of the fortress were damaged or destroyed during the Japanese colonial period and the Korean War, most of the walls were restored to their original state in the 1970s. Paths along them make the entire fortress accessible for exploration.

② Paldalmun Gate
달문

The twin of Hwaseong's main gate, Janganmun (p120), the south gate is remarkably well preserved, and still has a board engraved with the names of its stonemason and construction supervisor. Unfortunately, the same can't be said for its adjoining walls. The gate now stands in the middle of a busy roundabout.

Must See

③ Changnyongmun Gate and Hwaseomun Gate
화 창룡문 서문

Hwaseong's east and west gates, respectively, are also twins. They take the same form as their northern and southern counterparts, but have only one-story wooden pavilions. The open space north of Changnyongmun was used for military training. Hwaseomun is notable for its adjacent brick watchtower, the first such structure to be built in the Joseon era. Together, the tower and gate form one of the fortress's most iconic images.

④ Hwahongmun Gate
화홍문

Formally known as Buksumun, this gate was constructed as a military facility but in practice was used mainly as a pleasure pavilion. One look and you'll see why. The wooden structure sits atop a seven-arch stone bridge across the Suwoncheon Stream, which flows through the center of the fortress. Just outside the gate is Yongyeon, a small pond with a tiny island in its middle. The surrounding park is filled with gracefully drooping willows and is often crowded with picnickers.

⑤ Hwaseong Haenggung Palace
화성행궁

📍 825 Jeongjo-ro, Suwon
🕐 9am-6pm daily (May-Oct: until 9:30pm Fri-Sun)

Located in the center of the fortress, this was where Jeongjo stayed when visiting his father's tomb. Naknamheon, a banquet hall, and Noraedang, a room where Jeongjo relaxed, are original 1794 structures; the rest, largely destroyed in the 1920s, are reconstructions. Hwaseong Haenggung is especially pretty lit up at night. Just outside its north wall is Hwaryeongjeon, a shrine where memorial services for King Jeongjo were held.

⑥   Suwon Hwaseong Museum
수원화성박물관

📍 21 Changnyong-daero, Suwon 🕐 9am-6pm Tue-Sun 🌐 smuseum.suwon.go.kr

Suwon Hwaseong fortress was the largest and most technologically advanced construction project in Joseon history. Jeongjo also took a progressive approach to the people who built it, paying all his laborers a daily wage – previously commoners had simply been forced to provide free labor for such projects. Incredibly, it was completed in less than three years.

A couple of blocks east of the palace, this museum explores this remarkable history. There's a scale model of the fortress and city as they looked when completed, as well as displays like a cross section of the western watchtower. Models of building equipment dot the grounds outside.

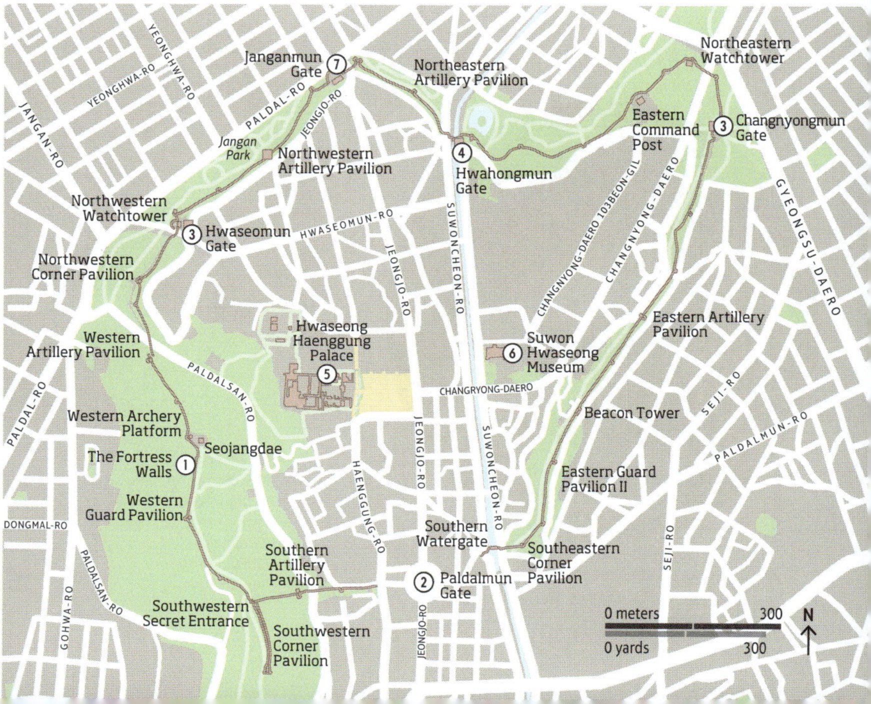

⑦ JANGANMUN GATE
장안문

At most Korean palaces and fortresses, the south gate is the main gate, but at Hwaseong it's the north gate, as King Jeongjo would arrive there first when visiting from the capital. Janganmun, whose name means "Gate of Perpetual Peace," was finished in 1794, the first of Hwaseong's gates to be completed. As handsome as it is imposing, it features a large stone base, a two-story wooden pavilion, and an *ongseong*, a semicircular defensive wall. The current wooden pavilion is a 1975 reconstruction; the original was destroyed during the Korean War.

> **INSIDER TIP**
> **Hot-Air Balloon Ride**
>
> Enjoy great views of Janganmun Gate and the fortress walls from 492 ft (150 m) up in Flying Suwon's tethered hot-air balloon. Tickets can be purchased online (flyingsuwon.com).

In the Japanese colonial era, this section of wall was torn down to expand the road linking Janganmun with Paldalmun Gate. It was partially restored in 2006.

↓ Illustration of Janganmun Gate

A semicircular defensive wall called an ongseong enabled troops to better defend the gate and to surround an enemy that breached the outer door.

↑ Looking toward the main entrance from beneath the two-story pavilion

Janganmun Gate was the main entrance to Hwaseong. This was where King Jeongjo and his retinue would pass on their way to Hwaseong Haenggung Palace (p119).

Must See

↑ Janganmun Gate, atmospherically lit up at night

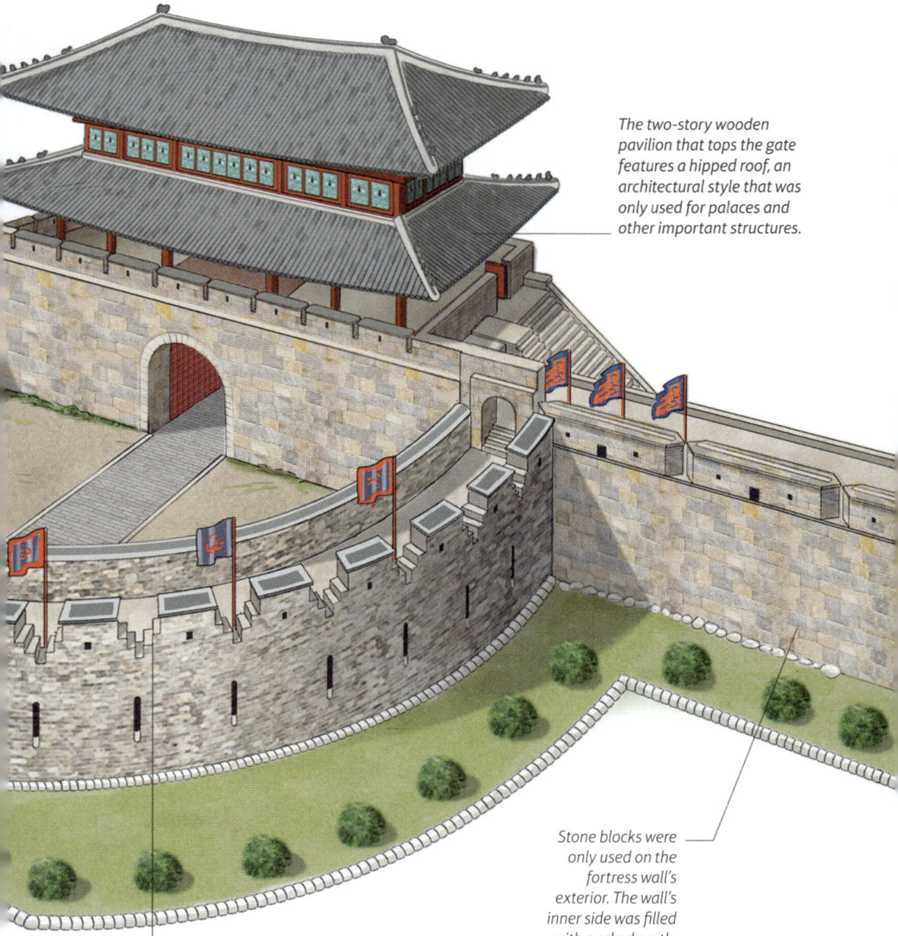

The two-story wooden pavilion that tops the gate features a hipped roof, an architectural style that was only used for palaces and other important structures.

Stone blocks were only used on the fortress wall's exterior. The wall's inner side was filled with packed earth.

Crenelations in the wall permitted archers to fire arrows down at approaching enemies.

121

The 17th-century Gwangseongbo Fort, site of the infamous Battle of Ganghwa

EXPERIENCE MORE

❹ Ganghwado Island
강화도

🅰 B2 🏠 34 miles (55 km) NW of Seoul 🚌 From Seoul, Incheon 🛈 43 Jungang-ro, Ganghwa; www.itour.incheon.go.kr

This large island's position where the Hangang River meets the Yellow Sea has long made it a place of both conflict and refuge. When the Mongols invaded in the 13th century, the Goryeo king Gojong relocated his capital here from Kaesong, in what's now North Korea. On the edge of the island's main town, Ganghwa-eup, the **Goryeogung Palace Site**'s (강화고려궁지) original buildings are gone, but a few Joseon-era structures still stand. Just up the road, the **Ganghwa History Museum** (강화역사박물관) tells the island's story since prehistoric times through excavated remains and folk items. The island's most arresting relic, though, is right outside: the Bugeun-ri Dolmen (부근리 지석묘), a 21-ft- (6.5-m-) long megalith resting atop two slightly smaller stones and marking a Bronze Age grave. It's only the most impressive of dozens of dolmens on the island.

Overlooking the strait separating the island from the mainland, **Gwangseongbo Fort** (광성보) was the site of a battle between Korean soldiers and American marines in 1871. A U.S. ship had attempted to force Korea open for trade, the Koreans burned the ship, and the Americans retaliated by attacking Ganghwado. Today you can view imposing gates, ramparts, and cannons at the fort, which was restored to its original condition in 1976.

Of course, Korea eventually opened to the outside world, and one of the most curious examples of the era's cultural mixing is the Ganghwa Anglican Church (성공회강화성당) at 10 Gwancheong-gil 27-beon-gil. Completed in 1900, its exterior was built in the Korean style, in the belief that would make locals more receptive to the foreign religion. If it weren't for the modest cross atop the traditional tile roof, you'd never know it was a church.

Confrontation is never far from mind on Ganghwado, which has only the Hangang to separate it from North Korea. At the island's northern tip is the **Ganghwa Peace Observatory** (강화평화전망대) where you can use a telescope to peer into the DPRK and view exhibitions on the country. Carry your passport when visiting.

On the opposite side of the island is **Jeondeungsa Temple** (전등사). Founded in 381 CE, it's Korea's oldest existing Buddhist temple, though most buildings date to the mid-Joseon period. The complex has a lovely setting within Samnangseong Fortress, and its buildings are decorated with intricate carvings.

> **Did You Know?**
> Over 500 people were needed to place the capstone on the Bugeun-ri Dolmen.

THE CARPENTER'S REVENGE

At the corners of Jeondeungsa's Daeungjeon Hall are a quartet of figures you wouldn't expect to find at a temple. Legend has it that a carpenter working on its construction fell in love with a local barmaid who then ran off with all his money. In an act of vindictiveness, he carved four figures of naked women in her likeness and placed them beneath Daeungjeon's eaves, to be forever condemned to hold up the hall's roof.

Southwest of the temple is another important, and even older, religious site. Sitting atop Mount Manisan (마니산), Chamseongdan is an altar where Dangun – the mythical founder of the Korean people when he established the kingdom of Gojoseon in 2333 BCE – is said to have made sacrifices to heaven.

Goryeogung Palace Site
394 Ganghwa-daero
9am-6pm daily

Ganghwa History Museum
994-19 Ganghwa-daero 9am-6pm Tue-Sun Jan 1, Seollal, Chuseok

Gwangseongbo Fort
833 Deokseong-ri

Ganghwa Peace Observatory
797 Jeonmangdae-ro 9am-6pm daily (Dec-Feb: to 5pm) ghss.or.kr

Jeondeungsa Temple
37-41 Jeondeungsa-ro Daily: summer 8am-6:30pm; winter 8:30am-6pm

⑤
Heyri Art Valley
헤이리예술마을

C2 70-21 Heyrimaeul-gil, Paju From Seoul Hours vary by venue heyri.net

Nearly 400 painters, sculptors, writers, and other artists live or work in Heyri Art Valley, a cultural complex that opened on the banks of the Imjingang River in 2003. Walking paths connect galleries, studios, and performance spaces, and exhibitions feature work by both domestic and international artists. With so much art on display, style and quality varies widely; some is astonishing, some is pure kitsch. As intriguing as the art is the architecture, with many of the village's eco-friendly buildings designed by top Korean architects. Numerous restaurants and cafés provide opportunities for breaks.

⑥
Paju Book City
파주출판도시

C2 145 Hoedong-gil, Paju From Seoul Hours vary, check website pajubookcity.org

With close to 1,000 publishing houses, bookbinders, libraries, bookshops, and other book-related businesses, Paju Book City is a reader's paradise, but bibliophiles needn't be Korean speakers to find inky charms aplenty. Peruse the **Book City Letterpress Museum** (출판도시 활판인쇄박물관), which displays printing equipment, including 35 million metal character blocks, or curl up with a good book in the Asia Publication Culture and Information Center's **Forest of Wisdom** (지혜의숲), a library with floor-to-ceiling shelves holding tens of thousands of titles.

Book City Letterpress Museum
9am-6pm daily Seollal, Chuseok letterpressmuseum.co.kr

Forest of Wisdom
10am-8pm daily forestofwisdom.or.kr

↑ The well-stacked shelves of the Forest of Wisdom, a haven for book lovers

↑ The Sky Way chairlift at Everland, linking the American and European Adventure zones

7

Nam June Paik Art Center
백남준아트센터

C2 ❏ 10 Paiknamjune-ro, Yongin Ⓜ Giheung Station
⏱ 10am–6pm Tue–Sun
🚫 Jan 1, Seollal, Chuseok
🌐 njp.ggcf.kr

Nam June Paik was Korea's most important modern artist, having more or less invented the medium of video art. Opened in 2008, two years after his death, this art gallery celebrates the visionary's art and influence in a large collection of his works, both digital and analog, alongside works by artists he inspired. Rotating exhibitions might look back at seminal creations in Paik's oeuvre or showcase performances by contemporary international artists who have picked up his boundary-pushing mantle. Admission is free, though special exhibitions attract a fee. Guided tours are conducted daily; they are only in Korean, but English-language audio guides are available.

8

Everland
헤리예술마을

C2 ❏ 199 Everland-ro, Yongin Ⓜ Jeondae-Everland Station
⏱ Hours vary, check website 🌐 everland.com

Samsung-owned Everland is Korea's biggest amusement park, a sprawling playground of rollercoasters, thrill rides, character parades, carnival games, and sugary snacks. The park is divided into five themed areas – Global Fair, American Adventure, European Adventure, Magic Land, and Zootopia – and hosts festivals throughout the year to celebrate spring flowers, Halloween, and the like. It's all great fun, but be prepared for some serious crowds if you show up on a summer weekend.

Right next to Everland is Caribbean Bay (캐리비안베이), a large water park with wave pools, waterslides, spa and sauna facilities, and plenty more. An indoor section means you can splash year-round.

Also on the resort grounds are the **Hoam Museum of Art** (호암미술관) and **Heewon Garden** (희원). The Hoam is the sister institution of Seoul's Leeum Museum of Art (p89) and displays the private collection of Samsung's founder, Lee Byung-chul. The impressive assembly focuses on Korean art and covers painting, furniture, and Buddhist sculpture. Outside the museum, Heewon is an exemplar of traditional garden design. Meander through the plum tree grove and past small ponds, and admire how the garden blends with its natural surroundings.

Hoam Museum of Art and Heewon Garden

❏ 38 Everland-ro 562-beon-gil, Yongin Ⓜ Jeondae-Everland Station
⏱ 10am–6pm Tue–Sun
🚫 Jan 1, Seollal, Chuseok
🌐 leeumhoam.org

> **Did You Know?**
> Nam June Paik coined the term "electronic superhighway" in 1974.

→ The Korean Folk Village, where *(inset)* visitors can see traditional music performed

> **INSIDER TIP**
> **Folk Festivities**
>
> On traditional holidays, the Folk Village celebrates the way Koreans used to, like serving red bean porridge on winter solstice and washing guests' hair with sweet flag-infused water during Dano festival.

9
Korean Folk Village
한국민속촌

C3 · 90 Minsokchon-ro, Yongin · From Seoul · Hours vary, check website · koreanfolk.co.kr

Bringing together 270 Joseon-era homes from around the country, the Korean Folk Village recreates a historic settlement authentic enough to have served as a film set for major TV productions like *Kingdom* and *Dae Jang Geum*. The site also features parades, exhibition halls, traditional music performances, amusement park rides, a working farm, and artisans who demonstrate how to make straw shoes and other crafts. Hands-on experiences making pottery and dyeing cloth help the past come alive for young visitors. Seasonal events include falconry demonstrations in winter and rice planting in spring.

10
Yangsu-ri
양수리

C2 · 24 miles (39 km) E of Seoul · Yangsu Station · 19 Dumulmeori-gil, Yangpyeong

The village of Yangsu-ri occupies a spit of land where two branches of the Hangang River meet before flowing through Seoul. Also known as Dumulmeori, this was long a busy port for merchants ferrying goods across the peninsula, but today it's a popular day-trip destination thanks to its beautiful natural setting. A gentle fog often hovers above the water at dawn, a 400-year-old zelkova tree stands sentry at the rivers' confluence, and traditional sailboats are sometimes moored just offshore. Even though you're only a 45-minute train ride from Seoul, you'll feel worlds, and centuries, away. Just over a pedestrian bridge is **Semiwon** (세미원), a garden known for its lotus flowers.

Semiwon

93 Yangsu-ro, Yangpyeong · Apr-Oct: 9am-6pm daily; Nov-Mar: 9am-6pm Tue-Sun · semiwon.or.kr

↑ Korean-style garden pond and pavilion at the Garden of Morning Calm

⓫ Garden of Morning Calm
아침고요수목원

▲C2 ⌂432 Sumokwon-ro, Gapyeong 🚌From Seoul ⏲8:30am-7pm daily 🌐morningcalm.co.kr

The Garden of Morning Calm takes its title from an old nickname for Korea, the "land of the morning calm." Set amid the mountains of eastern Gyeonggi-do Province, it contains some two dozen themed gardens, including one dedicated to roses of Sharon, the national flower. Come in spring for sky-kissing tulips and cherry blossoms (which stick around longer here, thanks to cooler temperatures), in summer for hydrangeas, or fall for crimson maple leaves and golden ginkgos. The garden is lovely in winter, too, when snow coats the ground and a festival of lights showcases bulbs of different colors.

⓬ Seoul Grand Park
서울대공원

▲C2 ⌂102 Daegongwongwangjang-ro, Gwacheon Ⓜ Seoul Grand Park Station ⏲10am-6pm Tue-Sun 🚫Jan 1, Seollal, Chuseok 🌐grandpark.seoul.go.kr

Despite its name, Seoul Grand Park is actually in the suburb of Gwacheon. Set around an artificial lake are several family-friendly attractions. **SeoulLand** (서울랜드) was the country's first theme park, and is still a good option for travelers with kids who don't have time to visit Everland (p124). **Seoul Grand Park Botanical Garden** (서울대공원 식물원) features themed gardens and a children's zoo with working border collies.

SeoulLand
 ⌂181 Gwangmyeong-ro Ⓜ Seoul Grand Park Station ⏲Hours vary, check website 🌐seoulland.co.kr

Seoul Grand Park Botanical Garden
Ⓜ Seoul Grand Park Station ⏲Daily: Mar, Apr, Sep & Oct 9am-6pm; May-Aug 9am-7pm; Nov-Feb 9am-5pm

---

⓭ Gyeonggi Museum of Contemporary Ceramic Art
경기도자미술관

▲D2 ⌂263 Gyeongchungdaero 2697-beon-gil, Icheon 🚌From Seoul ⏲10am-6pm Tue-Sun 🚫Jan 1, Seollal, Chuseok 🌐gmocca.org

You could make a strong argument that ceramics represent the height of

---

GREAT VIEW
Observatory

The observation tower in the Garden of Morning Calm's Hagyeong Garden provides a 360° view of the gardens' colorful flowers and manicured bushes, all backdropped by the green slopes of Mt. Chungnyungsan.

→
City views from the Namhansanseong Fortress

Korean artistic achievement, and for centuries, many of the country's finest pieces were produced in Icheon. The town remains an important center of pottery, with hundreds of ceramists calling it home. Visit this engaging museum to see how they're exploring the art form in the modern age. Exhibitions display pieces whose lineage you can clearly trace back to Goryeo celadon, alongside works that push the boundary of what clay can do. The museum shop sells both fine art pieces and functional ceramic goods. Docent tours (in Korean) are conducted at 2pm and 4pm.

Namhansanseong Fortress
남한산성

C2 731 Namhansanseong-ro, Gwangju From Seoul Apr-Oct: 10am-6pm; Nov-Mar: 10am-5pm Mon

Just southeast of Seoul, the UNESCO-listed Namhansanseong is a grand fortress that was built to serve as an emergency capital for the Joseon dynasty in times of trouble. The redoubt contained a temporary palace and could hold some 4,000 people. Buddhist monk-soldiers contributed to its construction and defense.

Today the site makes for an invigorating hike. Bargain on about four hours to circum-navigate the walls, which stretch for approximately 7.5 miles (12 km), and maybe a bit more if you linger to soak up the views of the capital from the west gate.

Donggureung
동구릉

C2 197 Donggureung-ro, Guri From Seoul Feb-May, Sep & Oct: 6am-6pm; Jun-Aug: 6am-6:30pm; Nov-Jan 6:30am-5:30pm Mon royal.khs.go.kr

More than a dozen Joseon royal tombs are scattered around Seoul and Gyeonggi-do Province, but this complex in Guri, just northeast of the capital, is the largest. Meaning "nine eastern tombs," Donggureung is actually the final resting place of seven kings and ten queens. Among them is King Taejo, the Joseon Dynasty's founder, whose tomb is covered in a fuzzy layer of silver grass from his hometown of Hamheung, in what's now North Korea.

STAY

Gyeongwonjae Ambassador
경원재 앰배서더

Within the Songdo district's lovely Central Park, this hotel is laid out like a palace and pairs modern amenities with traditional architecture and design.

B2 200 Technopark-ro, Incheon gyeongwonjae.com

Hotel Arte
호텔아르떼

A sleek, good-value stay, located amid a lively bar and restaurant district just a 10-minute bus ride from Hwaseong Fortress.

C2 37 Ingye-ro 108-beon-gil, Suwon artehotel.jalib.site

Golden Tulip Everyongin Hotel
골든튤립에버용인호텔

This family-friendly hotel is just steps from Everland. Watch the theme park's fireworks from the rooftop patio and pool.

C2 19-2 Jeondae-ro 78-beon-gil, Yongin gt-yongin.com

Giant seated Buddha, Singheungsa Temple

GANGWON-DO PROVINCE

Mountains cover more than 80 per cent of Gangwon-do, and the province's rough terrain has long kept it somewhat disconnected from the rest of the country – hard to traverse and hard to develop. With the minor exception of the period when Cheorwon served as the capital of the short-lived Later Goguryeo kingdom (901–918 CE), Gangwon-do has largely watched Korean history occur elsewhere. The most dramatic event in modern times came in the mid-20th century, when roughly one-third of it ended up in North Korea as a result of the peninsula's division at the end of World War II and the Korean War.

Beginning in the 1930s, Gangwon-do's staple industries, fishing and agriculture, were joined by coal mining. Communities such as Taebaek and Jeongseon prospered on the back of their mines for several decades, only to struggle when those mines started shutting down in the 1990s. More recently, the province has bolstered its economy through tourism, turning its rugged landscapes to its advantage by attracting hikers and skiers. This has been especially true since the International Olympic Committee announced that unheralded Pyeongchang would host the 2018 Winter Games. To prepare for the event, the government constructed several new roads and rail lines linking the province with Seoul, making it easier than ever for denizens of the capital region to escape to Gangwon-do's trails and beaches. Despite such development, though, the province remains a place defined by its small towns and soaring peaks.

GANGNEUNG
강릉

E2 139 miles (224 km) E of Seoul From Seoul From Seoul, Chuncheon, Daejeon, Ulsan, Pohang, Daegu 15 Haseulla-ro; www.visitgangneung.net

Gangneung was a popular retreat for Joseon-era artists, who braved the trek across the Taebaeksan Range to savor its natural beauty. Fortunately, getting here is now much easier, thanks to connections that were improved even further when the city hosted the 2018 Pyeongchang Winter Olympics' ice events.

①
Gyeongpoho Lake
경포호

Historically, this lake (actually an enclosed bay) has been regarded as one of the city's prettiest sites. Although it's now quite developed, the lake is still pleasant enough when its encircling cherry trees blossom in spring. The best views are from **Gyeongpodae Pavilion** (경포대), on the south-west shore. Built in 1326 and moved here in 1508, its eaves hold plaques with poetry by Joseon scholars and royals. On the southeast shore is the **Gyeongpo Aquarium** (경포아쿠아리움), home to a variety of marine animals, such as reef sharks.

Gyeongpodae Pavilion
 365 Gyeongpo-ro
 9am-6pm daily

Gyeongpo Aquarium
   131 Nanseolheon-ro 10am-6pm daily gg-aqua.com

②
Gyeongpo Beach
경포해변

This beach just in front of Gyeongpoho Lake is backed by pine trees and has excellent sand. It's one of Korea's most popular and gets packed with visitors from the capital on summer weekends. If things get too crowded for your liking, just head north. The beach stretches on for hundreds of meters, changing its name every so often. Korean-style sashimi restaurants line the road behind the beach.

③
Gangneung Coffee Street
강릉커피거리

The road immediately behind Anmok Beach is known as Gangneung Coffee Street. It's lined with cafés, many of which have large windows or, even better, terraces that look out over the sand and surf. Pull up a chair, grab a drink, and enjoy the view.

④
Seongyojang
선교장

 63 Unjeong-gil
 9am-6pm daily
 knsgj.net

Construction of Seongyojang began in the mid-1700s when, according to legend, a pack of weasels led the nobleman Lee Nae-beon to this site, which at the time was on the shores of Gyeongpoho. (The lake has

Must See

> **INSIDER TIP**
> **Hanok Stay**
>
> In the Joseon era, Seong-yojang regularly hosted traveling artists and scholars. Parts of the historic home function as a guesthouse today, continuing its long-standing tradition of hospitality (knsgj.net).

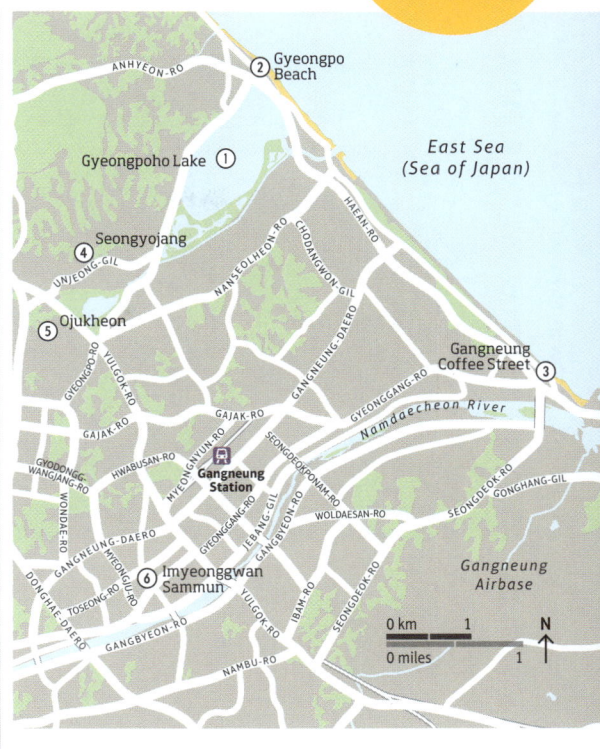

since contracted.) Expanded by descendants over the decades, it's one of Korea's largest remaining Joseon-era homes. Among its handsome buildings are Yeolhwadang, an 1815 hall with a pent roof that was a gift from a Russian diplomat, and Hwallaejeong, a pavilion overlooking a lovely lotus pond.

⑤ Ojukheon
오죽헌

24 Yulgok-ro 3139-beon-gil ◘ **9am–6pm daily**
🌐 **gn.go.kr/museum**

Erected in the early 1400s, Ojukheon is one of the oldest surviving houses in Korea. It's most famous for being the birthplace and home of Shin Saimdang, an accomplished artist who is today viewed as having embodied the ideal of Confucian motherhood, and her son, Yi I, one of the Joseon Dynasty's most revered scholars. The home is surrounded by beautiful, meticulously maintained grounds. Don't miss the elegant grove of black bamboo, from which the house takes its name. Also on site is the Gangneung Municipal Museum, which displays delicate ceramics, calligraphy, and drawings, including some by Shin.

> **Did You Know?**
>
> Ojukheon and Yi I are depicted on Korea's 5,000-won bill. Shin Saimdang is on the 50,000-won bill.

← Cherry trees blossoming on the shoreline of Gyeongpoho Lake

⑥ Imyeonggwan Sammun
임영관 삼문

6 Imyeong-ro 131-beon-gil ◘ **9am–6pm Tue–Sun**

Imyeonggwan Sammun's humble appearance belies its historical significance. The front gate to a guesthouse that once stood on the site, the rustic, unpainted structure is more than 1,000 years old, having been built in 936 CE. It looks sturdy enough to make another 1,000. Nearby is Chilsadang (칠사당), a building that dates to the late 1800s. Both structures were part of an old Goryeo and Joseon government complex. The other buildings on the site are reconstructions.

❷
SOKCHO
속초

🅰 E1 🚗 127 miles (205 km) NE of Seoul 🚌 From Seoul, Gangneung, Chuncheon ℹ 1-7 Subok-ro 201-beon-gil; www.sokcho.go.kr/ct/tour

The jumping-off point for excursions into Seoraksan National Park *(p136)*, Sokcho is an ideal place to experience Gangwon-do Province's briny coastal culture. Crabbing boats crowd the port, seafood restaurants abound, and visitors relax in soothing hot springs. The city also has a significant North Korean imprint, as it is home to a small fishing village established by Korean War refugees.

One of South Korea's northernmost towns, Sokcho lay inside North Korea when the peninsula was divided after World War II, only to end up south of the Military Demarcation Line at the end of the Korean War. It enjoys a beautiful setting, curling around two sizable lagoons, Yeongnangho (영랑호) and Cheongchoho (청초호), while Ulsanbawi Ridge forms a dramatic backdrop to the west.

Fishing is a major industry here, and the waterfront hums with seafood auctions, boats unloading their catches, and diners tucking into steamed snow crab at places like the Dongmyeong Seafood Center (동명활어센터). The basement in the Sokcho Tourist and Fishery Market (속초관광수산시장) is filled with sashimi restaurants where you can pick your dinner from the display tanks; other stalls specialize in salted seafood or *dalk-gangjeong*, fried chicken pieces tossed in a spicy sauce.

During the Korean War, many North Koreans from the Hamgyeong-do region fled south and settled in Sokcho, where they established a fishing community on an island in the harbor. Today, Abai Village, as it's known (*Abai* means

↑ Traveling to Abai Village aboard the wire-pulled *gaetbae* ferry

Sokcho's lovely setting aside Cheongchoho lagoon and *(inset)* a street-food stall in Abai Village

> # Must See
>
> # EAT
>
> ### Dancheon Sikdang
> 단천식당
> This well-established local favorite has been serving Abai *sundae* and *ojingeo sundae* (squid stuffed with meat, vegetables, and glass noodles) since 1978.
> 🅰 E1 🏠 17 Abaimaeul-gil, Sokcho
> 📞 033 632 7828
> ⓦⓦⓦ
>
> ### Mansuk Dakgangjeong
> 만석닭강정
> Head to Mansuk Dakgangjeong for Sokcho's local take on fried chicken, with pieces tossed in a tangy sweet-and-spicy sauce.
> 🅰 E1 🏠 9 Chodang-sundubu-gil, Sokcho
> ⓦ mansuk.kr
> ⓦⓦⓦ

"father" in the Hamgyeong dialect), has become a popular tourist destination, though it retains its charmingly unpolished feel. Its few streets are a good place to find places serving North Korean specialties like *naengmyeon* (cold noodles) with raw fish slices and Abai *sundae* (blood sausage with glutinous rice and glass noodles). You can reach the village by bridge, but the best way to get here is to step aboard the *gaetbae* ferry. The little boat is attached to a wire, and pilots shuttle it between the island and downtown by pulling it along the wire with a metal hook.

Beaches and Hot Springs

Sokcho isn't as much of a beach destination as some other east coast towns, but Sokcho Beach (속초해수욕장) is an excellent strip of white sand. Even more relaxing are the Cheoksan hot springs, on the city's west side. The mineral-rich spring water reaches temperatures of 113°F (45°C) and is said to be good for stress, arthritis, and other ailments. You can book a room at spa hotels like Cheoksan Spa (척산온천장) and Cheoksan Spatel (척산온천휴양촌) or pay a very modest fee to use their hot spring pools and saunas. The giant Hanhwa Resort Seorak Sorano (한화리조트 설악 쏘라노) even has a hot springs water park. For a bit of free indulgence, soak your feet at the public Cheoksan Foot Bath Park (척산족욕공원).

> ### JJIMJILBANG
>
> Korea has a few hot springs like Cheoksan, but almost anywhere you go you'll find *jjimjilbang* (찜질방), public bathhouses with gender-segregated bathing areas. Visitors can sweat in the saunas, soak in hot and cold pools, and get exfoliating scrubs from attendants, then relax in the co-ed common rooms, which typically have sleeping areas and TV lounges. Fancier places might even have salons, arcades, or karaoke rooms.

SEORAKSAN NATIONAL PARK

설악산국립공원

E1 ◆ 6 miles (10 km) W of Sokcho ◆ From Sokcho ◆ knps.or.kr

Mountains cover roughly 70 per cent of Korea's terrain, but seldom do they produce as much drama as they do in Seoraksan. Arguably the country's most beautiful park, this wild range of peaks is crisscrossed by hiking trails that lead to waterfalls, temples, and exhilarating views.

Seoraksan forms part of the Baekdudaegan range, the mountainous spine that runs from Baekdu Mountain on the North Korea-China border down to Jirisan Mountain *(p234)* in the peninsula's south. The park is an important ecological crossroads where flora and fauna from northern and southern regions intersect. It's home to conifers, bamboo, and more than 1,500 animal species, including Amur gorals. Mountain ridges divide the park into three parts: Oeseorak (Outer Seorak); Naeseorak (Inner Seorak), and Namseorak (South Seorak).

Outer Seorak

The eastern and most accessible area, Outer Seorak is where you'll find the park's most spectacular sights. Foremost among these is Ulsanbawi (울산바위), which may be the only rock formation in Korea famous enough to have its own website. From the coastal lowland, forested mountain slopes creep gradually upward before coming to an abrupt halt at this imperious granite spine. Also in this part of the park are 5,604-ft (1,708-m) Daecheongbong (대청봉),

> **Did You Know?**
>
> In 1982, Mount Seoraksan was declared Korea's first UNESCO Biosphere Reserve.

↑ Hikers scaling Ulsanbawi, with its spectacular views across the national park

↑ Giant seated Buddha statue at Sinheungsa Temple in Oeseorak, or Outer Seorak

Cheonbuldong Valley (천불동계곡), and three waterfalls: Biryong (비룡폭포), Yukdam (육담폭포), and Towangseong (토왕성폭포).

Inner and South Seorak

To the west, Inner Seorak's most significant sights are Daeseung Falls (대승폭포), which drops down a 289-ft (88-m) cliff (but only when there's been rainfall) and Baekdamsa Temple (백담사). Founded in 647 CE, it became famous in modern times as the temple where the poet and independence activist "Manhae" Han Yong-un was ordained in 1905, and infamous as the temple where the dictator Chun Doo-hwan lived for three years after stepping down from power in 1988.

Travelers visit South Seorak primarily for Osaek Springs (오색약수터). There's an iron-rich cold spring you can drink from, and in Osaek-ri Village, a cluster of basic inns get hot spring water pumped into their rooms.

TOP 4 HIKES IN SEORAKSAN

Ulsanbawi Course
울산바위코스
This 2.4-mile (3.8-km) route leads to rocky Ulsanbawi, Seoraksan's most famous site.

Daecheongbong Course
대청봉코스 (설악동)
A tough all-day thru-hike, this 10-mile (16-km) route summits Daecheongbong Peak.

Baekdamsa Course
백담사코스
A 4-mile (6.5-km) amble to a secluded temple makes for one of the park's easiest hikes.

Biryong Falls and Towangseong Falls Observatory Course
비룡폭포 (토왕폭전망대)
Visit two of the park's most impressive waterfalls on this 1.7-mile (2.8-km) hike.

EXPLORING SERAKSAN NATIONAL PARK

Spreading across 154 sq miles (398 sq km), Seoraksan is a brilliant place to hike, with loads of trails and panoramic views of green and gray mountain peaks set against the chilly blue of the East Sea. The park gets busy in fall, when the foliage sets its valleys aflame, but it's rewarding any time of year; winter, when snow blankets the slopes and waterfalls have frozen, is especially lovely. The terrain can make for challenging treks, but features such as stairs in tricky spots mean that you don't need any special skills to navigate the well-maintained trails. Outer Seorak is easily accessed by bus from Sokcho (p134) but Inner Seorak and South Seorak are best reached by car.

Baekdamsa's name means "Temple of the 100th Pool." According to legend, a monk dreamed he should build it next to the 100th pool of water he encountered while descending Daecheongbong Peak.

In the 10th century, **Daeseung Falls** was said to have been a favorite retreat of King Gyeongsun, the final king of the Silla Dynasty.

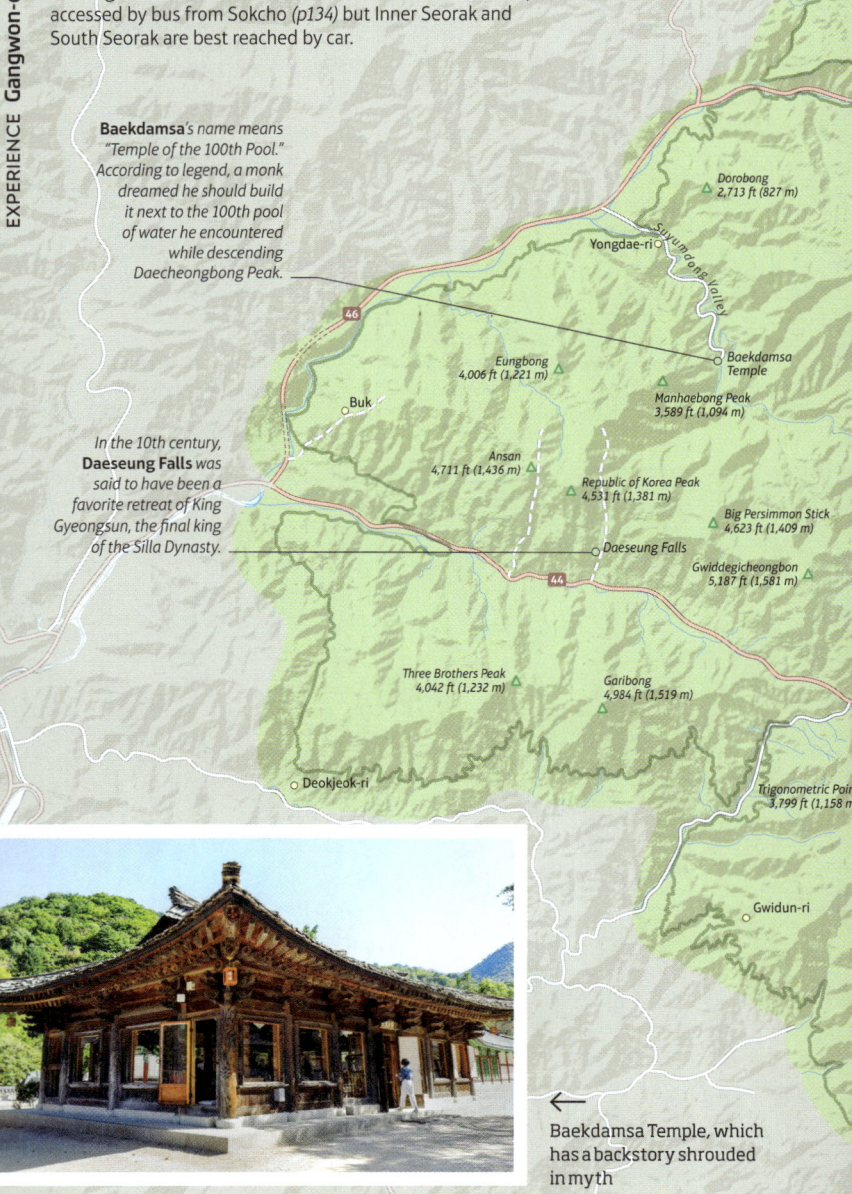

← Baekdamsa Temple, which has a backstory shrouded in myth

Must See

Biryong Falls, tumbling into an inviting cool, emerald-green pool

Seoraksan's most famous site is **Ulsanbawi** – its sawtooth peaks reach 2,953 ft (900 m).

Sinheungsa Temple's giant seated Buddha statue contains three pieces of the Buddha's sari, donated by the Myanmar government.

Meaning "Flying Dragon," **Biryong Falls** gets its name from a legend about a woman who was sacrificed to a dragon to end a terrible drought.

The **Towangseong Falls** descend a total of 1,050 ft (320 m).

The **Cheonbuldong Valley** got its name because its white cliffs and rugged peaks are said to resemble 1,000 Buddhist statues.

At 5,604 ft (1,708 m) high, **Daecheongbong** is South Korea's fourth-highest peak.

Osaek-ri Village has both a cold and hot spring, where the water reaches 108°F (42°C).

> **INSIDER TIP**
> **Seoraksan Shelters**
>
> Seoraksan is one of four national parks that have shelters where you can stay overnight on multi-day hikes. You can reserve your spots online (reservation. knps.or.kr).

EXPERIENCE MORE

Nami Island
남이섬

🅐 D2 🏠 Namiseom-gil 1, Chuncheon 🚢 Nami Island Wharf 🕐 Daily, check website for ferry times ℹ️ Namiseom-gil 1, Chuncheon; www.namisum.com

Set in the north branch of the Hangang River, Nami Island serves up an unusual combination of utopian idealism, marketing kitsch, and resort amenities. The island bills itself the Naminara Republic, having "declared cultural independence" from the rest of the country, and has its own flag and anthem.

To visit, you don't buy a ticket, you buy a "visa." Look past the cheesiness, though, and you're apt to find a place you just might consider emigrating to. The island is car-free and can only be reached by ferry (included in your "visa"), or, if you like your entrances dramatic, via a zip line. After you've crossed the "border," you can watch potters and glassblowers work in Nami Island Handicraft Studio; visit Nami Concours Gallery, a children's art gallery; relax in the Picture Book Lounge; or traverse the Forest Adventure TreeGo & TreeCoaster, a ropes course through the trees. Peacocks, ostriches, deer, and other animals roam the island. Nami is particularly popular with families and young couples, and most visitors opt for a decidedly relaxed sojourn, renting bikes to cycle the island's paths, getting drinks and desserts in its many cafés, and strolling its nearly two-dozen gardens. Hotel Jeonggwanru gives you the option of spending the night on the island – accommodations are limited, so book well in advance.

> 📷 **PICTURE PERFECT**
> **Snaps in Nature**
>
> Nami Island's colorful trees make an excellent background for selfies and group photos. Don't miss the pastel blossoms on Cherry Tree Lane in spring, or the gold leaves on Ginkgo Tree Lane in fall.

→

Twilight descending on the towering Soyanggang Maiden Statue in Chuncheon

Chuncheon
춘천

🅐 D2 Ⓜ Gyeongchun 🚆 From Seoul 🌐 tour.chuncheon.go.kr

Gangwon-do's capital has roots that stretch back to the 7th century, but the modern city is quite new, having been largely rebuilt after sustaining extensive damage in the Korean War. Although postwar construction of hydroelectric plants turned Chuncheon into an industrial hub, the city is best known for its cuisine, including *dakgalbi* (spicy stir-fried chicken) and *makguksu* (cold buckwheat noodles), and outdoor adventures in the surrounding mountains and lakes. Overlooking the water is also the 12-m (40-ft) tall Soyanggang Maiden Statue, a fictional character sung about in the popular folk song "Soyanggang Cheonyeo." Lyrics are inscribed on the base.

Southwest of downtown, the **Samaksan Mountain Lake Cable Car** whisks visitors over the Hangang

←

Enjoying a leisurely lunch by a serene waterlily pond on Nami Island

River to Samaksan Mountain, where hiking trails and the U-shaped Skywalk Observation Deck offer dreamlike views of the city, forested mountain ridges, and river islands. Northeast of town is Soyangho Lake, a massive reservoir created when the Soyang Dam was built in the late 20th century to control floods and provide power. It's best explored on a cruise departing from the Soyangho Lake Ilju Excursion Boat Terminal (*Sinsaembat-ro 1133*). From the terminus, it's a pleasant 2.5-mile (4-km) hike to **Cheongpyeongsa Temple** (청평사), one of Chuncheon's most popular sights. Families may want to make memories at the **LEGOLAND® Korea Resort**, on Hajung-do Island, situated in the river opposite the train station.

Samaksan Mountain Lake Cable Car

Sportstown-gil 245 Hours vary, check website samaksancablecar.com

Cheongpyeongsa Temple

Obongsan-gil 810
cheongpyeongsa.co.kr

LEGOLAND® Korea Resort

Hajungdo-gil 128 Hours vary, check website legoland.kr

Cheorwon
철원

C1 From Seoul
Taebong-ro 1825

This remote county, once part of North Korea, holds several Korean War sites, including the ruins of the **Workers' Party of Korea Building** (노동당사). Skeletal walls are all that remain of the structure where Communist officials once plotted guerilla attacks on the South. After the war ended in 1953, bones and bullets were found in a tunnel behind the building. Closer to the border is **Cheorwon Peace Observatory** (철원평화전망대), where you can peer into North Korea. A car or taxi is required to visit.

Workers' Party of Korea Building

Geumgangsan-ro 265
Nodongdangsa

Cheorwon Peace Observatory

Junggang-ri 588-14
9am-6pm, by guided tour only Tue

Chiaksan National Park
치악산국립공원

D2 Musoejeom-2-gil 26, Wonju Tteumbawi
Tteumbawi Daily
knps.or.kr

Chiaksan National Park spreads across 67.5 sq miles (175 sq km) in Gangwon-do's southwestern corner. It encompasses strange rock formations, plunging valleys, handsome waterfalls, and numerous mountain peaks, the tallest of which is the 4,225-ft (1,288-m) Birobong. In summer, azaleas paint the mountainsides, while fall brings reds and golds. There are plenty of hiking trails, including a 3.7-mile (6-km) route that departs from near the park office, passes Guryongsa Temple (구룡사), and continues up to Birobong's summit.

> **Chiaksan National Park encompasses plunging valleys, handsome waterfalls, strange rock formations, and numerous mountain peaks.**

↑ Studying historical exhibits at the DMZ Museum

8
DMZ Museum
DMZ 박물관

🅰 E1 📍 Tongiljeonmang-dae-ro 369, Goseong
🕐 Mar–Oct: 9am–6pm; Nov–Feb 9am–5pm 🚫 Mon, 1 Jan
🌐 dmzmuseum.com

Close to South Korea's northernmost point, the DMZ Museum explores the lasting impact of the Korean War through exhibitions on the peninsula's division, villages that still exist within the demilitarized zone, and, more optimistically, how the undeveloped strip of land has become a haven for rare birds and plants. Displays feature items such as antipersonnel mines and a war correspondent's typewriter. Outside is a boat that a North Korean family used to defect to the South in 2011 and a replica of DMZ barbed wire fencing that visitors can walk through. Just up the road from the museum, the Goseong Unification Observatory Tower (고성통일전망타워) offers views of North Korea's coast and Mount Geumgangsan. A car or taxi is required to visit, and you must first stop at the Civilian Control Line entry/exit reporting location (Geumgangsan-ro 481).

9
Yangyang
양양

🅰 E1 ℹ️ Donghae-daero 3094

A small east-coast town, Yangyang is the center of Korea's surfing scene. Crowds in wetsuits bob in the swells, urban escapees sip coffees in beachside cafés, and, after sundown, locals fire up barbecue grills. If you've never surfed but want to give it a try, Yangyang's a good place to do it. Waves are modest, there are lots of surf schools, and you definitely won't be the only novice in the water. Many places also provide the option to stand-up paddleboard or practice beach yoga.

Yangyang has two main beach areas. South of the town center is the 1-mile- (1.5-km-) long Hajodae Beach (하조대해수욕장), while about 4.5 miles (7 km) farther south are Jukdo (죽도해수욕장) and Ingu (인구해수욕장) beaches. The latter is where you'll find the largest concentration of surf schools, hotels, cafés, bars, and restaurants in the area. Alternatively, pray for gnarly barrels at **Naksansa** (낙산사), a lovely seaside temple north of Yangyang that traces its lineage back to 671 CE. A 52-ft (16-m) statue of the Avalokitesvara Bodhisattva stands sentinel above the waves.

Naksansa Temple
📍 Naksansa-ro 100
🌐 naksansa.or.kr

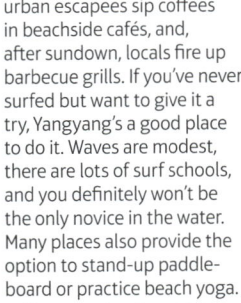

Did You Know?
Pro-South Korea propaganda broadcasts across the border can be heard 15 miles (24 km) away.

TOP 3 YANGYANG SURF SCHOOLS

Surfyy Beach
🏠 Hajodaehaean-gil 119
🌐 surfyy.com
Take lessons and enjoy camping facilities on a private strip of sand.

Surf Ocean
🏠 Saenaru-gil 43
🌐 surfocean.modoo.at
Join a group lesson, try a private lesson, or simply rent equipment.

Tyler's Longboard Shop
🏠 Ingujungang-gil 65
🌐 tyler.co.kr
Lessons include classes for couples and kids.

10

Jeongdongjin Beach
정동진해수욕장

📍 E2 🚉 Jeongdongjin Station

This long stretch of golden sand is one of the east coast's best beaches, and a popular place to watch the sun rise. Most days, there are a few people glimpsing the dawn, but those numbers balloon on New Year's Day, when it's become something of a local ritual to gather here. If you can manage to rouse yourself in time, it's a beautiful sight, although it's certainly difficult to overlook the enormous Sun Cruise, a hotel shaped like two cruise ships jutting out from atop a cliff.

Jeongdongjin is equally well known for its train station, which practically sits on the sand; it's been recognized by the *Guinness Book of World Records* as the closest station to a beach in the world. A high-speed train means visitors can go from Seoul to suntanning in just over two hours.

For something more active, you can pedal a two- or four-person rail bike alongside the beach, or lace up your walking boots and hike the scenic Jeondongsimgok Badabuchae Trail (정동심곡바다부채길). The 2-mile (3-km) path consists largely of walkways traversing the fanlike rock formations of a marine terrace that was created millions of years ago, when tectonic forces raised part of the seabed around 260 ft (80 m) above the waves.

11

Haesindang Park
해신당공원

📍 F3 🏠 Samcheok-ro 1852-6, Samcheok
🚌 Haesindang 🕐 Mar-Oct: 9am-6pm daily; Nov-Feb: 9am-5pm daily

This seaside park is filled with hundreds of penis statues, with many securing their place here after taking first prize at the Samcheok Phallus Sculpture Contest. Why are these artworks here? Supposedly, 500 years ago, a village girl drowned a virgin while collecting seaweed. Her spirit vented her frustrations by driving the fish away. Until, that is, a fisherman urinated off the side of his boat and the fish returned. From that point onward, locals began carving wooden phalli as offerings.

← Traditional architecture at Naksansa Temple, and *(inset)* its intricate interiors

 12

Odaesan National Park
오대산국립공원

🅰 E2 🏠 Odaesan-ro 2, Pyeongchang 🚌 Byeongan-samgeori 🌐 knps.or.kr

Odaesan National Park covers 127 sq miles (328 sq km) and centers on a line of five imposing peaks, of which Birobong is the tallest, at 5,128 ft (1,563 m). Its position at the heart of the Baekdudaegan, Korea's longest mountain range, makes it an important ecological site, home to water deer, mountain goats, otters, and other fauna. The park is equally important in the history of Buddhism on the peninsula, with two temples that date to the 7th century CE. Founded by the monk Jajang in 643 CE, **Woljeongsa Temple** (월정사) was burned down by the South Korean army to prevent DPRK troops from occupying it during the Korean War but was restored beginning in 1958. It's home to two designated national treasures: an octagonal nine-story pagoda and a seated stone bodhisattva. **Sangwonsa Temple** (상원사) would have been burned down, too, were it not for a brave monk who refused to abandon his post.

SEOPDARI BRIDGES

One of the most unusual things visitors to Odaesan may encounter are *seopdari* (섶다리). These traditional bridges are built in the fall, when water levels are low. After a frame of pine or willow logs is erected, brushwood is laid across the top and then covered with soil. Not a single nail is used in their construction. *Seopdari* stand until the next rainy season, when rising waters wash them away.

Unlike some of Korea's other national parks, Odaesan's mountains have relatively gentle slopes, making it a good place for casual hikers. A particularly popular trek is the 5.5-mile (9-km) Seonjaegil Trail, which links Woljeongsa and Sangwonsa temples.

Woljeongsa Temple
 🏠 Odaesan-ro 374-8, Pyeongchang 🌐 woljeongsa.org

Sangwonsa Temple
🏠 Odaesan-ro 1209, Pyeongchang

 13

Mona Yongpyong Ski Resort
모나 용평

🅰 E2 🏠 Olympic-ro 715, Pyeongchang 🚌 Yongpyong Resort ⏰ Hours vary, check website 🌐 monayongpyong.com

Mona Yongpyong is one of Korea's top ski resorts, and it hosted the 2018 Winter Olympics' slalom and giant slalom events. The resort features 28 slopes, 14 lifts,

← Sangwonsa Buddhist Temple, Odaesan National Park

→ The mirrored cascades of Ssang Falls in the Mureung Valley

and a terrain park. If you don't have your own skis or you want to try hitting the slopes for the first time, you can rent equipment in Mona Yongpyong, and the resort even provides English-language ski lessons. Other resort facilities include an indoor-outdoor water park, three golf courses, a bowling alley, a sauna, and a four-season sled hill. Lodging options here consist of a hotel, a hostel, and several condominiums.

Daegwallyeong Yangtte Ranch
대관령양떼목장

E2 Daegwallyeong-maru-gil 483-32, Pyeong-chang Daegwallyeong Yangtte Ranch May-Aug: 9am-6:30pm daily (Sep & Apr: til 6pm; Oct & Mar: til 5:30pm; Nov-Feb: til 5pm) yangtte.co.kr

This sheep ranch outside the little town of Hoenggye (횡계) might just be the most bucolic spot in all Korea. Visitors can stroll paths that wind across the farm's rolling hills to get up-close looks at flocks of grazing sheep, while all around, mountain ridges recede into the distance. Naturally, all the furry friends here make Daegwallyeong Yangtte Ranch a great destination for families. Kids will especially enjoy the chance to feed the lambs. Although the sheep mostly stay inside when it's cold, the ranch is equally enthralling in winter, when you can still access most of the trails and visit the sheep in their barn. The area's highlands get some of the country's heaviest snowfall, and Yangtte's trees are often coated in a layer of glimmering hoarfrost.

Did You Know?

The Korean word for hoarfrost (icy frost) is *nunkkot*, meaning "snow flower."

Mureung Valley
무릉계곡

E2 33 miles (53 km) S of Gangneung Mureung Valley Samhwa-ro 538, Donghae; www.dh.go.kr/english/index.do

How pretty is Mureung Valley? Pretty enough that a legend says Taoist fairies descended from the mountains to frolic in its pools and waterfalls. Carved by a stream flowing down Dutasan Mountain, Mureung does, in fact, feel a bit mythical. The water runs past Samhwasa Temple (삼화사), the jagged ridge of Baeteul Rock (베틀바위), and a broad slab of granite where scholars once etched their names. A 1.6-mile (2.5-km) trail leads up to Ssang Falls, mirrored cascades that tumble into a clear pool. The valley is a perfect place for a picnic, especially during Korea's humid summers, but if you don't want to pack food, there are plenty of cafés, restaurants, and stores near the entrance.

Jeongseon
정선

E2 42 miles (68 km) SW of Gangneung From Seoul, Wonju, Gangneung Jeongseon-ro 1357-1, Jeongseon; www.jeongseon.go.kr/tour

Jeongseon-gun County (정선군) is rugged, rural, and a hub for leisure sports. The popular Jeongseon Rail Bike (정선 레일바이크) operates on a 4.5-mile (7-km) track that once carried freight trains laden with coal. From Gujeol-ri Village, visitors can pedal along a river, through tunnels, and past a pair of cafés shaped like a fish and grasshoppers before arriving at the hamlet of Auraji. For aerial adventure, head to **Arii Hills** (아리힐스) resort, whose glass-floored Skywalk offers views of a horseshoe bend in the Donggang River from 1,912 ft (583 m) up. There's also a zip line that shoots down to the river valley. Besides being one of Korea's prettiest rivers, the Donggang is also its best for white-water rafting. Most trips begin in Jeongseon and end in adjacent Yeongwol-gun County, usually pulling ashore in Geoun-ri Village. In between adrenaline rushes, make sure to visit the charming **Jeongseon Arirang Market** (정선아리랑시장) in Jeongseon-eup Town, where vendors sell local specialties like buckwheat crêpes.

Arii Hills
청평사

Byeongbangchi-gil 235, Jeongseon 9am-6pm daily (winter: 10am-5pm) ariihills.co.kr

Jeongseon Arirang Market

40 Siljang-gil, Jeongseon 9am-6pm daily

Hwanseongul Cave
환선굴

F2 Hwanseon-ro 800, Samcheok Hwanseongul 9am-5pm (Nov-Feb: 9:30am-4pm) 18th of each month 82 33 541 9266

Formed some 530 million years ago, Hwanseongul is the biggest cave in Korea – 3.85 miles (6.2 km) long and 98 ft (30 m) high in some places. Around a quarter is open for exploration, and within that span, a series of walkways provides access to waterfalls, stalagmites, stalactites, and

ARIRANG

Jeongseon is considered the birthplace of Arirang, Korea's most beloved folk song. Arirang has no fixed melodies or lyrics, save for a refrain of "*Arirang, arirang, arariyo*." Throughout history, it's been used to express sentiments as varied as a longing for one's hometown and resistance to Japanese colonization. Its most common form, however, is an achingly beautiful lament expressing the sorrow of a separated lover. In all, there are some 60 regional versions and 3,600 variations. You can listen to the song at the Arirang Center (아리랑센터) in Jeongseon-eup Town.

curious rock formations. The cave maintains a consistent temperature of 50–60°F (10–15°C), so dress appropriately. From the ticket office, it's a 30-minute uphill hike to the cave, or, for a small additional fee, a quick monorail ride.

High1 Resort
하이원리조트

E3 Highone-gil 424, Jeongseon High1 Resort Entrance Hours vary, check website high1.com

High1 gives skiers and snowboarders 20 runs to choose from, spread across three peaks above 4,100 ft (1,250 m). Perched on the highest summit is High1 Top, a restaurant that rotates 360 degrees and serves up fine views of the Baekdudaegan mountain range. Skiers with specific requirements will find accessible facilities and a ski school catering to their needs, the first of its kind in Korea. Other leisure facilities include an 18-hole golf course, an indoor archery center, karaoke rooms, yoga, and meditation courses. Families in particular will appreciate the indoor-outdoor water park with water slides and wave pools.

Taebaeksan National Park
태백산국립공원

E3 Beonyeong-ro 59, Taebaek Hak Village knps.or.kr

Taebaeksan is one of South Korea's newest national parks, having only been designated in 2016. At 5,141 ft (1,567 m), the titular mountain is among the country's tallest; on a clear day, you can make out the East Sea from its summit. The mountain slopes take on a pink blush in spring, thanks to blooming rhododendrons and azaleas, but Taebaeksan is most renowned for its dramatic winter beauty, when it's blanketed in heavy snow. More than 2,500 animal species live in these epic environs, including 22 that are considered endangered.

Taebaeksan is also one of the country's most sacred mountains. According to legend, this is where Hwanung, the son of the King of Heaven, descended to found a city and teach people how to live. Located near the summit is Cheonjedan (천제단), a complex of three altars where shamans regularly perform ceremonies; the largest of which are held on October 3, Korea's National Foundation Day.

Until the 1980s, mining was the principal industry in the area. Visitors can unearth this local history at the **Taebaek Coal Museum** (태백석탄박물관), located near the park's main entrance. Exhibitions include the equipment used by miners.

Taebaek Coal Museum
Cheonjedan-gil 195, Taebaek 9am–6pm daily taebaek.go.kr

> **Did You Know?**
> South Korea's longest (Nakdonggang) and largest river by volume (Hangang) begin in Taebaeksan.

← Hiking through a winter wonderland in Taebaeksan National Park

A DRIVING TOUR
GANGWON NATURE ROAD COURSE 6

Length 83 miles (134 km) **Stopping-off points** Gangneung, for coffee and the city's renowned soft tofu
Terrain Paved roads

Mountains or beaches? Gangwon-do answers the old traveler's dilemma with a clear "both." This is Korea's most mountainous province, yet it's also home to some superb strips of sand – and you really need to visit both to get the full Gangwon experience. This driving route, part of the larger Gangwon Nature Road touring course, starts with a long cruise up the east coast, passing golden beaches and the welcoming city of Gangneung, before darting inland and heading straight for the heart of the Baekdudaegan range.

Wind between peaks home to water deer and wild goats at **Odaesan National Park** (p144).

Hairpin bends lead to **Jingogae Pass** – and access to a hiking trail.

Woljeongsa Temple (p144), founded in 643 CE, is home to a pair of designated National Treasures.

Rural Pyeongchang hosted the 2018 Winter Olympics and is home to several good ski resorts.

Odaesan Food Village restaurants serve buckwheat noodles, dried pollack, and bibimbap.

INSIDER TIP
BTS Bus Stop

K-pop fans might want to make a 5-mile (8-km) detour to Jumunjin Beach for a photo at the BTS Bus Stop, featured on the cover of their album *You Never Walk Alone*.

→ Woljeongsa Temple in Odeasan, covered in a heavy dusting of snow

Locator Map
For more detail see p130

↑ A decorative sign marking the start of the Isabu Road

In **Gangneung**, break for coffee at Anmok Beach's Gangneung Coffee Street (p132).

Jeongdongjin Beach (p143) is one of the best places in Korea to watch the sunrise.

East Sea (Sea of Japan)

The **Dojjaebigol Sky Valley** complex features a Skywalk with sweeping East Sea views.

Check out slender **Chuam Candlestick Rock**, just offshore, and walk above the waves on a suspension bridge.

The coastal **Isabu Road** to Samcheok Beach is known as one of Korea's most beautiful drives.

Aerial view of the pretty Chungjuho Lake

CHUNGCHEONG-DO PROVINCE

Situated in South Korea's middle, Chungcheong-do Province has long been something of a crossroads. This is true even geographically, as eastern mountains gradually give way to western plains. Ancient Chungcheong-do was occupied by the tribes of the Mahan Confederacy and later formed a core part of the Baekje kingdom. When Goguryeo invasions forced Baekje to abandon its capital in what's now Seoul, the dynasty relocated here, first to Gongju, in 475 CE, and then to Buyeo, in 578. It was during the Joseon Dynasty (1392–1897), when the province was famed for its large population of noblemen, that Chungcheong-do adopted its current name, a combination of the cities of Chungju and Cheongju.

Chungcheong-do's status as a central meeting place for people from Jeolla-do, Gyeongsang-do, and the capital means it doesn't have a strong regional identity. Instead, it's developed as a place of connection. Its largest city, Daejeon, grew from a small village to an important educational center, something akin to Korea's Silicon Valley. The neighboring city of Sejong, built from scratch in the early 2000s, was initially conceived of as a new capital that would take over from Seoul but it settled for becoming a major administrative hub, home to a number of government ministries.

Crowds watching a spectacular sunset at Kkotji Beach

① TAEANHAEAN NATIONAL PARK

B3 9 Gwisil-gil, Taean Namsan-3-ri Gwisil knps.or.kr

Historically free of natural disasters and with a mild climate, the park has led a charmed existence, befitting a place that means "peaceful and comfortable." The good times were furthered in 1987 by the decision to designate parts of the Taean Peninsula, Anmyeondo Island, and dozens of outlying islands, a national park. This has helped preserve the area's tidal flats, sand dunes, and beaches along 145 miles (230 km) of coast.

Did You Know?

When Taean suffered an oil spill in 2007, 1 million people volunteered to help clean up.

Sinduri Coastal Sand Dune
태안 신두리 해안사구

201-54 Sinduhaebyeon-gil, Taean Sinduri-Sinduri Sagu Center 9am–6pm daily (Nov–Feb: to 5pm)

The wind has spent 15,000 years shaping the gentle undulations of Korea's largest sand dune, which measures just over 2 miles (3 km) in length and nearly 1 mile (1.5 km) in width. In certain places, it can feel as if you're in the Sahara, but most of the dune is actually covered in a variety of grasses that offer perches for dragonflies and launchpads for grasshoppers. A variety of walking trails take different courses across the dune and down to a beach that grows exponentially at low tide. As you walk on the sand and wooden boards, keep an eye out for Mongolia racerunners and dung beetles.

Mallipo Beach
만리포해수욕장

Mohang-3-ri-Mallipo

Mallipo is the Taean Peninsula's most popular beach. Lying just outside the national park boundaries, it's also the most developed, lined with hotels, restaurants, cafés, convenience stores, and even a few surf schools. It gets busy in summer, but its ample length means it never feels

 Must See

📷 PICTURE PERFECT
Sunset at Kkotji Beach

Along the sidewalk at Kkotji Beach's north end is a small plaza and reflecting pool where you can snap the sun setting between Halmibawi and Harabibawi rocks.

overcrowded. The beach has some of the best sand on the west coast, and the very gradual drop-off makes it ideal for families with kids. Buses 202 and 210 travel here from downtown Taean and take about an hour.

③
Gijipo Beach
기지포해수욕장

 Changgi-6-ri-Teulmusi-Gijipo Beach

Gijipo Beach is the complete opposite to Mallipo beach: a secluded stretch of sand whose facilities don't extend beyond an information center and some bathrooms. It's a wonderful place to reset and reconnect with nature after time spent in Korea's busy cities. The beach is backed by a copse of *gomsol* pine trees, and there's a small sand dune covered in Siberian sea rosemary, sand sedge, and other vegetation. Gijipo sits near the northern end of Anmyeondo Island, which was connected to the mainland until 1638, when a channel was dug to facilitate shipping.

④
Kkotji Beach
꽃지해수욕장

 Kkotji Beach

Farther down from Gijipo is this beautiful 3-mile (5-km) stretch of golden sand. The beach has become famous for its incredible sunsets as well as a pair of islets known as Halmibawi and Harabibawi, or Grandmother and Grandfather rocks. A local legend says that when her husband was sent into battle, a woman named Mido waited for him atop one of the rocks. She died waiting in vain and after her death a second rock appeared alongside the one she waited on. At low tide, a land bridge appears, connecting the islets and allowing you to walk out to them.

↑ An aerial view of Gungnamji Pond in Seodong Park

❷
BUYEO
부여

C4 38 miles (62 km) E of Daejeon From Seoul, Daejeon
247-9 Seongwang-ro; www.buyeo.go.kr/html/tour

It may not be obvious today, but the unassuming city of Buyeo was once one of the peninsula's most powerful cities. From 538 to 660 CE, it was the capital of the Baekje kingdom; today, its museums and historic sites preserve this halcyon era of the culturally influential dynasty.

Did You Know?

The Baekje kingdom introduced Buddhism to Japan.

①
Buyeo National Museum
국립부여박물관

5 Geumseong-ro
Dongnam Apartments
9am-6pm Tue-Sun
buyeo.museum.go.kr

This large museum provides the ideal introduction to the achievements of the Baekje Dynasty (18 BCE–660 CE). Though the kingdom was established in what is now Seoul, it was during the 120 years that the capital was located in Buyeo, then known as Sabi, that its cultural hegemony reached its zenith. The collection of this museum focuses on the dynasty's art and history. Among the highlights here is the beautifully decorated Baekje gilt-bronze incense burner. Its base is shaped like a dragon, and a phoenix perches on top. Its intricately designed lid depicts a series of mountain peaks, several immortals, a number of musicians, and some imaginary wild beasts.

← A decorated gilt-bronze incense burner

②
Jeongnimsa Temple Site and Museum
정림사지, 정림사지박물관

83 Jeongnim-ro
Jeongnimsa Temple Site Temple: 9am-10pm daily (Nov-Feb: to 9pm); Museum: 9am-6pm Tue-Sun (Nov-Feb: to 5pm) Jan 1, Seollal, Chuseok
jeongnimsaji.or.kr

Buddhism flourished under the Baekje Dynasty, and one of its most important temples stood on this site. Sadly, all that remains today is a five-story granite pagoda, along with a Stone Seated Buddha, which was built during the later Goryeo Dynasty (918–1392). A designated National Treasure, it's one of just two remaining Baekje pagodas. A museum on the grounds offers an indcation as to how impressive the complex once was and displays various excavated temple relics. Be sure to note the Mona Lisa-esque "Baekje smile" that many Baekje depictions of the Buddha possess.

Gungnamji Pond
궁남지

Dongnam Apartments

Commissioned by King Mu in 634 CE, this pleasure pond in Seodong Park was the first artificial pond created in Korea. Today, a small footbridge provides access to an island in the pond, where you'll find a wooden pavilion. It makes for a lovely spot from which you can admire the willows along the shore and the lotus flowers in the pond. These generally bloom in late spring, prior to the annual Buyeo SeoDong Lotus Festival held here in July.

Busosanseong Fortress
부소산성

31 Buso-ro **9am-6pm daily (Nov-Feb: to 5pm)**

On a small mountain next to the Baengmagang River is this rammed-earth fortress, built during the Baekje Dynasty. The fortress was used to defend the adjoining palace in times of war. Visitors can follow shady walking paths that run across the slopes and past the foundations of historic gates and pavilions. The fortress's most famous spot is Nakhwaam, "Falling Flowers Rock." Legend says that when the Silla kingdom and its Tang China allies laid siege to the palace in 660 CE, Baekje's court ladies, rather than be taken captive, jumped off the cliff. As they plunged toward the river, their fluttering clothes were said to resemble falling petals.

⑤   Baekje Cultural Land and Baekje Historical Museum
백제문화단지
백제역사문화관

455 Baekjemun-ro **Baekje Historical Museum** **9am-6pm Tue-Sun (Nov-Feb: to 5pm)** **Jan 1** **bhm.or.kr**

Baekje Cultural Land may be Korea's largest history-themed park, but there are no theme-park rides here. Instead, the complex has re-created Baekje buildings to give an idea of how these places would have looked. Visitors can explore a reconstructed Buyeo palace, a royal temple with an imposing five-story pagoda, and a Baekje village. These homes represent the abodes of actual historical figures, from a celebrated general to a blacksmith and a brewer. There's also a museum that displays some of the excavated relics and uses videos and graphics to depict various important historical sites.

Must See

EAT

Goodoorae Dolsodbap
구드래돌솥밥

Hearty meals of *dolssambap*, rice and vegetables cooked in a hot stone pot, amid a rustic country atmosphere.

31 Naruteo-ro **0418369259.modoo.at**

Yeonkkot Iyagi
연꽃이야기

This cute place alongside Gungnamji Pond serves *yeonipbab*, rice wrapped in lotus leaves, a local specialty.

22 Seongwang-ro **041 833 3336**

EXPERIENCE MORE

③
Cheongju
청주

D3 85 miles (137 km) S of Seoul From Seoul, Daejeon 38 Sangdang-ro 69-beon-gil; www.cheongju.go.kr

Cheongju, the capital city of Chungcheongbuk-do Province, doesn't see many tourists, but it has a trio of sights that more than merit a visit. The **Cheongju Early Printing Museum** (청주고인쇄박물관) stands on the spot where, in 1377, Buddhist monks created the world's oldest surviving book printed with movable metal type, seven decades before Gutenberg and his Bible. **Cheongju National Museum** (국립청주박물관) explores regional culture and history through its collections. Highlights here include a gold crown excavated from a royal tomb. On the east edge of town is **Sangdansanseong Fortress** (상당산성), whose 2.5 miles (4 km) of walls mostly date back centuries, to around the 1710s. Restaurants just inside the east gate serve hearty food.

Cheongju Early Printing Museum
713 Jijkji-daero Cheongju Early Printing Museum & Heungdeoksaji 9am-6pm Tue-Sun Jan 1, Seollal globaljikji.org

Cheongju National Museum
143 Myeongam-ro Cheongju National Museum 9am-6pm Tue-Sun cheongju.museum.go.kr

Sangdansanseong Fortress
5 miles (8 km) NE of Cheongju Sanseongnammun, Sangdangsanseongjongjeom

④
Daecheongho Lake
대청호

D4 9 miles (15 km) S of Cheongju From Cheongju

Chungcheongbuk-do is Korea's only landlocked province, but it still has plenty of waterfront thanks to this many-armed lake – formed in 1982 by the Daecheong Dam – that sprawls across several counties. Near

INSIDER TIP
Visiting Cheongnamdae

To visit Cheongnamdae, purchase a ticket at the ticket office *(148-31 Micheon-ri, Munui-myeon)*. Tickets to drive to the complex can be bought online, but only by residents of Korea.

its northern tip is the **Munui Cultural Heritage Complex** (문의문화재단지). Sites that would have been flooded by the dam were moved or re-created here, among them a 17th-century government guesthouse. There's also an exhibition hall and art gallery. Additionally, the lakeshore is home to **Cheongnamdae** (청남대). Once a presidential villa, the scenic complex is now open to the public, letting you explore the grounds and former presidential quarters.

Munui Cultural Heritage Complex
721 Daecheonghoban-ro, Cheongju Munui Cultural Heritage Complex Terminal 9am-6pm Tue-Sun (Nov-Feb: to 5pm) Jan 1, Seollal, Chuseok

Cheongnamdae
148-31 Micheon-ri, Munui-myeon Munui Hyanggyo Feb-Nov: 9am-6pm; Dec-Jan: 9am-5pm Mon, Jan 1, Seollal, Chuseok chnam.chungbuk.go.kr

⑤
Chungjuho Lake
충주호

D3 7 miles (11 km) E of Chungju From Chungju

Another massive lake created by 1980s dam construction, Chungjuho is a popular place

↑ The walls of Cheongju's Sangdansanseong Fortress at sunset

Chungjuho Lake surrounded by colorful fall foliage

for fishing, boating, and waterskiing. The best way to soak up its scenery is on one of the lake cruises operated by the **Chungjuho Cruise Company** (충주호크루즈). There are three piers on the lake, but Chungju Naru, near the dam, is the most convenient if you don't have a car, as buses run from the nearby city of Chungju. Cruise schedules vary based on the time of year and water levels, so it's best to reserve tickets in advance.

Chungjuho Cruise Company, Chungju Naru Pier
🏠 882 Jideung-ro, Chungju
🚌 Chungju Naru Rest Stop
🕘 9am–6pm daily 🌐 chungjuho.com

Songnisan National Park
속리산국립공원

📍 D4 🏠 84 Beopjusa-ro, Boeun 🚌 Sangpan
🌐 knps.or.kr

Right in the middle of the country, Songnisan National Park follows a ridgeline that runs north to south and reaches 3,471 ft (1,058 m) at its highest point. It's a remarkably beautiful preserve of towering peaks and plunging valleys, and provides refuge to almost 3,000 different animal species, rare black woodpeckers, and flying squirrels among them. As far as flora goes, the park's most interesting specimen is a 600-year-old pine tree near the main entrance. According to legend, back in the 1400s it raised its branches to allow King Sejo's palanquin to pass, and in gratitude the king named it a minister of the second rank.

Many visitors come to Songnisan not for nature, but to see **Beopjusa** (법주사), which was founded no later than 553 CE and is among Korea's most impressive Buddhist temples. Its main hall is one of only a few in the country that are two stories, and it possesses a rare wooden pagoda, the five-story Palseongjeon, completed in 1626. Most eye-catching is the temple's 110-ft- (33-m-) tall gilded Buddha statue. Starkly set amid the dark green of the surrounding mountains, the temple appears as if it's been beamed in from another dimension.

Beopjusa Temple
🏠 405 Beopjusa-ro, Boeun
🚌 Songnisan
🌐 beopjusa.org

> **Did You Know?**
> Beopjusa's huge 8th-century CE iron cauldron could prepare enough soup to feed 30,000 people.

A Maitreya Buddha statue at Beopjusa Temple

⑦ Woraksan National Park
월악산국립공원

🅐 D3 🏠 1647 Mireuk-songgye-ro, Jecheon 🚌 Samsindang-ap 🌐 knps.or.kr

Bordering Chungjuho Lake's southern shore, Woraksan National Park marks the intersection of the Songnisan and Sobaeksan mountain ranges. Within its boundaries are more than 20 peaks, pine and Mongolian oak forests, and rare Amur gorals.

Most of Woraksan's main attractions are found in the western part of the park. The Mireukdaewon Stone Temple Site (충주 미륵대원지) holds the atmospheric remains of a temple destroyed by the Mongols in the 1200s, highlighted by a 35-ft (10.5-m) stone Buddha statue. The Joseon-era Deokjusanseong Fortress (덕주산성) once guarded a strategic mountain pass. Today, the main access point at Deokjugol bus stop is also the start of a popular 3-mile (5-km) hiking route to Yeongbong, Woraksan's highest peak at 3,593 ft (1,095 m). Hikers who reach the summit are rewarded with views of Chungjuho.

Did You Know?
Haneuljae Pass (하늘재), in Woraksan National Park, is one of Korea's oldest roads, built in 156 CE.

⑧ Daejeon
대전

🅐 D4 🏠 100 miles (162 km) S of Seoul 🚆 From Seoul, Busan, Gwangju, Jeonju & Daegu 🚌 From Seoul, Incheon, Gwangju & Jeonju ℹ️ 7 Daehak-ro; www.daejeontour.co.kr

Daejeon is one of Korea's most thoroughly modern cities. Barely a village until two major rail lines were joined here in 1914, it's boomed in the years since, but has few tourist sights. Its most recognizable building is the **Hanbit Tower** (한빛탑), a shimmering silver observatory that was constructed for Taejon Expo '93 and resembles a speared UFO. A short distance from the tower is the **National Science Museum** (국립중앙과학관). Geared toward kids, it has a planetarium and plenty of hands-on exhibits centered on natural history and future tech, among other subjects. Also on this side of town is the riverside Hanbat Arboretum (한밭수목원), where visitors can amble among themed forests, gardens, and artificial ponds and streams. On Daejeon's eastern edge is the city's most notable sight, **Uam Historical Park** (우암사적공원), where the renowned Joseon scholar Song Si-yeol (pen name: Uam) lived and taught in the 1600s. Near the entrance to the park is Namganjeongsa (남간정사), a picturesque classroom built over a brook that empties into a small pond. After exploring Daejeon's sights, enjoy a relaxing soak at the Yuseong Hot Springs. Try one of the many nearby hotel spas or public baths or dip your feet in the free Yuseong Foot Bath (족욕체험장) in Yuseong Oncheon Park (유성온천공원).

Hanbit Tower
 🏠 480 Daedeok-daero 🚌 Hanbit-tap 🕘 9:30am–5:40pm

Admiring the colorful landscape in Woraksan National Park

National Science Museum
481 Daedeok-daero National Science Museum 9:30am-5:30pm Tue-Sun Jan 1, Seollal, Chuseok science.go.kr

Uam Historical Park
53 Chungjeong-ro Uam Historical Park Summer: 5am-9pm daily; winter: 6am-8pm daily

Danyang
단양

D3 105 miles (170 km) SE of Seoul From Busan & Seoul From Seoul & Jecheon 43 Darian-ro; www.danyang.go.kr

Danyang has been something of a tourist town for centuries, long feted by Joseon poets for its ample natural beauty. Much of their verse was devoted to the so-called Eight Scenic Views of Danyang (단양 팔경). Contemporary travelers may find some of these sights overhyped by the poets, but a visit to them is still an enjoyable way to soak up the region's rural charms.

Dodam Sambong (도담삼봉) is a trio of jagged islets in the Namhangang River north of central Danyang. If you can, visit when the islets are beautifully shrouded in the morning mist or lit up at night. Just upstream is Seongmun (석문), a stone arch. Buses run to these sites from downtown; be sure to get off at Dodam Sambong bus stop.

Gudambong (구담봉) and Oksunbong (옥순봉) are cliffs fuzzed with greenery that rise up from the shore of Chungjuho Lake. They're best viewed from one of the tour boats that depart from Janghui Naru pier. Take bus 402, 403, 404, or 405 to get to the pier. Over to the south of town is Sainam (사인암), a reddish, perfectly vertical cliff on a stream. Take bus 521, 522, 523, or 532 to Jikti bus stop, from where it's a short walk.

Not one of the great eight, but still deserving of a visit, is **Gosu Cave** (고수동굴), which stretches for more than a kilometer underground and contains stalactites, waterfalls, and small pools. It's a simple 25-minute walk or a quick bus ride from central Danyang.

Gosu Cave
8 Gosudonggul-gil Gosu Cave Ipgu 9am-5pm daily gosucave.co.kr

Independence Hall of Korea
독립기념관

C3 1 Dongnipgin-yeomgwan-ro, Cheonan Independence Hall of Korea 9:30am-6pm Tue-Sun (Nov-Feb: to 5pm) i815.or.kr

From 1905 until 1945, Korea was a protectorate and then colony of Japan. It was a period of exploitation,

> **KOREA'S INDEPENDENCE MOVEMENT**
>
> After protestors gave a public reading of the Korean Declaration of Independence on March 1, 1919 in Seoul's Tapgol Park, demonstrations spread across the country. Though the Japanese violently suppressed them, it energized the movement. Yet it took until 1945 and Japan's defeat in World War II for Korea to regain its independence.

one whose scars have yet to fully heal. The giant Independence Hall of Korea explores the history of this era in great detail and memorializes those who fought for independence. Across seven exhibition halls, it provides reminders of the repression Koreans faced during this period, like being forced to take up Japanese names. Alongside these repressive acts, the museum documents the efforts of individuals to defend their freedom and culture, whether by taking up arms or secretly compiling a Korean dictionary. You can explore the hall on your own or, if you prefer, request a docent-led tour by phone *(041 560 0500)*.

The partially frozen Namhangang River and Dodam Sambong

Boating by the scenic Dodamsambong Peaks in Danyang

⑪ Gongju
공주

C4 86 miles (138 km) S of Seoul From Gwangju, Seoul & Yeosu From Seoul & Daejeon 280 Ungjin-ro; www.gongju.go.kr/tour/

Gongju's modest size belies its historical importance. The town was the capital of the Baekje kingdom for several decades in the 5th and 6th centuries, when it was known as Ungjin, or "Bear Port." It's in this area where Gongju's main attractions are found.

Overlooking the Geumgang River is the **Gongsanseong Fortress** (공산성). The original Baekje structure was a packed-earth fortification, but the stone walls visible today were constructed in the Joseon era. Visitors can walk the 1.5 miles (2.5 km) of walls to explore what remains of the presumed Baekje palace site and take in lovely river views from the pavilions. West of the fortress are the seven ancient royal Baekje tombs in **Songsan-ri** (공주 무령왕릉과 왕릉원), the most important of which belonged to King Muryeong (r. 501–23). Its discovery in 1971 was one of Korea's most important archaeological finds, revealing over 4,600 artifacts. Many of these items are now on display in the **Gongju National Museum** (국립공주박물관), including a stone guardian animal that resembles a flying pig and a sword with dragon and phoenix decorations.

Ancient Tombs in Songsan-ri
37 Wangneung-ro
Ungjin Doseogwan
9am–6pm daily (Nov–Feb: to 5pm)
Jan 1 & public hols

Gongsanseong Fortress
280 Ungjin-ro
Gongsanseong 9am–6pm (Nov–Feb: to 5pm)
Jan 1 & public hols

Gongju National Museum
34 Gwangwangdanji-gil
Gongju National Museum
9am–6pm Tue–Sun
Jan 1, Seollal, Chuseok
gongju.museum.go.kr

⑫ Sejong
세종

C4 86 miles (138 km) S of Seoul From Daejeon & Seoul sejong.go.kr

Sejong was founded as a planned city in the early 2000s with the intent that it would become South Korea's new capital, thus easing Seoul's warping economic and social dominance. That didn't happen, but many government ministries did relocate here, and the city functions as an important administrative center. It lacks the vibrancy typical of Korean cities, though, and walking its broad avenues, among uniformly new towers, feels like navigating a real-world simulator. Its one destination of note is the **Sejong National Arboretum** (국립세종수목원), which displays more than

---

DRINK

Blue Whale Brew House
블루웨일 브루하우스
This microbrewery has ales, IPAs, stouts, and more on tap at its Chungju pub. Perfect after a long day on Chungjuho Lake.
D3 109 Sajik-ro, Chungju whalebrew.kr

Champspace Coffee Roasters
챔프스페이스 커피로스터스
Impeccable coffees are made here by an award-winning barista. Be sure to try the Champ's Einspanner, with its added ground nuts.
D4 97 Suhyang-gil, Daejeon
0507 1425 5388

Bameu
바므
Chestnuts are a Gongju specialty, and this café adds chestnut ice cream to a flat white.
C4 3-2 Jemin 2-gil, Gongju
0507 1339 4904

→ A glasshouse of colorful flowers at the Sejong National Arboretum

The interior of the Sudeoksa Temple and *(inset)* the temple's facade

4,000 plant species over some two dozen themed gardens, including ones that recreate a palace garden and the garden of a traditional rural home.

Sejong National Arboretum

136 Sumogwon-ro ⊠ Sejong National Arboretum ⊙ 9am–6pm daily ⌂ sjna.or.kr

---

Sudeoksa Temple
수덕사

B3 79 Sudeoksaan-gil, Yesan ⊠ Sudeoksa

Set on the southern slopes of Deoksungsan Mountain, Sudeoksa Temple was likely founded in the latter half of the 6th century. The primary reason to visit is to see the temple's main hall. Built in 1308, it's the oldest wooden building in the country, yet unlike most Buddhist temple structures, the hall is largely unpainted and possesses a rustic, austere beauty. Inside is a wooden Buddhist triad that also dates to 1308.

Magoksa Temple
마곡사

C4 966 Magoksa-ro, Gongju ⊠ Magoksa ⌂ magoksa.or.kr

Founded in 640, Magoksa is one of Korea's best preserved Buddhist monasteries. Thanks to its secluded location, which is remote even by Buddhist temple standards, it escaped the Japanese invasions of the 16th century and the Korean War relatively unscathed. The only major reconstruction was necessitated after a fire in the mid-1600s. The temple has northern and southern sections, split by a stream that flows through the temple. Cross the stone bridge over the stream and pause amid timeworn buildings. It can make you feel as though you've entered another realm (you might even say nirvana, though the monks would be quick to correct you).

Magoksa is one of seven mountain temples in Korea collectively recognized by UNESCO and contains five designated National Treasures. Among these is the regal two-story Daeungbojeon Hall, which houses three golden Buddha statues (Past, Present, and Future) and overlooks the rest of the sprawling complex.

> **TEMPLESTAY**
>
> Magoksa is an ideal place to take part in a Templestay. This well-regarded program lets visitors experience Buddhist monastic life by participating in meditation, meals, tea ceremonies, and other activities. Stays are offered at 156 sites across the country, 28 of which conduct activities in English. Each temple takes a slightly different approach: some provide an authentic monastic experience while others focus on rest and relaxation. Reservations can be made on the Templestay website *(www.templestay.com).*

15

Haemieupseong Fortress
서산 해미읍성

B3 143 Nammun-2-ro, Seosan Mar-Oct: 5am-9pm daily; Nov-Feb: 6am-7pm daily Haemisioe

Unlike *sanseong*, or "mountain fortresses," *eupseong* are lowland fortresses built around settlements that functioned as both military bases and administrative centers. Constructed between 1417 and 1421 to defend the area against Japanese pirates, Haemieupseong is one of the best-preserved examples of a Joseon-era *eupseong*. Be sure to visit its south gate, which is original, and Cheongheojeong Pavilion, where officials rested and composed poetry.

Besides its architectural significance, the fort has an important, and gruesome, place in the history of Korean Christianity. In the 1860s, when the country was going through a period of violent persecution of Catholics, more than 1,000 believers were imprisoned and executed here.

16

Gyeryongsan National Park
계룡산국립공원

C4 86 Donghaksa-2-ro, Gongju Donghaksa-ipgu knps.or.kr

Gyeryongsan's peculiar name (meaning Chicken Dragon Mountain) supposedly derives from the fact its ridgeline resembles a dragon wearing a rooster's comb. While this mythical cosplay isn't easy to make out, the real history of the mountain is just as interesting. Its excellent feng shui meant the site was nearly chosen over Seoul to be the royal capital in the Joseon era. Instead, Gyeryongsan became Korea's second national park, in 1968. Though it's only 25 sq miles (65 sq km), it packs in granite rock domes, tumbling waterfalls, bucolic valleys, and 16 mountain peaks, of which Cheonhwangbong (2,779 ft/ 847m) is the tallest. Eleven endangered species are also found here, including otters and black woodpeckers.

The park also contains two important Buddhist temples. In the east, and easily accessed from Daejeon, is **Donghaksa** (동학사), home to a community of female monks. In spring, the valley leading to the temple from the park office is famous for its cherry blossoms. In the west of the park is **Gapsa** (갑사). The temple has existed since 420 and possesses a lovely mix of spirituality and natural beauty. A popular 6-mile (10-km) trail links the two temples via Gwaneumbong Peak.

Donghaksa Temple
462 Donghaksa-1-ro, Gongju Donghaksa

Gapsa Temple
567-3 Gapsa-ro, Gongju Gapsa gapsa.org

> Constructed between 1417 and 1421 to defend the area against Japanese pirates, Haemieupseong is one of the best examples of a Joseon-era *eupseong*.

← Hiking past a temple in Gyeryongsan National Park

Did You Know?

Western missionaries built a resort complex at Daecheon Beach in the 1930s.

Daecheon Beach
대천해수욕장

🅐 B4 📍 110 miles (175 km) SW of Seoul 🚌 Mud-gwangjang ℹ️ 116 Daehae-ro, Boryeong & 123 Mud-ro, Boryeong; www.brcn.go.kr

Take a bus around three hours from Seoul, or two hours from Daejeon, to reach this beach, the largest on Korea's west coast, in the city of Boryeong. It's already an expansive area at high tide, 2 miles (3.5 km) long and 330 ft (100 m) wide, but grows even bigger when the tide goes out. As the sea retreats, it exposes some vast mudflats.

While other Chungcheong-do Province beaches have a rustic, almost-off-the-grid charm, Daecheon leans hard in the opposite direction. Resort complexes for Western missionaries first popped up here in the 1930s, and today the streets beyond the sand are lined with hotels, bars, cafés, and row upon row of restaurants serving sashimi and grilled shellfish. The area is now popular all summer, but reaches fever pitch during the annual Boryeong Mud Festival (www.mudfestival.or.kr), held over two weeks in July and August. This festival was started in 1998 as a way of promoting cosmetics made from the local mud, which has an exceptionally high mineral content, but the event has since grown into one of Korea's biggest parties. Today it includes K-pop concerts from some of the biggest stars and various mud-related events, including actual mud slides, mud dance parties, mud obstacle courses, and much more besides. There's also a family zone with more gentle activities just for kids. Visitors can purchase festival tickets on the website or in person. If visiting during the festival, lodging should be booked well in advance.

→ People partaking in an event at the Boryeong Mud Festival

SHOP

Boryeong Mud Theme Park
보령머드테마파크

Pick up soap, masks, cleansing foam, and other products made from the renowned local mud at this center near Daecheon Beach.

🅐 B4 📍 55 Gojam 2-gil, Boryeong 🌐 bmtp.or.kr

Geumsan Ginseng Market
금산국제인삼시장

The largest ginseng market in Korea, it's *the* place to buy ginseng roots, infused liquor, and red ginseng.

🅐 B4 📍 11-7 Jungdo-ri, Geumsan 📞 041 752 1815

Sungsimdang
성심당

Expect to wait in line for cakes, *twigim soboro* (fried streusel buns), and other treats at this uber-popular Daejeon bakery.

🅐 D4 📍 15 Daejong-ro 480-beon-gil, Daejeon 🌐 sungsimdang.co.kr

A DRIVING TOUR
CHUNGJUHO LAKE

Distance 69 miles (111 km) **Stopping-off points** Cafés and restaurants cluster just south of the Cheongpung Cultural Heritage Complex and in Seongam-ri Village **Terrain** Paved roads

Locator Map

For more detail see p152

Created by the damming of the Namhangang River, Chungjuho Lake sprawls every which way as it usurps the river's course between Danyang and Chungju. The lake's channels create an endless series of bays, inlets, and narrow peninsulas, while the surrounding mountains and observatories provide stunning views. This drive links some of the finest lake vistas while also taking you to parts of the country that few travelers explore. At the end, you're rewarded with Korea's best hot springs.

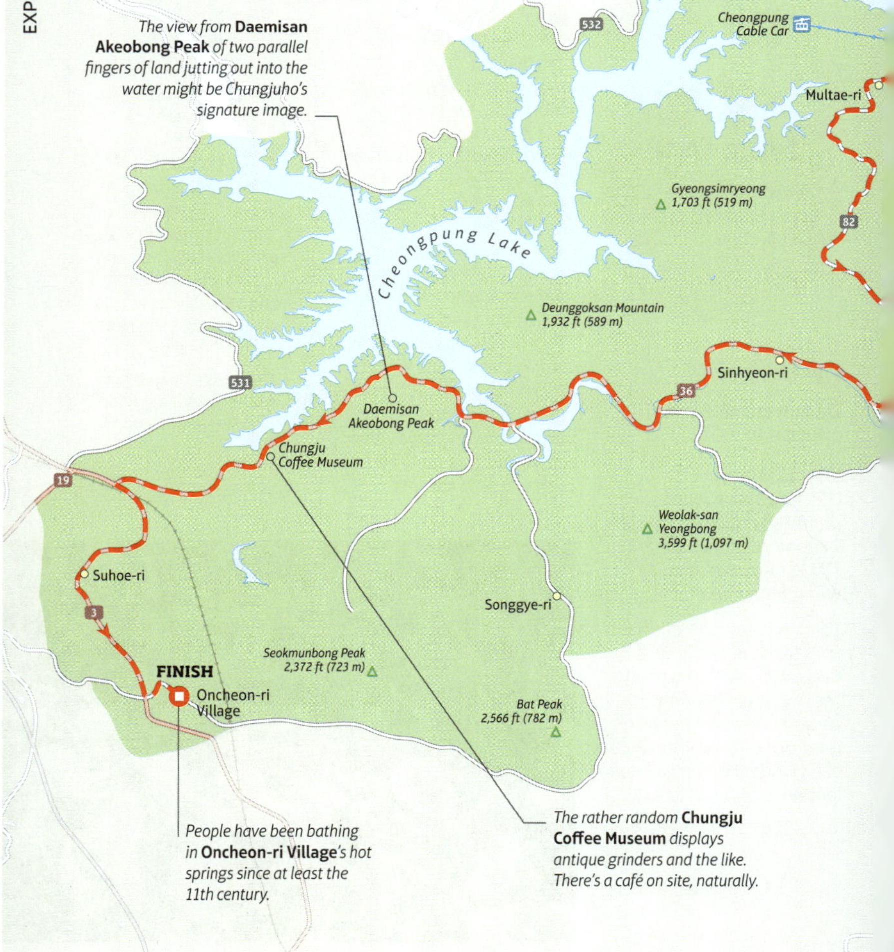

*The view from **Daemisan Akeobong Peak** of two parallel fingers of land jutting out into the water might be Chungjuho's signature image.*

*People have been bathing in **Oncheon-ri Village**'s hot springs since at least the 11th century.*

*The rather random **Chungju Coffee Museum** displays antique grinders and the like. There's a café on site, naturally.*

Cheongpung Cultural Heritage Complex preserves buildings moved here when the Chungju Dam was built.

↑ Stunning views down over Danyang from the Mancheonha Skywalk

The **Oksun Bridge Observatory**, reached by a short hike from the bridge itself, provides epic views of Oksunbong Cliff.

The impressive, glass-floored **Mancheonha Skywalk** looks over Danyang and Sobaeksan Mountain.

Start in the tourist town of **Danyang** (p161), which draws visitors with its Eight Scenic Views.

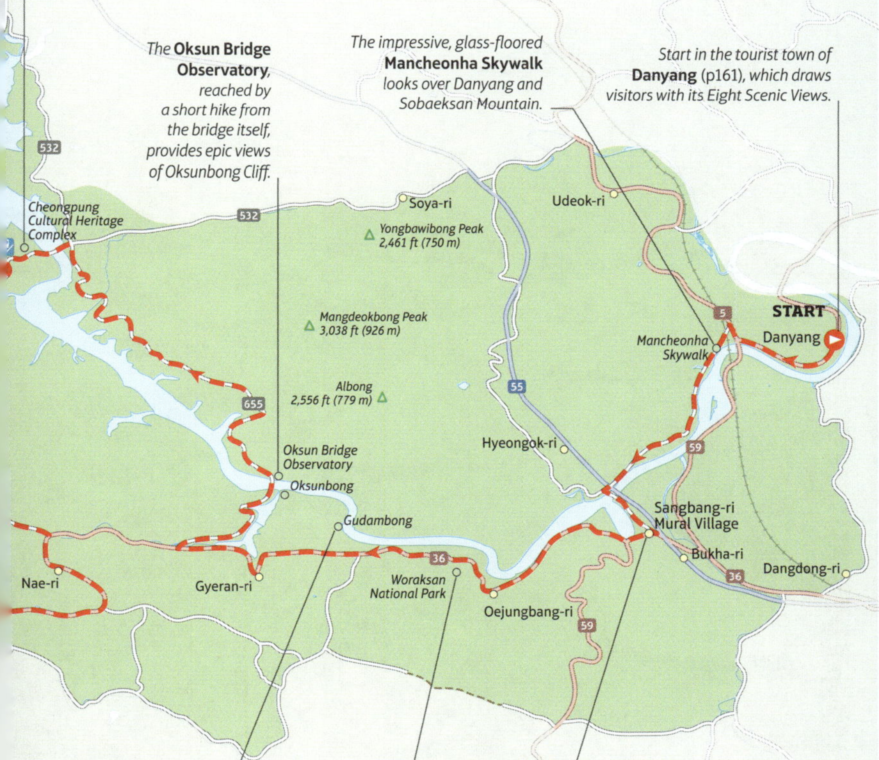

A roadside trail leads up to **Gudambong** and **Oksunbong**, two cliffs that rise from the lakeshore.

Woraksan National Park (p160) is where the Songnisan and Sobaeksan mountain ranges come together.

Walls in **Sangbang-ri Mural Village** are painted with traditional farming scenes.

GREAT VIEW
Cheongpung Cable Car

It seems unfair to single out a particular view, but nothing compares to the aerial angle you get from Cheongpung Cable Car (cheongpungcablecar.com).

169

The Joseon-era Naganeupseong Folk Village

JEOLLA-DO PROVINCE

The land that now makes up Jeolla-do has been home to thriving communities for millennia, as evidenced by the thousands of Neolithic and Bronze Age dolmens that dot the province. Later, Jeolla-do spent the first centuries of the Common Era as part of the Baekje kingdom before joining the rest of the peninsula under the subsequent banners of Silla, Goryeo, and Joseon.

Jeolla-do's foremost feature is the broad Honam Plain, a productive agricultural area that's long been Korea's rice basket. The plain, together with a 3,800-mile (6,100-km) coastline that facilitated fishing and maritime commerce, made Jeolla-do a prosperous region during the Joseon Dynasty and, for a time, the kingdom's most populous.

Though Jeolla-do's agricultural character has proven less advantageous in modern times, with industrial development focused elsewhere, it still has a reputation for fantastic local cuisine. Jeolla-do is also known for its association with the arts. Prized celadon pottery was created here during the Goryeo era, and the musical genre *pansori* emerged from the province in the 18th century. Today, the city of Gwangju has become a significant creative center, attracting artists and designers from across the globe and hosting the country's most important art biennial.

JEOLLA-DO PROVINCE

Must Sees
1. Jeonju
2. Byeonsanbando National Park
3. Gwangju
4. Juknokwon
5. Suncheonman Wetland

Experience More
6. Gunsan
7. Deogyusan National Park
8. Maisan Provincial Park
9. Geumsansa Temple
10. Gochang
11. Naejangsan National Park
12. Unjusa Temple
13. Mokpo
14. Jindo Island
15. Heuksando Island
16. Hongdo Island
17. Ttangkkeut Village
18. Songgwangsa Temple
19. Boseong
20. Naganeupseong Folk Village
21. Yeosu

Overlooking the traditional roofs of Jeonju Hanok Village

①
JEONJU
전주

C4 135 miles (215 km) S of Seoul From Seoul, Daejeon From Seoul, Gwangju, Daejeon, Yuseong, Busan 69 Girin-daero; www.tour.jeonju.go.kr

Jeonju is, without question, the best food city in Korea. Anyone who fancies themselves even a casual foodie can feast on bibimbap, *kongnamul gukbap* (bean sprout and rice soup), and more besides. The city is also a repository of traditional culture, which visitors can experience at the National Intangible Heritage Center and throughout the atmospheric Jeonju Hanok Village.

①
Jeonju Hanok Village
전주한옥마을

hanok.jeonju.go.kr

After Bukchon (p72) in Seoul, Jeonju Hanok Village is the best known cluster of *hanok* (p74) in Korea. Most of its 735 *hanok* date to the 1920s and 30s and many have been converted into guesthouses, galleries, and cafés. The main streets of Taejo-ro and Eunhaeng-ro can feel a bit carnivalesque, with stalls, shops, and people dressed in *hanbok* (traditional clothes) but significant historical sites are scattered throughout the village. Near to the entrance is the Romanesque **Jeondong Cathedral** (전동성당), built where the Catholic martyr Yun Ji-chung was beheaded in 1791.

Opposite is the 15th-century Gyeonggijeon Shrine (경기전), which holds the memorial portrait of Yi Seong-gye, who founded the Joseon Dynasty in 1392. Climb the hill to the Omokdae(오목대)pavilion,where Yi celebrated victory over Japanese invaders in 1380, to look over the black waves of tiled roofs below. On the south side of the village is **Jeonju Hyanggyo** (전주향교), one of Joseon's most important Confucian schools, which dates back to 1354. It's especially beautiful in fall when the ginkgo trees turn gold.

Learn about local history at **Jeonju Hanok Village History Hall** (전주한옥마을역사관), or visit the **Jeonju Korean Liquor Museum** (전주전통술박물관) to explore traditional brewing methods and drinking games.

Jeondong Cathedral
51 Taejo-ro 9am-5pm daily jeondong.or.kr

Jeonju Hyanggyo
139 Hyanggyo-gil Nov-Feb: 10am-5pm Tue-Sun; Mar-Oct: 9am-6pm Tue-Sun jjhyanggyo.or.kr

Jeonju Hanok Village History Hall
17-10 Choimyeonghui-gil 10am-6pm Tue-Sun

> **Did You Know?**
>
> The ginkgo trees in Jeonju Hyanggyo's main courtyard are more than 600 years old.

Jeonju Korean Liquor Museum

 9 Choimyeonghui-gil
May-Oct: 10am-8pm Tue-Sun (to 6pm Nov-Apr)
urisul.net

② National Intangible Heritage Center
국립무형유산원

95 Seohak-ro
9:30am-5:30pm Tue-Sun
Jan 1 nihc.go.kr

This center hosts captivating performances and exhibitions dedicated to Korean culture. Performing arts, ceremonies, rituals, and games, from tug-of-war to Buddhist dance, are all exhibited. English explanations are lacking, but the displays are presented so vividly, and with helpful videos and interactive features, that the emotions underlying these art forms are clear. Outside of such shows, visitors can hold abalone shells or step in front of a digital screen to have a *pansori* master sing to them.

③ Pungnammun Gate
풍남문

1 Pungnammun-3-gil

Just west of Jeonju Hanok Village is Pungnammun, the only surviving gate of the old city walls; the others were destroyed in 1905. The gate has a two-story wooden superstructure and is protected by a semicircular *ongseong* wall. It was first erected in 1734, but was partially rebuilt after suffering major fire damage in the 1760s, and required further restoration in the late 1970s.

④ Samcheon-dong Makgeolli Alley
삼천동막걸리골목

Jeonju has three streets filled with taverns specializing in *makgeolli* (a cloudy, unrefined rice wine). Of these, the alley in Samcheon-dong neighborhood, along Geomasan-ro, is the biggest. The dining experience here is something like a pub-food banquet. At any of the alley's ten or so taverns, even the smallest order comes with a kettle of *makgeolli* and half a dozen other dishes. These might include grilled fish, braised pork and kimchi, pork trotters, and mussel soup. It's one of Korea's best eating experiences.

EAT

Yongjinjip Makgeolli
용진집막걸리

This is a particularly good pick on Samcheon-dong Makgeolli Alley.

14 Geomasan-ro
063 224 8164

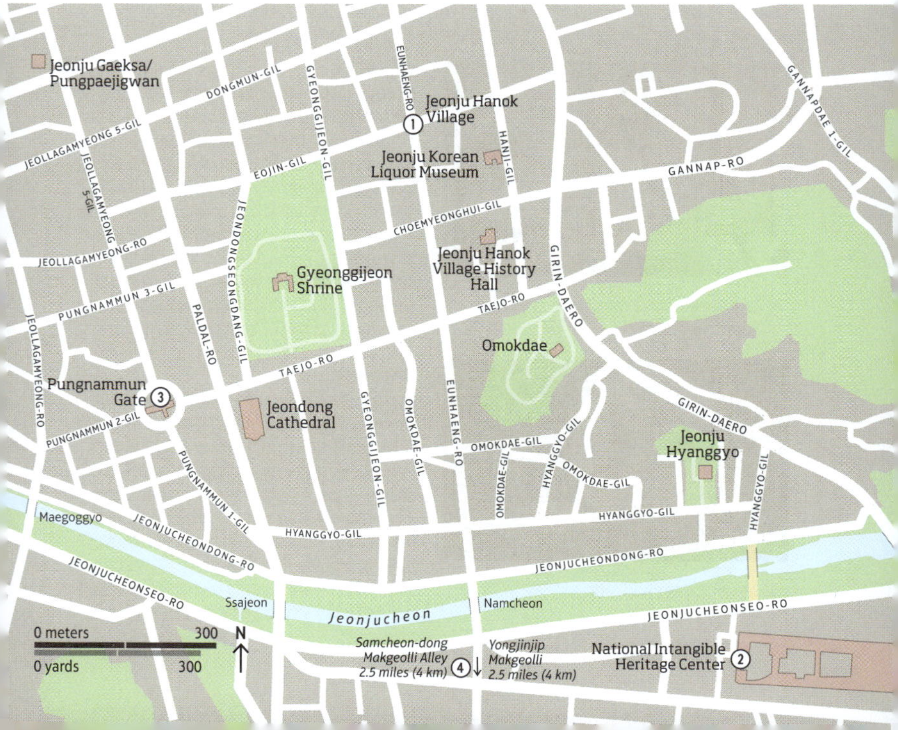

Must See

TRADITIONAL PERFORMANCE

Artistic performance seeps into Korean life in all manner of ways, whether through singing competitions on TV, the Seoul metro melody, or the K-pop singalongs that are ever-present today. But those are just modern iterations of a performing tradition that stretches back to the era of royal court music and bawdy masked dramas.

↑ An ensemble of musicians playing *jeongak* music

JEONGAK

Jeongak is formal music that was originally performed at the royal palace, government offices, and gatherings of the upper-class, typically on the occasion of a banquet, Confucian ceremony, or sacrificial rite. It's performed by a soloist or small ensembles of musicians on instruments including the *gayageum*, a type of zither; the *daegeum*, a large flute; and the *janggu*, an hourglass-shaped drum. Occasionally a singer accompanies the musicians.

↑ A performer and drummer in a *pansori* show

PANSORI

Pansori is a relatively young form of traditional art, having developed in the 1700s in Jeolla-do Province. Joined by a drummer, a lone performer sings, narrates, and acts out an epic drama. These revolve around one of five pieces that are based on a folk tale or historical event, and celebrate values like justice, loyalty, and filial piety. While performances traditionally lasted for several hours, today they're usually abbreviated.

TOP 3 TRADITIONAL PERFORMANCE VENUES

National Intangible Heritage Center *(p175)*
A celebration of rituals, crafts and games.

Jindo National Gugak Center *(p194)*
Enjoy live performances of traditional music.

Andong Hahoe Folk Village *(p232)*
Watch tea ceremonies or a Hahoe Mask Dance performance.

Masked actors dancing on stage as part of an elaborate *talchum* show and *(inset)* a collection of *talchum* masks

NONGAK
Meaning "farmers' music," *nongak* (also called *pungmul*) developed in agricultural communities as a way to lighten the load of village labor, appeal to the gods for a good harvest, and scare off evil spirits. Shows are loud, percussive, and a good time as performers sing, dance, and bang out rhythms on the *kkwaenggwari* (a small gong) and *janggu*. Most performers wear costumes that include either *goggal* (hats decorated with large, colorful balls of paper flowers), or *sangmo* (hats whose long ribbons are swirled in elaborate patterns).

SEUNGMU
Seungmu (known as "the monk dance") arose some 500 years ago from Buddhist tradition but is recognized more as an art form than a religious ritual. Performers, be they monks or laypeople, wear a conical white hat and a white top whose sleeves extend far beyond their hands. The dance's movements, which recall those found in Buddhist rituals, are considered some of the most beautiful in all of Korean dance.

TALCHUM
Talchum is a collective term for masked performances that include music, dance, and theater. While they vary across Korea, almost all forms are irreverent displays that use masks to satirize the foibles of corrupt aristocrats, lecherous monks, and foolish scholars. *Talchum* performances traditionally occurred wherever a village had a bit of open space, and involved plenty of jeering and cheering from the audience.

JULTAGI
Jultagi, or tightrope walking, originated in performances at the royal court to mark holidays and entertain guests. Over time it migrated out of the palace and into the villages. The Korean version involves not just balance, but acrobatics, singing, and lots of jokes. The tightrope walker, who performs while holding a fan for a bit of added flair, is supported by a clown who adds their own comic remarks and works to liven up the crowd.

BYEONSANBANDO NATIONAL PARK

변산반도국립공원

📍 B5　🚗 36 miles (58 km) SW of Jeonju　🚌 From Buan　🌐 knps.or.kr

This national park on the Byeonsanbando Peninsula has a bit of everything: dramatic cliffs, ancient temples, vast mudflats, mist-wrapped mountains, and sunset-blessed beaches. It's also one of Korea's most important and fascinating geological sites, home to a thriving wildlife.

A national park since 1988, the impressive Byeonsanbando spans 59 sq miles (154 sq km). It can be roughly divided into two parts. Oebyeonsan (Outer Byeonsan) is where beaches dotted with crabs and hungry seabirds meet the Yellow Sea, while Naebyeonsan (Inner Byeonsan) is a mountainous area filled with Buddhist temples, picturesque waterfalls, and challenging hiking trails. For keen walkers, these walking routes are best accessed from the village of Seokpo-ri.

In addition to being a national park, Byeonsanbando is part of a UNESCO Global Geopark. Intense volcanic and tectonic activity during the Cretaceous period left the area with a permanent record of the upheaval in the form of columnar joints, recumbent folds, and other formations that are on display at places like Jikso Falls and the Chaeseokgang Cliffs.

Jeokbyeokgang River, which flows through Byeonsanbando National Park

Must See

1 Boats crowded around Gyeokpo Port.

2 Statues of Buddhist Gods holding musical instruments at Naesosa Temple, built in 633.

3 Steps leading up to the Daeungjeon Hall of the Buddhist Gaeamsa Temple.

Did You Know?

Byeonsanbando National Park is home to more than 2,600 animal species and 1,100 plant species.

EXPLORING BYEONSANBANDO NATIONAL PARK

Byeonsanbando is rural and remote by Korean standards, and the best way to explore it is by car. If you have the time and a bit of patience, though, most of its main sights can be reached by bus from the town of Buan. Highway 30 is the main road for trips around the peninsula's perimeter, but Byeonsanhaebyeon-ro, which runs close to the coast between Buan and Gyeokpo Port, is more scenic. To see more of the park's interior, follow Local Road 736.

The popular **Byeonsan Beach** (변산해수욕장) is bookended by rocky headlands. At low tide, vast mudflats appear, blurring the distinction between land and sea.

The 1-mile (2-km) **Gosapo Beach** (고사포해수욕장) is the peninsula's longest. The pine forest, a natural windbreak, creates idyllic conditions.

With shallow water and many cafés nearby, **Gyeokpo Beach** (격포해수욕장) is great for families.

The 98-ft- (30-m-) tall **Jeokbyeokgang Cliffs** (부안적벽강), and their natural features, are best seen from the shore.

Chaeseokgang Cliffs (채석강) were formed by sediments deposited in an ancient lake, then eroded by the waves.

Walking along part of the Gosapo Beach

Try delicacies such as jeoneo (gizzard shad) and jjukkumi (webfoot octopus) at **Gyeokpo Port** (격포항).

Near to the small **Mohang Beach** (모항갯벌해수욕장) are unusual rocks formed by volcanic activity.

Must See

> **INSIDER TIP**
> **Time the Tide**
>
> A visit to Chaeseokgang Cliffs can be completely different depending on the tide. Low tide exposes a trail around the cliffs along with sea caves in the cliff face.

Close to **Gaeamsa Temple** (개암사) is Ulgeumbawi Rock. Legend says when a monk named Wonhyo moved into one of its caves, water gushed out of the ground.

A 1.5-mile (2.5-km) hike from Seokpo-ri Village, the lovely **Jikso Falls** (직소폭포) drop 98 ft (30 m) into a circular pond below.

Founded in 633, **Naesosa Temple** (내소사) has a beautiful mountain backdrop. The approach is famed for its pine trees, and the cherry trees that blossom in spring.

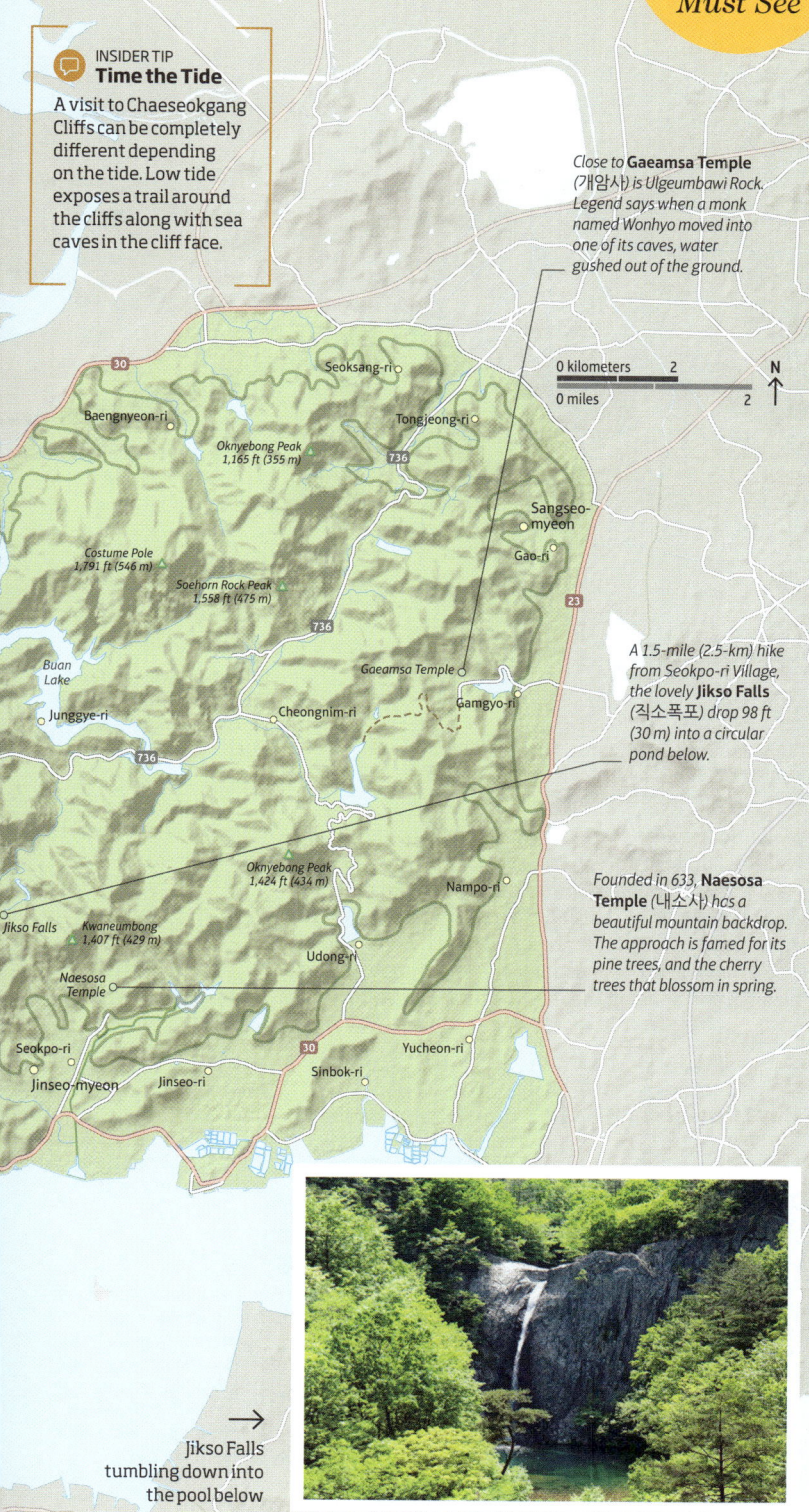

→ Jikso Falls tumbling down into the pool below

↑ The vast Asia Culture Center, bordered by trees

③ GWANGJU
광주

C6 185 miles (297 km) S of Seoul From Seoul, Daejeon From Seoul, Daejeon, Jeonju, Busan 904 Mujin-daero; www.tour.gwangju.go.kr

Jeolla-do Province's largest city, Gwangju holds a hallowed place in Korean history as the site of the May 18, 1980 Gwangju Uprising, a student-led protest against martial law that set the country on the path to democracy. In recent decades, Gwangju has developed into a major arts hub, hosting Asia's most important art biennial and opening the massive Asia Culture Center.

① May 18 Democracy Square
5.18민주광장

 Culture Complex

This plaza was the epicenter of the 1980 Gwangju Uprising. After protests spread from Chonnam National University, demonstrators converged on the now former Jeollanam-do Provincial Office (옛전남도청), on the square's southwest side. This was also where the city's citizen militia made its last stand before the military retook control of Gwangju.

Numerous memorials in the square commemorate the citizens killed during the uprising. Today, the square frequently hosts festivals and other events.

② Asia Culture Center
국립아시아문화전당

38 Munhwajeondan-ro Culture Complex 10am–6pm Tue-Sun Jan 1 acc.go.kr

Occupying the eastern part of May 18 Democracy Square, this massive – and massively fun – complex celebrates modern Asian culture and creativity. The labyrinthine campus includes theaters, a children's space, and public artworks. The Asia Culture Museum's permanent exhibition ranges from Vietnamese pop music to Indochinese independence struggles, while the ACC Creation building hosts rotating exhibits that display interactive pieces, video art, and multimedia epics.

THE GWANGJU UPRISING

In December 1979, General Chun Doo-hwan seized power in a coup and declared martial law. When paratroopers assaulted Gwangju student protesters on May 18, 1980, the brutality only caused the demonstrations to spread. Citizen militias held the city until May 27, when the military crushed the uprising. Tragically, hundreds were killed, but the uprising energized Korea's pro-democracy movement, which ultimately succeeded in 1987.

Must See

Did You Know?
Gwangju is the hometown of Han Kang, winner of the 2024 Nobel Prize in Literature.

③ Jungoe Park
중외공원

This large park is the site of several important cultural institutions. Foremost is the **Gwangju Biennale Exhibition Hall** (광주비엔날레전시관), the main venue for Korea's biggest event on the international art calendar, generally held in the fall of even-numbered years.

Nearby, the **Gwangju Museum of Art** (광주시립미술관) has a collection of more than 5,000 pieces, primarily from modern Korean and Jeolla-do artists. This being Gwangju, rotating exhibitions often touch on themes of democracy and human rights. Between these two facilities is the **Gwangju History & Folk Museum** (광주역사민속박물관), which is devoted to the regional culture of Jeollanam-do Province. In the park's southwest corner is the **Gwangju Arts Center** (광주예술의전당), the city's primary venue for ballet, opera, classical music, and *changgeuk*, a traditional form of musical theater.

Gwangju Biennale Exhibition Hall
 111 Biennale-ro
🕐 10am–6pm Tue-Sun during Biennale dates
🌐 gwangjubiennale.org

Gwangju Museum of Art
📍 52 Haseo-ro
🕐 10am–6pm Tue-Sun
🚫 Jan 1, Seollal, Chuseok
🌐 artmuse.gwangju.go.kr

Gwangju History & Folk Museum
📍 48-25 Seoha-ro
🕐 10am–6pm Tue-Sun
🚫 Jan 1, days after public hols
🌐 gwangju.go.kr/gjhfm

Gwangju Arts Center
📍 60 Bukmun-daero
🕐 Hours vary, check website
🌐 gjart.gwangju.go.kr

④   Gwangju National Museum
국립광주박물관

📍 110 Haseo-ro
🕐 10am–6pm daily (Apr-Oct: til 8pm Sat)
🚫 Jan 1, Seollal, Chuseok, 1st Mon of Apr & Nov
🌐 gwangju.museum.go.kr

Just north of Jungoe Park, the Gwangju National Museum shares the history and culture of the people who have lived in Jeollanam-do Province, beginning in the Paleolithic era. The museum's highlight is a haul of 24,000 objects, including ceramics, incense and metalware, that were recovered from a Chinese ship that sank off Korea's southwest coast in 1323. It was later excavated between 1976 and 1984.

⑤ Mudeungsan National Park
무등산국립공원

📍 5 Dongsan-gil 7-beon-gil
🌐 knps.or.kr

Immediately east of the city, Mudeungsan is Gwangju's guardian mountain. This 29-sq-mile (75-sq-km) national park makes for a convenient escape for locals, who fill its gently sloping hiking trails. The mountain is especially pretty in spring, when bright pink royal azaleas bloom. Mudeungsan's highest peak is the 3,894-ft- (1,187-m-) high Cheonwangbong. Make it to the summit and you'll get a good look at rock formations that exhibit columnar jointing.

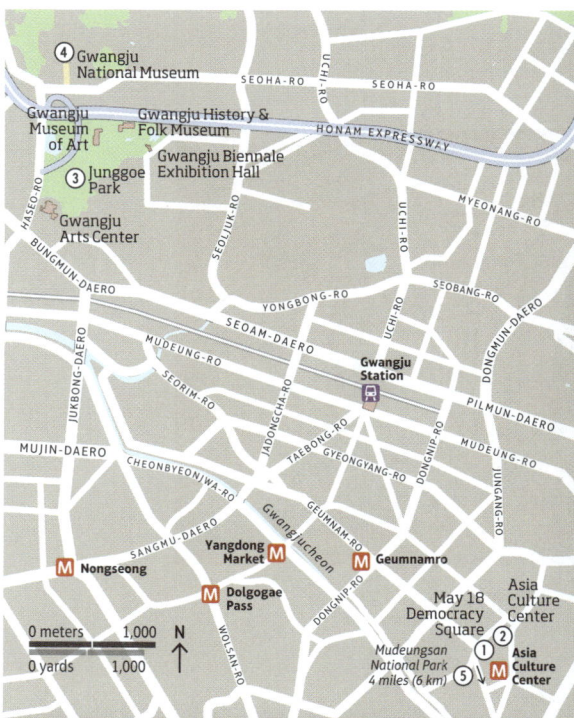

EXPERIENCE Jeolla-do Province

A SHORT WALK
GWANGJU ART WALK

Distance 1.5 miles (2.5 km) **Time** 40 minutes
Nearest metro Culture Complex

Gwangju's art isn't just contained inside its museums and galleries. Since 2011, the Gwangju Folly program has commissioned public artworks for the city's downtown streets by the likes of Dutch architect Rem Koolhaas, Korean architect Seung H-Sang, and Chinese artist Ai Weiwei. While some pieces could use a touch-up, these outdoor installations provide delightful moments of serendipity as you stroll the city streets. Embrace Gwangju's artistic spirit on this downtown walk, which takes travelers past several follies and other notable sights before wrapping up near to the Asia Culture Center.

Flow Control links Geumnam-ro, Gwanju's main avenue, with a plaza, where there's a memorial to Korea's comfort women (p100).

A digital art banner titled "**Vote**" hangs across this alley, asking visitors a question. Walk under the banner in the "yes," "no," or "maybe" lane to respond.

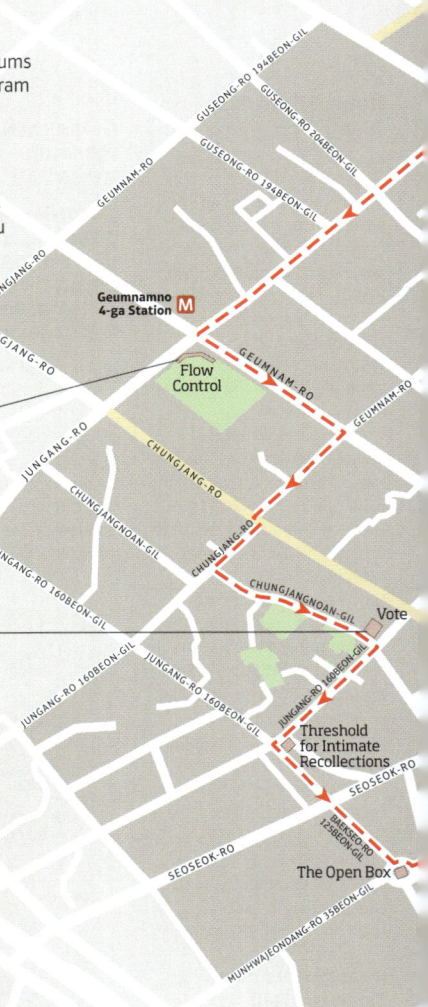

↑ The striped View Folly observation platform

184

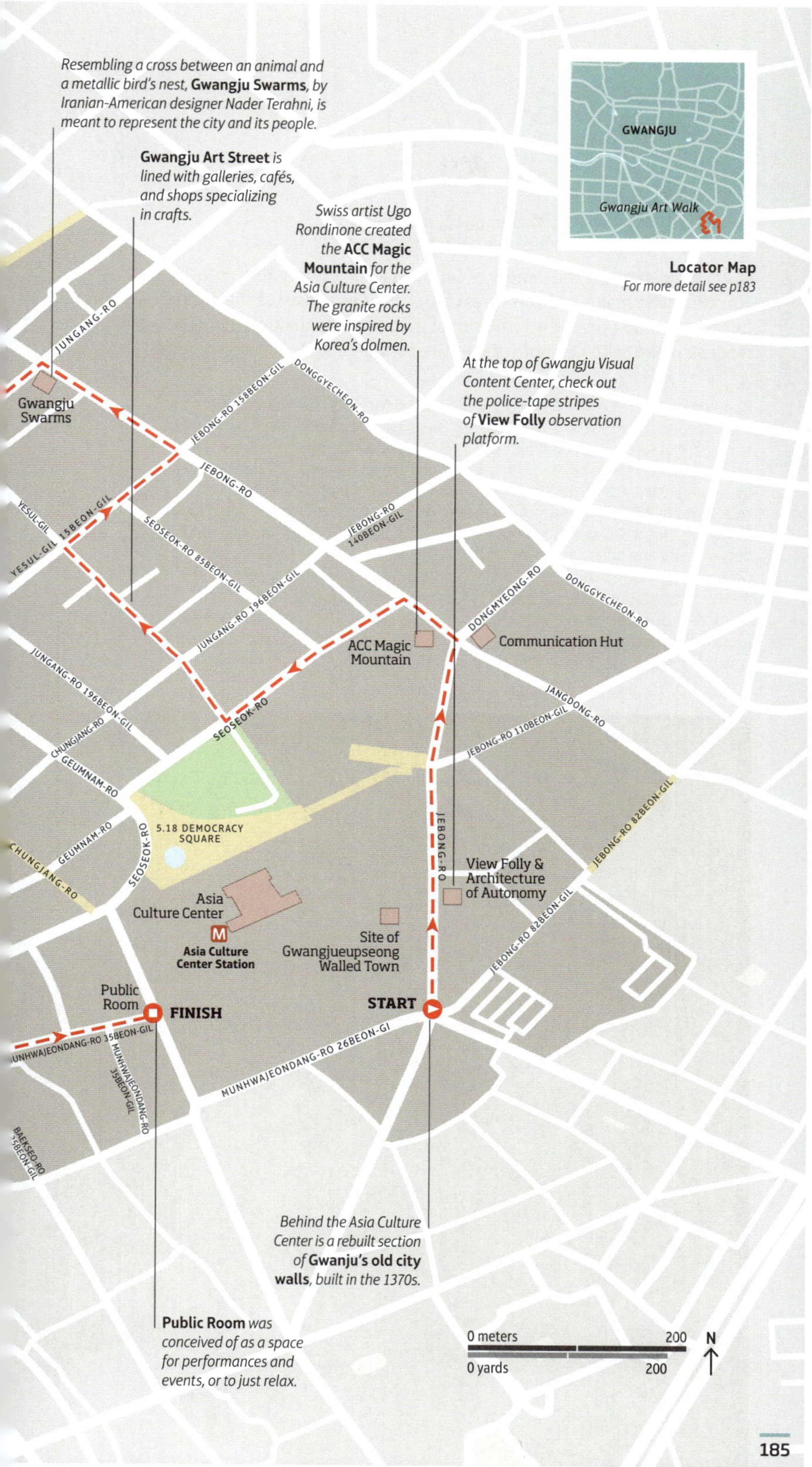

Resembling a cross between an animal and a metallic bird's nest, **Gwangju Swarms**, by Iranian-American designer Nader Terahni, is meant to represent the city and its people.

Gwangju Art Street is lined with galleries, cafés, and shops specializing in crafts.

Swiss artist Ugo Rondinone created the **ACC Magic Mountain** for the Asia Culture Center. The granite rocks were inspired by Korea's dolmen.

At the top of Gwangju Visual Content Center, check out the police-tape stripes of **View Folly** observation platform.

Locator Map
For more detail see p183

GWANGJU

Gwangju Art Walk

Gwangju Swarms

ACC Magic Mountain

Communication Hut

5.18 DEMOCRACY SQUARE

Asia Culture Center

Asia Culture Center Station

Site of Gwangjueupseong Walled Town

View Folly & Architecture of Autonomy

Public Room

FINISH

START

Behind the Asia Culture Center is a rebuilt section of **Gwanju's old city walls**, built in the 1370s.

Public Room was conceived of as a space for performances and events, or to just relax.

0 meters 200
0 yards 200

N

JUKNOKWON
죽녹원

C5 119 Juknokwon-ro, Damyang Juknokwon
9am-7pm daily (Nov-Feb: to 6pm) juknokwon.go.kr

Poets have extolled the beauty of Damyang-gun County for centuries. Travelers who make it to this rural corner can get a taste of the region's famed bamboo groves and traditional gardens at Juknokwon, where reconstructed scholars' huts add to the feeling of an East Asian reverie.

Bamboo grows better in Damyang than anywhere else in Korea. The best place to do a bit of forest bathing amid this graceful plant is Juknokwon, a large bamboo garden just across the Yeongsangang River from central Damyang. Dirt walking paths wind between soaring bamboo groves, and when the wind sighs through their feathery canopy, the effect is quite magical. Besides just strolling the grounds, you can soak your toes in a bamboo vinegar foot bath – said to be good for blood circulation – near the garden's entrance, check out bamboo-themed work at an art center, and take in the views over a coffee or ice cream at either of two *hanok* cafés.

In the northern part of Juknokwon is Siga Culture Village. In the Joseon era, many out-of-favor scholars and officials retreated to Damyang, where they developed a form of lyrical poetry called *gasa*. This complex re-creates the homes and leisure pavilions of some of the area's most famous writers.

Must See

 Trishaws lining up along a riverside pathway

Bonghwangru Pavilion, rising above one of the area's lush bamboo groves ↓

 PICTURE PERFECT
Bonghwangru
Across from the entrance to Juknokwan is a plaza where you can snap a photograph that makes it seem as if Bonghwangru Pavilion is floating atop the garden's bamboo.

↑ Walking through a towering bamboo grove at Juknokwon

Suncheonman's reed fields and mudflats, seen from Yongsan Observatory

SUNCHEONMAN WETLAND
순천만습지

D6 513-25 Suncheonman-gil, Suncheon ▪ Suncheonman Wetland ▪ 8am-7pm daily (Mar, Apr, Sep & Oct: to 6pm; Nov-Feb: to 5pm) ▪ scbay.suncheon.go.kr/wetland

The marshes of Suncheon Bay make up one of the five largest coastal wetlands in the world. Travelers can explore the ecologically important region by boat or by boardwalk at this preserve just outside the city of Suncheon, where migratory birds, hide-and-seek crabs, and vast reed fields await.

The Suncheon Bay wetlands began to appear at the end of the last Ice Age, when rivers deposited sediment and organic matter at the mouth of the bay, creating salt marshes and tidal flats. Today, those flats cover more than 8.5 sq miles (22 sq km) and – as a UNESCO Biosphere Reserve – provide refuge for some 230 bird species, more than two dozen of which are endangered.

The easiest place to commune with all this nature is at Suncheonman Wetland, which sits at the innermost part of the bay and is home to Korea's largest reed field. It's a gorgeous spot, especially in fall, when the tawny reed tops contrast with the bright blue sky and green mountains. Boardwalks meander through the grasses, providing visitors with an intimate look at the wetlands. As you walk, listen for birdcalls and keep an eye out for mudskippers and fiddler crabs. You can also experience the wetlands from the water; boats depart several times a day from a pier near the reed-field entrance for 30- or 60-minute tours along Suncheonman's S-shaped waterway.

Must See

GREAT VIEW
Yongsan Observatory

A trail at the end of a boardwalk leads to this observatory, where you can look over tentacles of brown-green reeds, yellow rice fields, and the gnarled peaks of surrounding mountains.

Did You Know?

Until the 1970s, people cut Suncheonman's reeds to sell as sunshades for ginseng fields.

1 A boardwalk meandering through a field of reeds in Suncheonman Wetland.

2 Visitors gathering around a windmill during the colorful annual flower festival in Suncheon Bay.

3 Hooded cranes taking flight; the birds are one of several crane species that overwinters in Suncheonman Wetland, along with whooper swans and gulls, while sandpipers and Far Eastern curlews visit the preserve in spring and fall.

Hikers tackling a trail in the snow-covered Deogyusan National Park

Sinheung-dong Japanese House (Hirotsu House)

17 Guyeong-1-gil · Gunsan Yeogo · 10am–5pm · Mon

⑦ Deogyusan National Park
덕유산국립공원

D5 · 159 Gucheondong-1-ro, Muju · Gucheondong bus stop · knps.or.kr

The Deogyusan National Park is one of the largest parks in Korea at 88 sq miles (230 sq km), and is famous for its winter scenery, vibrant springs, and important subalpine ecosystem. The park lies within a range of soaring mountains, including Hyangjeokbong (향적봉) peak, the fourth-highest in Korea at 5,295 ft (1,614 m). The mountains are ideal for skiing in winter and the **Muju Deogyusan Resort** (무주 덕유산 리조트) has Korea's longest and steepest ski runs. Just to the southeast, are the revered ponds, waterfalls and cliffs of the Gucheondong Valley (구천동 계곡). During the warmer months, the valley is filled with hikers, who follow a river through the valley.

EXPERIENCE MORE

⑥ Gunsan
군산

C4 · 27 miles (44 km) NW of Jeonju · From Seoul & Daejeon · 19 Guyeong-6-gil; www.gunsan.go.kr/tour

Until the 20th century, Gunsan was a small west-coast fishing village, but that changed in 1899 when it opened to international trade. The village was soon dominated by Japanese colonists who transformed it into a key trading port. Many Japanese buildings from that era remain, making the city an intriguing portal to the past. Among these are the **Sinheung-dong Japanese House (Hirotsu House)** (신흥동일본식가옥), the best-preserved Japanese home in Korea, and the **Dongguksa Temple** (동국사), the country's only surviving Japanese-style temple. The somewhat plain look of the temple presents a stark contrast to its colorful Korean counterparts.

The later introduction of Western architecture can best be seen on Gunsan's Modern History Street. A walk along here takes visitors past several sites including the red-brick Gunsan Modern Architecture Exhibition Hall (군산근대건축관) and the Old Gunsan Customs Office (호남관세박물관), with its unusual mix of Romanesque windows, Gothic roof, and light blue English-style doors. Farther down the same street is the **Gunsan Modern History Museum** (군산근대역사박물관), which features a re-created 1930s street, exhibitions on the city's history as a port, and its role in the independence movement.

Dongguksa Temple
16 Dongguksa-gil · Myeongsan Sageo-ri

Gunsan Modern History Museum
240 Haemang-ro · Modern History Museum · Mar-Oct: 9am–6pm Tue-Sun (Nov-Feb: to 5pm) · Jan 1, public hols · museum.gunsan.go.kr

> **Did You Know?**
> Starting in Gunsan, the Saemangeum Seawall is the longest such wall in the world at 20 miles (34 km).

The famous horse-ear mountains in Maisan Provincial Park

> Mireukjeon Hall has been designated a National Treasure and is considered one of the country's greatest architectural achievements.

Muju Deogyusan Resort
 185 Manseon-ro, Muju Baebang (Resort)
Hours vary, check website
mdysresort.com/english

8

Maisan Provincial Park
마이산도립공원

D5 130 Maisan-ro, Jinan Maisan Bukbu

Maisan is a park famous for the twin outcroppings of Ammaibong (암마이봉) (2,254 ft /687 m) and Sutmaibong (숫마이봉) (2,234 ft/681 m). These were thrust up from a lakebed some 70 million years ago and are Korea's most striking geological formations due to the fact they look like a pair of equine ears (Maisan means Horse Ear Mountain).

Equally unique is **Tapsa Temple** (탑사), just south of the peaks, famous for its stone pagodas built by the hermit Yi Gap-nyong. Starting in the 1880s, he spent over 30 years building pagodas, up to 44 ft (13.5 m) tall, through stacking rocks by hand. Despite not using anything to bind the stones together, none of the around 80 pagodas have collapsed from natural causes.

Tapsa Temple
 367 Maisannam-ro, Jinan Maisan Nambu
9am–6pm daily

9

Geumsansa Temple
금산사

C5 11 Muak-15-gil, Gimje Geumsansa
geumsansa.org

Geumsansa was founded in 599 CE, but, like many other temples, was burned to the ground during the Japanese invasions of the 1590s. Most of its structures date to a 1635 reconstruction. Among these is Mireukjeon Hall, Korea's only temple building with three stories. The building has been designated a National Treasure and is considered one of the country's greatest architectural achievements. In addition to Mireukjeon, the temple is home to ten other official treasures, including a five-story stone pagoda from the late 10th century.

DRINK

Teasoha
티소하
Café culture meets fine dining here through offerings such as plum tea, coconut cordial, and melon oolong cocktails.

C6 151-17 Donggyecheon-ro, Gwangju
0507 1351 8186

Gunsan Beer Port
군산비어포트
Overlooking the Geumgang River, this community-run space brings together four Gunsan craft breweries.

C4 146-24 Hae-mang-ro, Gunsan
070 4179 0101

The World of Spreading Green Leaves
초록잎이 펼치는 세상 티하우스
Sample a variety of green tea drinks as you enjoy sweeping views over mountains, tea fields, and a small lake.

C6 613 Nokcha-ro, Boseong
0507 1375 7988

Deogyusan National Park, dusted in snow

❿ Gochang
고창

▲C5 🏠27 miles (43 km) NW of Gwangju 🚌From Seoul, Jeonju, Gwangju
ℹ️133 Eupnae-ri; www.tour.gochang.go.kr

During the Neolithic and Bronze ages, dolmens – tombs generally formed of large capstones laid across two smaller stones – proliferated on the Korean Peninsula. More than 30,000 such dolmens have been found across the country, with the largest cluster at the UNESCO-listed **Gochang Dolmen Site** (고창고인돌유적), just west of central Gochang. Around 440 dolmens dot a field here. Just to the south is a smaller cluster and the **Gochang Dolmen Museum** (고창고인돌박물관), which delves into life during the Bronze Age and dolmen construction.

Modern by comparison is **Gochangeupseong Fortress** (고창읍성), constructed in the 1450s to protect a Joseon government complex from Japanese pirates. Visitors to this well-preserved downtown site can explore the original gates, see the reconstructed government buildings, and walk along the 1-mile (2-km) walls. These ramparts were once the site of an important spring event for local women. They would carry heavy stones on their heads and their weighted footsteps would compact, and thus strengthen, the earthen fortifications. The stones would then be used for repairs or as part of the artillery. Today, a festival celebrating this tradition is held annually during October, featuring women in brightly colored traditional dress and lively *pansori* music.

Gochang Dolmen Site
🏠668 Jungnim-ri 🚌Gochang Dolmen Museum ⏰Daily

Gochang Dolmen Museum
♿♻🏠74 Goindolgongwon-gil ⏰Mar-Oct: 9am-6pm Tue-Sun (Nov-Feb: to 5pm) 🚫Jan1 🌐gochang.go.kr/gcdolmen/index.gochang

Gochangeupseong Fortress
♿🏠125-9 Eupnae-ri 🚌Jungang-dong ⏰5am-10pm daily

> More than 30,000 dolmens have been found across the country, with the largest cluster at the UNESCO-listed Gochang Dolmen Site.

 PICTURE PERFECT
Ssanggyeru Pavilion

Stepping stones across a small pond in front of Baegyangsa offer the perfect angle to snap Ssanggyeru Pavilion and Baekhakbong Peak as their reflections shimmer in the water.

⓫ Naejangsan National Park
내장산국립공원

▲C5 🏠328 Naejanghoban-ro, Jeongeup, Jeonbuk-do 🚌 🌐knps.or.kr

With no peaks above 2,503 ft (763 m), Naejangsan doesn't hit the heights of some other national parks, but its steep, dramatic ridgelines and spectacular fall colors make up for any shortcomings. Indeed, the park has some of Korea's most vivid fall foliage, with colors typically peaking in early November. Within the park are a number of waterfalls, including the Dodeokpokpo Falls and the Geumseonpokpo Falls, as well as two Buddhist temples of note: **Naejangsa** (내장사) and **Baegyangsa** (백양사). Both temples were founded in the 7th century, and both had to be rebuilt after being burned to the ground in the Korean War. They are also among the best spots for visitors to take in the fall reds and golds. Near to Naejangsa, the Naejangsan Cable Car (내장산 케이블카) runs up to a ridgeline observatory and provides stunning aerial views of the park's scenery.

Naejangsa
🏠1253 Naejangsan-ro 🚌Naejang Terminal Rest Stop 🌐naejangsa.or.kr

Baegyangsa
🏠1239 Baegyang-ro 🚌Baegyangsa

↑ Baegyangsa Temple, Naejangsan National Park

Seafaring exhibits in the Mokpo National Maritime Museum

12 Unjusa Temple
운주사

C6 91-44 Cheontae-ro, Hwasun Unjusa

Unjusa might be Korea's most mysterious temple. No one is entirely sure when it was built, though best guesses put it somewhere between the 9th and early 11th centuries. Even more mystifying are the 101 Buddha statues and 22 stone pagodas scattered across the valley, many seeming to be unfinished. The most peculiar are two Buddhas lying flat on the ground. Legend says that originally there were 1,000 Buddhas, 1,000 pagodas, and a Zen master who called down fairies to build them.

← One of the many stone Buddha statues found at Unjusa Temple

13 Mokpo
목포

B6 44 miles (70 km) SW of Gwangju From Seoul, Gwangju, Daejeon From Seoul, Gwangju, Jeonju, Busan 122 Yudal-ro; www.mokpo.go.kr/toureng

Mokpo holds a somewhat unique location, squeezed between a river mouth and the Yellow Sea. As such, it has historically been tied to the water and was the country's main naval base during the Joseon Dynasty. Though the base was razed during the Japanese occupation, it's been partially restored as Mokpojin History Park (목포진역사공원), with some reconstructed stone walls and a guest house for officials.

The best view of the rebuilt port comes from the top of Mount Yudalsan (유달산). It's possible to hike this 748-ft (228-m) peak, which also offers sweeping views of downtown, multiple ports, and islands as far as the eye can see. To learn about the city's naval history, visit the **Mokpo National Maritime Museum** (목포해양유물전시관), found inside the National Research Institute of Maritime Heritage (국립해양유산연구소). The museum explores Korea's seafaring history through exhibits on the construction of traditional ships, maritime trade, and artifacts recovered from 16 shipwrecks.

Away from the water, Mokpo has several well-preserved Japanese buildings, a legacy of the Japanese enclave that existed during the colonial period. Two of the buildings, originally the Japanese consulate and the local branch of the Oriental Development Company, now serve as the **Mokpo Modern History Museum** (목포근대역사관). Together they house displays on Mokpo's 1897 establishment as an open port, the colonial-era, and the city's independence movement.

Mokpo National Maritime Museum
136 Namnong-ro
National Research Institute of Maritime Heritage
9am–6pm Tue–Sun
seamuse.go.kr

Mokpo Modern History Museum
6 Yeongsan-ro 29-beon-gil & 18 Beonhwa-ro
Yudalsan Post Office & Yudal Elementary School
9am–6pm Tue–Sun
mmhm.modoo.at

14 Jindo Island
진도

🅐 B7 📏 30 miles (49 km) SW of Mokpo 🚌 From Seoul, Mokpo, Gwangju, Busan ℹ️ 8478 Jindo-daero; www.jindo.go.kr/tour/main.cs

Though far removed from Seoul and other traditional centers of power, Jindo claims an important place in Korean culture. This large island is a center of *gugak* (p47), or traditional music, which encompasses everything from *pansori* (narrative chanting) to court music and Buddhist dance. Visitors can take in the sounds and spectacles at the **Jindo National Gugak Center** (국립남도국악원), which holds concerts every Saturday from March to November. Jindo's most beloved contribution to Korean culture, however, is its eponymous breed of dog. Known for their loyalty, intelligence, and hunting ability, Jindos were designated an official Natural Monument in 1962. Learn about them and watch training sessions at the **Jindo Dog Theme Park** (진도개테마파크) in Jindo-eup.

The island also attracts nature lovers. Tides here are some of the world's most dramatic, and a few times a year, the ebb tide off the southeast coast is so extreme that a nearly 2-mile- (3-km-) long path appears in the sea. Depending on how extreme the tide is, the path can be up to 130-ft (40-m) wide and allows visitors to walk to neighboring Modo Island, a quiet isle farther southeast. The local tourism office organizes the local Jindo Miracle Sea Road Festival (신비의 바닷길축제) to coincide with the phenomenon.

Jindo National Gugak Center
 🏠 3818 Jindo-daero 🚌 Gwiseongni ⏰ Performances Mar-Nov: 3pm Sat 🌐 jindo.gugak.go.kr

Jindo Dog Theme Park
🏠 35 Seongjukgol-gil ☎️ Jindo Office of Education ⏰ 9am-5pm daily; performances 10am & 3pm Mon-Fri, 11am Sat & Sun

15 Heuksando Island
흑산도

🅐 A6 📏 63 miles (101 km) W of Mokpo 🚌 From Mokpo ℹ️ 41-23 Yeri-1-gil; www.tour.shinan.go.kr

When a Joseon official ran afoul of the king, they were often exiled to Heuksando, a remote island 58 miles (93 km) west of Mokpo. Thankfully it's a far more accessible place today, with three daily ferries from Mokpo Ferry Passenger Terminal (목포항여객터미널), and many make the trip here to take a break. The best way to explore the island is to either hire a taxi or take one of the (infrequent) buses. Follow the ring road around

---

BATTLE OF MYEONGNYANG

The narrow Myeongnyang Strait, which separates Jindo Island from the mainland, was the site of one of history's most famed naval battles in 1597. Korean Admiral Yi Sun-sin faced an invading armada of at least 120 Japanese warships with only 12 vessels of his own to command. To even the odds, Yi lured the Japanese into the strait, where tidal forces are so severe they cause the current to reverse every three hours. As the Japanese fleet foundered, Yi attacked, destroying 31 ships and forcing the enemy to retreat. No Korean ships were lost.

← The hills of Jindo Island looming over a village at dusk

17 Ttangkkeut Village
땅끝마을

B7 77 miles (124 km) S of Gwangju From Haenam 70-7 Ttangkkeutmaeul-gil; www.haenam.go.kr/eng

Ttangkkeut means "land's end," and this inviting little village marks the southernmost point of mainland Korea. It was traditionally a fishing settlement but over the past decade it has become a destination for urbanites seeking relaxation. Besides enjoying the village's cafés and sashimi restaurants, visitors can hike or ride a monorail up to the **Ttangkkeut Observation Deck** (땅끝전망대), at the top of Sajabong Peak, which presents vistas of southern islands and seaweed farms. On the west side of Ttangkkeut's peninsula is Songho Beach (송호 해수욕장), whose half a mile (1 km) of fine sand is backed by a copse of 200-year-old pine trees.

Ttangkkeut Observation Deck

100 Ttangkkeutmaeul-gil, Haenam Ttangkkeutmaeul 9am–5:50pm daily

Did You Know?

In spring and fall, more than 370 species of migrating birds stop on Heuksando.

the island to explore fishing villages and the mountainous interior. Alternatively, take to the water with a Seojin Naksi *(ezbuilder.co.kr)* sightseeing or fishing excursion and marvel at the rugged coastline.

only 4 miles (6km) wide and much of it is off-limits to visitors, given over to a nature preserve for the island's roughly 170 animal species. However, anyone who makes it out here will still find plenty to do. Tour boats can take visitors up close to the island's spectacular red cliffs, and a roughly 2-mile (4-km) hiking trail runs from the port to the northern tip of Hongdo, taking visitors along a mountain ridge that serves up stunning sea views.

Ferries run from Mokpo to Hongdo twice a day, stopping at Heuksando en route. There are basic guesthouses and restaurants near the port.

16 Hongdo Island
홍도

A6 94 miles (152 km) W of Mokpo From Mokpo 36 Hongdo-1-gil; www.tour.shinan.go.kr

If a remote escape is on the agenda, head farther west to reach the mountainous Hongdo Island. The island is

→ The Ttangkkeut Observation Deck on Sajabong Peak, which can be reached by monorail

18

Songgwangsa Temple
송광사

C6 100 Songgwangsa-gil, Suncheon
songgwangsa.org

This large monastery on Mount Jogyesan is one of the "Three Jewel Temples" along with Haeinsa (p230) and Tongdosa (p241) of the Jogye order, Korean Buddhism's largest sect. It's Korea's most important *seon* (zen) meditation site, training monks from all across the country in its tranquil environs. Since it was founded in the 10th century, Songgwangsa has been destroyed and rebuilt several times, the most recent of which occurred in the 1980s. Despite these disasters, Songgwangsa has amassed a stunning array of some 8,000 Buddhist artifacts, which is more than any other temple in the country. Many of these items, including a Goryeo-era bronze bell and Joseon-era paintings, can be seen among the exhibits in the on-site museum.

> **INSIDER TIP**
> **Steep in Green Tea**
>
> Soak in a spa pool that combines seawater and the local green tea at Yulpo Haesu Nokcha Center, in the coastal village of Yulpo-ri, just south of the Daehan Dawon tea fields.

19

Boseong
보성

C6 40 miles (65 km) SE of Gwangju From Gwangju, Busan From Seoul, Gwangju, Mokpo 769 Nokcha-ro, Boseong-eup; www.boseong.go.kr/

Boseong, which is also known as Boseong-gun, is Korea's main tea-growing region, producing some 90 per cent of the country's green tea, or *nokcha*. Of the region's plantations, the oldest, largest, and most well known is **Daehan Dawon Boseong Green Tea Field** (대한다원보성녹차밭). Rows of tea plants wind in neat curves across over 2 sq miles (4 sq km) of steep hills, broken up by thick copses of fir and cypress trees. Walking paths permit visitors to immerse themselves in the greenery. The best time to visit is spring, when workers spread across the fields to pluck leaves, and a heady aroma of tea fills the air. Near to the entrance, a café infuses green tea into shaved ice and *affogatos*, while a restaurant adds green tea to bibimbap, pork cutlets, and other dishes.

Nearby is the **Korea Tea Museum** (한국차박물관). Here, visitors can learn about tea history and culture and view artifacts such as Joseon-era tea tables and bronze spoons from the Goryeo dynasty.

Daehan Dawon Boseong Green Tea Field
 763-65 Nokcha-ro Daehan Dawon Mar-Oct: 9am-6pm (Nov-Feb: to 5pm) dh-du.com

Korea Tea Museum
 775 Nokcha-ro Daehan Dawon 10am-5pm Mon, Jan 1, Seollal, Chuseok boseong.go.kr/tea

20

Naganeupseong Folk Village
낙안읍성

C6 13 miles (21 km) W of Suncheon From Suncheon suncheon.go.kr/nagan

Naganeupseong is Korea's best-preserved Joseon-era walled town, with over 200 traditional buildings, protected by a stone wall that has stood since the 1620s. Inside the ramparts, most of the

← A pair of Buddhist monks entering a hall of the Songgwangsa Temple

↑ An aerial view of Yeosu and nearby islands

> **GREAT VIEW**
> **Folk Village**
>
> Climb the set of stairs on Naganeupseong village wall's west side to gaze over a sea of brown thatch roofs spreading across the plain. You'll spot Mount Obongsan rising up in the background.

buildings have thatched roofs, unlike at Andong Hahoe Folk Village *(p232)*. But a few of the official buildings, including a jail and government guesthouse, have tiled roofs. Many buildings are still occupied, either by the roughly 200 people who still live here, or by restaurants and inns where visitors can spend the night. Try your hand at or watch demonstrations of straw weaving, calligraphy, and more at the village's traditional craft exhibition centers.

Yeosu
여수

◮ D6 ◮ 75 miles (120 km) SE of Gwangju ◮ From Seoul, Suncheon, Daejeon ◮ 2 Mangyang-ro; www.yeosu.go.kr/tour

Perched at the tip of a peninsula between mountains and 365 islands, Yeosu enjoys arguably the most beautiful setting of any city in Korea. The city is just three hours from Seoul by high-speed rail and trains pull into a station on the grounds of the 2012 Expo. Several of the event's facilities remain open and are now major tourist attractions. The 220-ft (67-m) **Sky Tower** (스카이타워) observation deck provides a great view over the Expo site and beyond, while some 280 species, including beluga whales and Baikal seals, can be seen at the Aqua Planet (아쿠아플라넷) aquarium.

Connected to the Expo grounds by a long breakwater is Odongdo Island (오동도). It's most famous for the roughly 3,000 camellia trees that paint the island red from January to March, but it also possesses lovely pine forests, a lighthouse, and walking paths leading to rocky headlands. Near the entrance to the breakwater is the Yeosu Cable Car (여수해상케이블카), which floats over the sea for just under 1 mile (1.5 km) and links Jasan Park with Dolsando Island. From the car people can look down on fishing boats and islands in the bay.

Dolsando Island is best known for the **Hyangiram Hermitage** (향일암), which has stood since 644 CE, perfectly balanced atop a granite cliff at the island's southern edge. It has undergone several reconstructions, most recently in 2009 after a devastating fire, and has since become a popular spot for both sunrises and sunsets.

Back on the mainland, **Jinnamgwan** (진남관) is Yeosu's other historical structure of note. It was erected in 1599 on the site of a former naval base and the massive hall served as a guesthouse for government officials. Jinnamgwan was rebuilt in 1718 and is today the largest one-story wooden building in the country.

Sky Tower
◮ 1 Bangnamhoe-gil
◮ Yeosu Expo Station
◮ 10am–10pm daily
◮ expo2012.kr

Hyangiram Hermitage
◮ 60 Hyangiram-ro
◮ Impo (Hyangiram)
◮ hyangiram.or.kr

Jinnamgwan
◮ 11 Dongmun-ro
◮ Jinnamgwan ◮ Summer: 9am–6pm daily; winter: 9am–5pm daily

> **Odongdo Island is most famous for the roughly 3,000 camellia trees that paint the island red from January to March, but it also possesses lovely pine forests.**

EXPERIENCE Jeolla-do Province

A LONG WALK
NAMPARANG-GIL COURSE 55

Distance 10 miles (16 km)
Terrain Paved walking paths, sidewalks
Nearest bus stop Yeosu United Port (Yeosu Marine Park)

Yeosu's *(p199)* gorgeous setting on a peninsula that forks around the island-dotted Gamakman Bay practically begs for a long, slow walk. You'll get to see a bit of the city and lots of incredible ocean views on this roughly five-hour ramble, which makes up just one small part of the Namparang Trail, a 913-mile (1,470-km) route across Korea's south coast – which, in turn, makes up just one part of the Korea Dulle Trail that encircles the country. The route is almost perfectly flat, and you're never far away from a restaurant or a café.

Restored buildings mark the former site of **Seonso Village***, which began building ships in the Goryeo era and crafted some of Yi Sun-sin's Geobukseon.*

Your last steps on this walk are above the water, on the **Soho Dongdong Bridge***.*

A footbridge leads to **Jangdo Island***, which has an art gallery, a sculpture garden, and an observation deck over Gamakman Bay.*

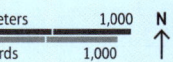

HENDRICK HAMEL

At the start of the walk, you'll no doubt notice the bright red Hamel Lighthouse, named for one of Korea's most notable foreign residents. Hendrick Hamel was an employee of the Dutch East India Company who was shipwrecked on Jeju Island in 1653. Held by the Joseon authorities, he lived in Jeju, Seoul, Gangjin, and, finally, Yeosu, until 1666, when he managed to escape and sail to Nagasaki. He later published an account of his time in Korea that was largely responsible for introducing the country to the West. You can learn more about him at the Hamel Museum, next to the lighthouse.

View of the bridge to Jangdo Island in Gamakman Bay

Locator Map
For more detail see p172

Jeolla-do Province
Namparang-gil Course 55

Get a plate of sashimi at **Yeosu Seafood Market** *or* **Yeosu Fisheries Specialty Market**, *which face each other across the Yeondeungcheon Stream.*

Yi Sun-sin Square commemorates Korea's naval hero, who had his base in Yeosu during the Imjin War (1592–98).

The alleyways of **Goso 1004 Mural Village** *are filled with colorful paintings of seascapes, hanbok-wearing cats, and many other cheery images.*

A memorial marks the former **Station of the 14th Regiment**, *which, in 1948, mutinied rather than follow orders to put down the Jeju Uprising (p257).*

In the atmospheric **Gukdong Port**, *fishing boats are moored while awaiting their next trip out to sea.*

Jongpo Marine Park *is especially lively at night, when its promenade is filled with buskers and food stalls.*

201

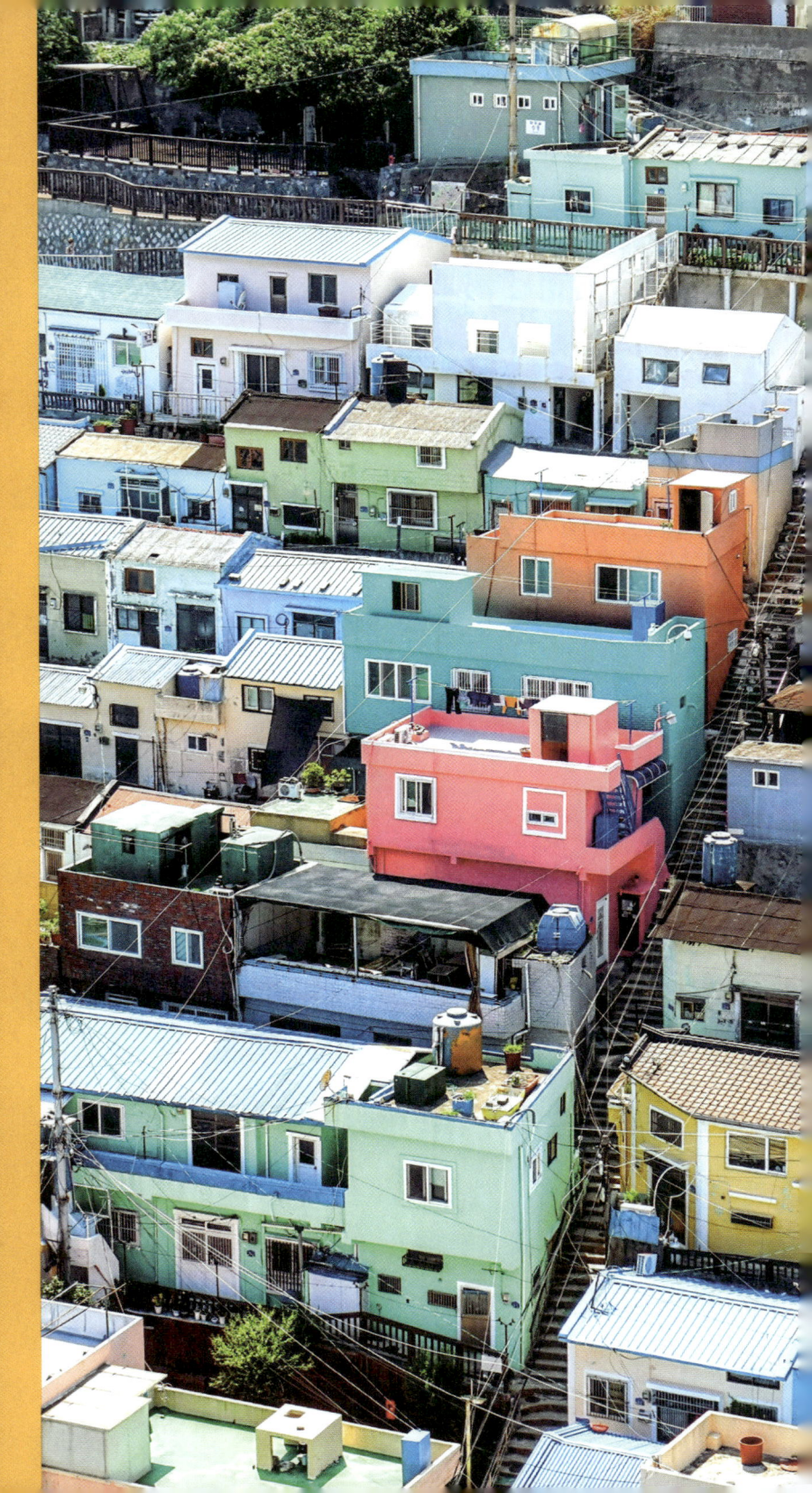

Colorful homes in Gamcheon Culture Village

BUSAN

The land Busan occupies was for a time the domain of one of Korea's lesser-known polities, the Gaya Confederation. This collection of city-states emerged along the Nakdonggang River in 42 CE, developing a flourishing culture based on ironworking and maritime trade before eventually being absorbed into the Silla kingdom in 532. Settlements here remained tied to the sea, and to nearby Japan, over the ensuing centuries, for better or worse. During the Joseon Dynasty, Busan was a significant port, but it also bore the brunt of the Imjin War invasions of the 1590s.

A similar pattern followed in the modern era. The Japan–Korea Treaty of 1876 reopened international trade, making it a gateway for modern culture but it also facilitated Japan's eventual colonization of Korea. Busan's finest hour came during the Korean War (1950–53). South Korean troops were pushed back as far as the Nakdonggang River. The South's last redoubt, Busan not only became the country's provisional capital but also absorbed half a million refugees.

In the country's postwar years, Busan experienced enormous population and economic growth. Today, it's Korea's second-largest city, with 3.5 million people, and a major tourist destination. Shipbuilding, electronics, and chemicals have emerged as major industries, their fortunes aided by the city's port, the seventh-busiest in the world.

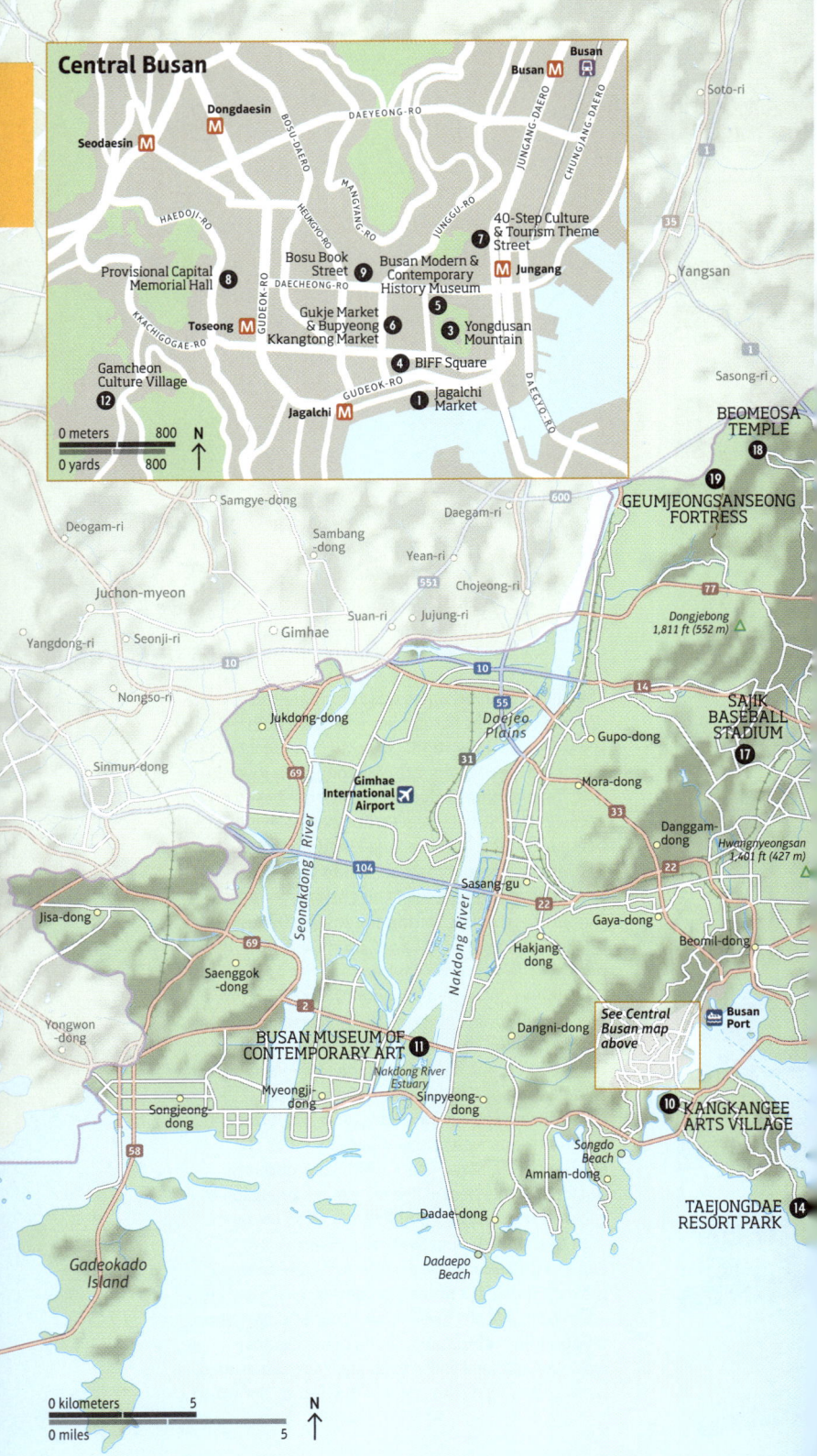

JAGALCHI MARKET
자갈치시장

E6 52 Jagalchihaean-ro **M** Jagalchi, Nampo **5am–9pm daily** 1st, 3rd, & 5th Tue of the month, Seollal and following day, Chuseok and following day **w** bisco.or.kr/jagalchimarket

Jagalchi Market is the soaking-wet heart of Busan. Much of the seafood that the city's fishing fleet pulls out of the East Sea ends up here, where workers in Wellington boots and rubber aprons scale it, slice it, and serve it up to hungry customers.

Jagalchi, Busan's largest seafood market, was established in 1970. Its name is a combination of the word for the seaside gravel (*jagal*) the first stalls were built atop, and a suffix (*-chi*) that's used with the names of fish. In 2006, it moved into a gleaming new building, where the main market occupies the first floor. Perpetually wet aisles are lined by glass tanks of clams and crabs, slippery rows of squid and mackerel, and bubbling tubs of eels and sea squirts. Pick something for dinner, and the restaurants on the second floor will turn it into sashimi or a spicy seafood stew. Upstairs is also where you'll find shops specializing in dried fish: packs of leathery squid, boxes of anchovies sorted by size, and tiny shrimp for sale by the scoop.

TOP 3 JAGALCHI SPECIALTIES

Hagfish
꼼장어
Called *ggom-jangeo* in Korean, these pink-ish, eel-like fish are marinated in a spicy sauce and roasted over charcoal.

Hoe
회
Pronounced "hway," this delicious Korean-style sashimi can be prepared from just about any of the fish displayed in the market's glass tanks. Prepare to be stunned by the silky texture.

Crab
게
Snow crabs (대게) and blue crabs (꽃게) are steamed or marinated in soy sauce, seasoned, and served raw as *ganjang-gejang* (간장게장).

↑ Glass tanks displaying the day's catch in Jagalchi's main market hall

Must See

1. Myriad varieties of fish and seafood are on sale at Jagalchi. The market handles almost a third of Korea's fish production.

2. Steaming bowls of seafood soup, packed with shrimps, crabs, clams, and vegetables, are among the tempting specialties on offer.

3. The modern market building sits right on Busan's lively harborfront.

GREAT VIEW
Busan Harbor

Head up to Jagalchi Market's rooftop terrace (9am–10pm daily) for great views spanning Namhang Bridge, boats cruising through the harbor, and the ship repair yards of Yeongdo Island.

HAEUNDAE
해운대

🅐 F6 Ⓜ Haeundae

This trendy neighborhood on Busan's east side is home to luxury hotels, upscale dining, and boisterous nightlife. At the center of it all is Haeundae Beach, the country's most popular strip of sand.

Haeundae is Korea's poshest neighborhood outside of Seoul. High-end apartment towers pierce the skyline, yachts bob in the harbor, and every fall, movie stars walk the red carpet at the Busan Cinema Center *(p217)*. However, its top attraction is completely free. Haeundae Beach (해운대해수욕장) is one of the nicest swaths of sand in Korea. The only problem is everybody knows it – the beach gets crowded in summer, when visitors flock here to lay out their towels. Nonetheless, the throngs of people and the surrounding high-rises create an urban beach vibe you'll be hard-pressed to find elsewhere.

At the beach's west end is Dongbaekseom (동백섬), or Camellia Island, a scenic spot named for the camellias that bloom red every winter. Hiking along the coastal path here offers some great views. Near the southeast shore is a rock with three characters thought to have been carved by the 9th-century poet Choi Chi-won.

The streets between Haeundae Station and Haeundae Beach are chock-full of hotels, bars, restaurants, clubs, and cafés. If you're after something a bit quirkier, head to the Haeridan-gil (해리단길) neighborhood, just north of the station, where hip places to eat and shop attract a young crowd.

DRINK

Galmegi Brewing Co
갈매기브루잉
On a mission to bring world-class brews to Busan, Galmegi was the city's first craft brewery. It also has taprooms near Gwangalli Beach and Jagalchi Station.
🅐 F6 🅐 9 Haeundae-haebyeon-ro 265-beon-gil
🅦 galmegibrewing.com

Momos Coffee
모모스커피
Sip coffee here made by a World Barista Championship winner, at this café in the Marine City complex.
🅐 F6 🅐 91 Marine City-1-ro
🅦 momos.co.kr

↑ Haeundae Sky Capsule, an elevated railway running along a 1.2-mile (2-km) stretch of Busan's coastline

Must See

7,937

The number of beach umbrellas set up at Haeundae Beach one day in 2008 – a world record.

↑ Haeundae's mile-long sandy beach at night, illuminated by the bright city lights

EXPERIENCE MORE

③
Yongdusan Mountain
용두산

E6 Nampo, Jungang
bisco.or.kr/
yongdusanpark

This small mountain pokes up out of central Busan to provide an accessible green space amid the downtown bustle. The park's main attraction is the 394-ft (120-m) **Busan Tower** (부산타워), whose observatory looks out over the port, Yeongdo Island, and ships steaming out to sea.

The steep climb provides a good way to get your bearings in this sprawling, disjointed city. If you want to spare your legs, take the escalator that leads up to the park from Gwangbok-ro, at its intersection with Gudeok-ro 22-beon-gil.

Busan Tower

37-30 Yongdusan-gil
10am-10pm daily

④
BIFF Square
비프광장

E6 Jagalchi Jagalchi Station & BIFF Square

BIFF Square was the hub of the Busan International Film Festival (BIFF) until it moved into the fancy Busan Cinema Center (p217) in 2011. A few BIFF films still screen here, and BIFF Square-ro is lined with plaques featuring the handprints of Korean movie stars – Busan's answer to the Hollywood Walk of Fame – though today the square and its surrounding streets are mainly a center of shopping, dining, and nightlife. Most stores can be found along Gwangbok-ro, with bars and restaurants in the side streets. Both are especially fun places after dark.

> **INSIDER TIP**
> **Ssiat Hotteok**
>
> Street stalls in BIFF Square are famous for their *ssiat hotteok*, small pancakes filled with a delicious mix of seeds, cinnamon, and brown sugar that caramelizes as it cooks – ideal for a winter's day.

⑤
Busan Modern and Contemporary History Museum
부산근현대역사관

E6 104 & 112 Daecheong-ro Jungang
9am-6pm Tue-Sun
Jan 1 busan.go.kr/mmch

True to its name, this museum covers the city's history since the late 19th century. You can peruse old photos, learn about the opening of the port, and walk along a re-creation of the street in front of the museum as it was in colonial times. The museum is split between two

↑ Busan Tower, looming over Yongdusan Park on a sunny winter's day

↑ A busy alley lined with stalls at Bupyeong Kkangtong Market

buildings, and the annex is itself an important part of Busan's modern story. Built in 1929 as the local branch of Japan's Oriental Development Company, after World War II it served for half a century as the U.S. Cultural Center.

❻
Gukje Market and Bupyeong Kkangtong Market
국제시장 & 부평깡통시장

🅰 E6 Ⓜ Jagalchi 🕐 Gukje: 9am–8pm daily 📅 First & third Mon of every month; Bupyeong: hours vary 🌐 bupyeong-market.com

These twin markets flank Junggu-ro, south of Daecheong-ro. Gukje, or "International," Market has its roots in 1945, when Japanese colonists sold off possessions before departing, and returning Koreans hawked goods they'd procured overseas. Kkangtong (meaning "Can") Market developed during the Korean War as a place for refugees to sell canned food and other goods smuggled off U.S. military bases. After the war, the two markets became hubs for imported and black market goods. Today the markets supplement their stalls with cafés and photo studios, and are a great place to snack on *eomuk* (fish cakes), a Busan specialty.

❼
40-Step Culture & Tourism Theme Street
40계단 문화관광테마거리

🅰 E6 Ⓜ Jungang

The street and staircase that make up this site may appear underwhelming, but the history they represent is rich with drama. Stretching west from Exit 11 of Jungang Station, they form a commemorative space that pays tribute to the more than 100,000 refugees who fled to Busan in the first months of the Korean War, as North Korean troops swept south. Many of them settled in this area, where they built shantytowns, improvised markets, and traded news of missing family members. Statues of exhausted porters, a man making *bbeongtwigi* (puffed rice snacks), and other denizens of the period line the road and steps.

→ Statue of a refugee at 40-Step Culture & Tourism Theme Street

SHOP

Asteroid B612 Souvenir Shop
소행성 B612 기념품숍

The place to find winsome crafts and souvenirs from Gamcheon Culture Village like diffusers, sticky notes, and bracelets.

🅰 E6 📍 133 Gamnae-2-r ☎ 0507 1399 1156

Docomoto
도코모토

Gukje Market has a number of vintage shops, and this one is among the best. Score old jeans, classic jackets, and lots more.

🅰 E6 📍 22-1 Junggu-ro 34-beon-gil, B1F 🌐 docomoto.com

Pretty Whale
고래서이빼

This charming boutique sells cute, mostly ocean-themed handmade gifts like plush otter keychains, seashell magnets, and whale-shaped chopstick rests.

🅰 E6 📍 15-1 Udong-1-ro 38-beon-gil ☎ 0507 1479 2302

8 Provisional Capital Memorial Hall
임시수도기념관

E6 45 Imsisudoginyeom-ro Toseong 9am-6pm Tue-Sun Jan 1 busan.go.kr/monument

One of the only cities under South Korean control for the entirety of the Korean War, Busan served as the country's provisional capital for most of the conflict. At that time, this stately red-brick house was the home of President Syngman Rhee. It's been restored to its wartime appearance, and visitors can walk through the living room, bedroom, study, and other rooms. A separate residence displays exhibits on the conflict, the lives of refugees, and wartime life in Busan.

9 Bosu Book Street
보수동책방골목

E6 Jagalchi Hours vary bosubook.com

For lovers of the written word, the fact that this tiny alleyway still exists in a world of AI feels like a small miracle. Running diagonally off the northwest corner of Daecheong Intersection, it's lined with more than two dozen used bookstores stocking everything from middle school textbooks and comics to novels and magazines. You can even find foreign-language books here.

The alley goes back to the early days of the Korean War, when shops began popping up to meet the needs of refugee students and displaced bookworms. Three quarters of a century on, it remains a charming throwback to another era.

↑ Books piled high at one of Bosu Book Street's many stores

10 Kangkangee Arts Village
깡깡이예술마을

E6 36 Daepyeong-buk-ro; www.kangkangee.com

This neighborhood, whose nickname mimics the sound of hammers knocking shellfish and rusted paint off boat hulls, has been a center of shipbuilding and repair since the late 1800s. In 2015, an urban regeneration project began installing artworks here to inject a bit of life into the old port. Grab a map at the Kangkangee Information Center and wander the salty streets, exploring the art and watching boats get touch-ups at the handful of shipyards that still exist. Don't miss the **Kangkangee Village Museum** (깡깡이마을박물관), which shows old videos of workers – mainly middle-aged women – hammering away at ship hulls as they dangle precariously from ropes.

Kangkangee Village Museum

  6 Daepyeong-ro 27-beon-gil 10am-6pm Tue-Sun

↑ Pastel-painted stores and cafés in Gamcheon Culture Village

11 Busan Museum of Contemporary Art
부산현대미술관

E6 1191 Nakdongnam-ro 10am-6pm Tue-Sun Jan 1 busan.go.kr/moca

The Busan Museum of Contemporary Art (MoCA) opened in 2018. Its five galleries display pieces from the museum's permanent collection alongside rotating exhibitions that explore themes ranging from technology to the connection between humans and the environment. The latter is a strong focus at MoCA, as the

> **HIDDEN GEM**
> ### Eulsukdo Ecological Park
> Occupying most of the island Busan MoCA sits on, this beautiful reserve's marshes form an important migratory bird habitat, not to mention a refreshing escape from the city.

museum sits near the northern tip of Eulsukdo, an island in the mouth of the Nakdonggang River where reed fields host snipes and plovers in spring and fall, and swans and spoonbills in winter. Even the building drives the point home. MoCA's facade is covered in a vertical garden of 175 indigenous plant species; it was installed by the French artist and botanist Patrick Blanc. It seems to turn the concrete and glass box into a living object and gives the museum an appearance that changes with the seasons.

Gamcheon Culture Village
감천문화마을

E6 | 203 Gamnae-2-ro; www.gamcheon.or.kr

Gamcheon is Busan's unlikeliest tourist attraction. In the 1950s, Korean War refugees and followers of a fringe religious movement settled in this out-of-the-way neighborhood at the bottom of a narrow bay, where they built a dense jumble of homes that run up the mountainside like a LEGO® amphitheater. For a long time, Gamcheon languished in relative poverty and obscurity. Then, in 2009, a public art project began installing murals and statues throughout the village, and empty homes were swiftly converted into art galleries and workshops.

The result was a revitalized neighborhood filled with cafés, souvenir shops, and artist residencies that makes for a whimsical and nostalgic place to explore. Near the top of the village, the Little Museum (작은박물관) displays old Gamcheon photos and household goods, and the Haneul Maru (하늘마루) observation deck offers sensational views of the village's colorful houses and Gamcheonhang Port.

The two main roads of Gamnae-1-ro and Gamnae-2-ro are where visitors will find most shops and the biggest crowds, but the tiny, steep alleyways reward spontaneous exploration, turning up hidden ateliers, the odd neighborhood cat, and other surprises. As you explore, though, don't forget that Gamcheon remains a place where people live and sleep. Respect private spaces and mind your voice level in residential areas.

> ### MOON VILLAGES
> Gamcheon Culture Village is Korea's most famous *dal dongnae*, or "moon village": poor, improvised settlements nicknamed for their mountain locations, close to the moon. The first moon villages emerged after the Korean War, as internal migrants flooded cities in search of work. Later ones sprang up as a result of evictions from more desirable neighborhoods marked for redevelopment.

STAY

Good ol'days Hotel
굿올'데이즈 호텔

A centrally located, design-forward boutique hotel just east of Jagalchi Market, with wonderful details like Blackwing pencils and art supplies in each room. There is also an excellent café.

E6 5 Jungang-daero 41-beon-gil
0507 1320 3278

Hotel 1
호텔 1

Right on Gwangalli Beach, Hotel 1 brings five-star views to backpackers: there are luxe options, but even some capsule rooms look out on Gwangan Bridge.

E6 203 Gwanganhaebyeon-ro
hotel1.me

La Valse Hotel
라발스호텔

Occupying a glassy tower on the channel separating Yeongdo Island from downtown Busan, this handily located hotel serves up panoramic views of boat docks, bridges, and the coastal skyline.

E6 82 Bongnaenaru-ro
lavalsehotel.com

↑ Terarosa Coffee at F1963, serving up first-rate brews in industrial-chic surroundings

F1963
깡깡이예술마을

E6 20 Gurak-ro 123-beon-gil Mangmi
Hours vary, check website f1963.org

F1963 is a multipurpose art, culture, and dining space that occupies a converted wire factory that dates back to 1963. It's somewhat removed from other Busan sights, but its facilities, diverse programming, and cool architecture make it well worth a trip.

Culture vultures will appreciate the Busan branch of Seoul's well-regarded **Kukje Gallery**, which exhibits a wide range of thought-provoking work by both domestic and international artists, as well as the Gum Nanse Music Center, a chamber music

→ The golden sands of Gwangalli Beach, one of the city's prime summer hotspots

venue whose glass walls make its concerts available even to F1963's casual visitors. The large, jack-of-all-trades Sukcheon Hall might be holding a car show, art exhibition, or fashion show at any given time. There's also an open-air event space, an art library, and an exhibition hall operated by Hyundai, though the latter functions mostly as a high-concept PR exercise.

Before a show or between exhibitions, visitors can peruse a large used bookstore, stroll through the outdoor bamboo grove, or relax at one of F1963's restaurants and cafés. These include the Czech-style brewpub Praha993, Ahbo Seasonal Food Lab, which makes its own soy sauce and soybean paste, and Terarosa Coffee, where you'll find the wire factory's original generator, a bar and tables made from old steel plates, and excellent coffee.

Kukje Gallery
10am-6pm Tue-Sun
kukjegallery.com

> **Shady walking paths wind along a small mountain and above the rocky coastline, looking out over fishing boats and shipping vessels.**

14

Taejongdae Resort Park
태종대 유원지

F6 24 Jeonmang-ro
Mar-Oct: 4am-midnight daily; Nov-Feb: 5am-midnight daily
bisco.or.kr/taejongdae

Out on Busan's very edge, Taejongdae (ignore the "resort" in its name) occupies the dramatic southern tip of Yeongdo Island. Shady walking paths wind along a small mountain and above the rocky coastline, looking out over fishing boats and shipping vessels. The best views are at the Taejongdae Observation Deck and Yeongdo Lighthouse.

If you'd rather not hike, hop on the trolley called the Danubi Train, which runs in a loop from the park entrance, stopping at the observation deck, the lighthouse, and the Taejongsa Temple. There are also sightseeing boats, which depart from a dock just south of the trolley station for 40-minute tours.

15

Gwangalli Beach
광안리해수욕장

F6 Gwangan

This 0.9-mile (1.4-km) strip of sand is one of Busan's best and most popular beaches. It draws major crowds in summer, when people come not just for the sun and sand, but for the many surrounding bars, clubs, cafés, and restaurants. The beach is also frequently the setting for performances and festivals, among them late fall's explosive Busan Fireworks Festival. Gwangalli's signature sight is Gwangan Bridge, which spans the bay in front of the beach. The graceful suspension bridge is especially beautiful at night, lit up and shining against the pitch-black sea.

The shoreline temple of Haedong Yonggungsa and *(left)* votive figurines scattered across the rocks

Haedong Yonggungsa Temple
해동용궁사

 F6 📍 86 Yonggung-gil
⏰ 4:30am-8:30pm daily
🌐 yongkungsa.or.kr

First built in 1376, this temple has undergone a few reconstructions and name changes over the years. Its current moniker stems from a monk's dream in which a bodhisattva ascended to the sky on dragonback. Haedong Yonggungsa possesses Busan's flair for the cinematic. Walk down the 108 steps to its entrance and you'll encounter a complex of shrines and prayer halls stacked atop a rocky headland, practically hovering above the sea. Few scenes in Korea rival standing atop the temple's stone bridge as waves crash below you and the sound of monks' chants fills the air.

> 📷 **PICTURE PERFECT**
> **Temple Above the Waves**
>
> North of Haedong Yonggungsa is an outcrop with a gold bodhisattva statue. From here you've got a clear shot of the temple, its stone bridge, and waves breaking over the rocks.

Sajik Baseball Stadium
사직야구장

 E6 📍 45 Sajik-ro
🚇 Sajik, Sports Complex
🌐 giantsclub.com

Baseball is Korea's most popular sport, but even if you're not a fan, a trip to the ballpark makes for a fun – and raucous – day out. Korean baseball games are much livelier than their U.S. counterparts, with fans singing songs for each player, cheerleaders doing K-pop dances, and home runs punctuated with showstopping back flips. The Busan Lotte Giants may be perennial underachievers, but their fans are Korea's most passionate, making Sajik the best place in the country to catch a game. Tickets can usually be bought at the stadium on game days.

Beomeosa Temple
범어사

 F5 📍 250 Beomeosa-ro
⏰ 8am-5pm daily
🌐 beomeo.kr

Officially, Beomeosa is in Busan. Spiritually, it's several planes of existence away. High up the wooded Mount Geumjeongsan on the city's northern fringe, this *seon* meditation-focused temple was founded in 678 CE, though it had to be rebuilt following Japanese invasions in the 1590s. A legend that a golden fish living in a well filled with golden water would ride clouds down from the mountaintop to play here gave the temple its peculiar name, which means Temple of the Fish from Heaven. The

main hall and the low-slung, kaleidoscopically painted Jogyemun Gate are designated National Treasures.

19
Geumjeongsanseong Fortress
금정산성

 E5 geumjeong.go.kr

Ringing Mount Geumjeongsan, Geumjeongsanseong is Korea's largest fortress, with a circumference of almost 12 miles (19 km). Its current walls were constructed in 1703, and for a long time it was one of the country's most important military outposts. Today it's an excellent urban escape, with plenty of hiking. A good route runs for about 3 miles (5 km) from Beomeosa Temple, past the fortress's north gate, to Geumjeongsanseong Foods Village (금정산성마을 먹거리촌), a collection of restaurants and cafés. Black goat *bulgogi* and the local Geumjeongsanseong *makgeolli* (rice wine) are village specialties.

20
Busan Cinema Center
영화의전당

F6 120 Suyeong-gangbyeon-daero Centum City Hours vary, check website dureraum.org

Sheltered under its striking cantilevered roof, the Busan Cinema Center (BCC) has been the main venue for the Busan International Film Festival (BIFF) since its completion in 2011. The 4,000-seat outdoor theater hosts BIFF's opening and closing ceremonies, while a two-screen cinema, a pair of theaters dedicated to classic and indie films, and a theater for stage performances hold events year-round. The dramatic-looking center also houses a film library, where ardent cinephiles can thumb through film books and magazines, listen to movie soundtracks, and watch classic Korean films and past BIFF selections in the multimedia room.

Did You Know?
The BCC has the world's longest cantilevered roof, extending 279 ft (85 m) from its support.

> **Ardent cinephiles can thumb through film books and magazines, listen to movie soundtracks, and watch classic Korean films.**

→ Busan Cinema Center, an iconic space for Korea's most important film festival

A SHORT WALK
HISTORIC BUSAN

Distance 1.8 miles (2.9 km) **Time** 1 hour
Nearest metro Jungang Station

Busan sprawls over a large area between bays and mountains, but its downtown core is relatively compact. This walk through the streets encircling Yongdusan Mountain provides a crash course in the city's modern history, from the colonial period through the Korean War and up to Busan's development as an important center for film. It also turns up plenty of opportunities to eat local specialties like savory fish cakes, *ssiat hotteok* (pancakes filled with seeds and brown sugar), and sashimi. Partway through, an optional spur provides an opportunity to scale Yongdusan and get a bird's-eye view from Busan Tower.

Bosu Book Street (p212) *is a delightful alley lined with dozens of used bookstores, a legacy of Korean War-era shops that supplied displaced students.*

In the postwar years, **Bupyeong Kkangtong Market** (p211) *was filled with black market goods and canned food "liberated" from U.S. army bases. Today it's an atmospheric traditional market and a street-food hotspot.*

TOP 3 BUPYEONG KKANGTONG STREET FOODS

Eomuk
Fish cakes (also called *odeng*) dipped in or brushed with soy sauce.

Tteokbokki
The Busan version of rice cakes in spicy sauce. Bigger rice cakes and spicier sauce.

Yubu Jumeoni
Fried tofu pockets stuffed with glass noodles in a warm broth.

The former center of Busan's cinematic universe, **BIFF Square** (p210) *and its surrounding streets remain a lively hub of shopping and nightlife.*

Busan's biggest seafood market, **Jagalchi Market** (p211) *has hundreds of vendors selling anything that swims.*

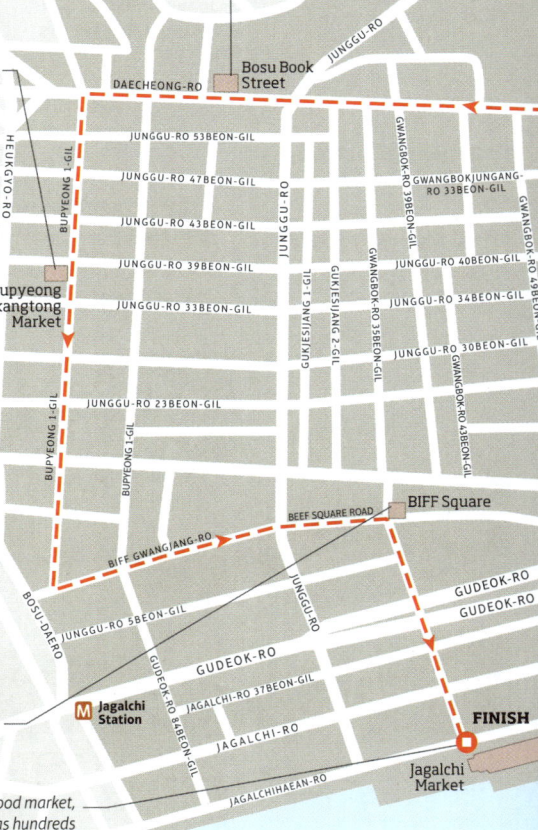

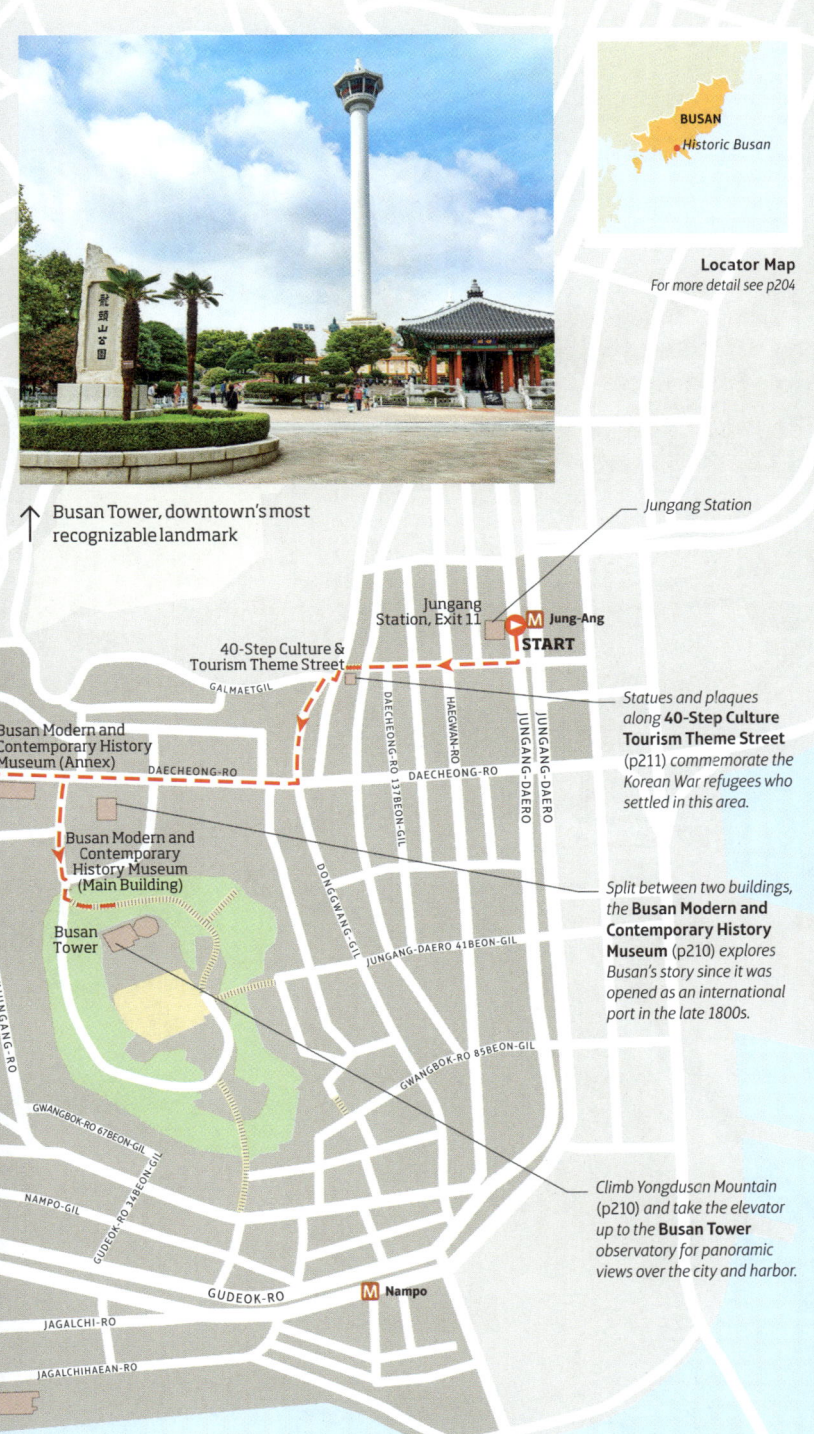

Hwaeomsa Temple at the base of Jirisan Mountain

GYEONGSANG-DO PROVINCE

Despite its relative distance from Seoul, the southeastern province of Gyeongsang-do has wielded an outsize influence on Korean history. Founded in Gyeongju in 57 BCE, the Silla kingdom became the first to unite the peninsula, subduing the last of its rivals in 668 and ruling until the mid-10th century. During the Joseon era, Gyeongsang-do – and the town of Andong in particular – produced many of the officials who guided the Confucian Dynasty, among them Yi Hwang (1501–70), the most important scholar and philosopher of his time. In 1860, the region gave birth to Donghak ("Eastern Learning"), a neo-Confucian ideology that evolved into the Cheondogyo religion, which many early 20th-century independence activists adhered to.

Following the Korean War, Gyeongsang-do witnessed some of the country's most aggressive industrialization, much of it focused on its southeastern coast. Away from the coast and the Daegu metropolitan area, however, Gyeongsang-do is largely rural and mountainous, dotted with farms. While aging and population decline are problems that nearly all regions of Korea are facing, they're especially acute in Gyeongsang-do's countryside. It's still a political powerhouse, though. In modern times, the province has yielded eight of Korea's 13 presidents, forming a staunch base for the nation's conservative parties.

Ulleungdo Island

GYEONGSANG-DO PROVINCE

Must Sees
1. Gyeongju
2. Haeinsa Temple
3. Andong
4. Jirisan National Park

Experience More
5. Daegu
6. Palgongsan National Park
7. Pohang
8. Yangdong Folk Village
9. Mungyeongsaejae Provincial Park
10. Buseoksa Temple
11. Juwangsan National Park
12. Ulleungdo Island
13. Ulsan
14. Tongdosa Temple
15. Upo Wetland
16. Jinhae
17. Jinju
18. Geojedo Island
19. Oedo Botania
20. Tongyeong

↑ The ancient tombs at Daereungwon, also known as Tumuli Park

①
GYEONGJU
경주

▲F5 🚗 53 miles (85 km) N of Busan 🚆 From Seoul, Busan, Ulsan, Pohang & Daegu 🚌 From Seoul, Busan, Ulsan, Pohang & Daegu ℹ️ 6 Taejong-ro 685-beon-gil; www.gyeongju.go.kr/tour

For nearly a millennium, Gyeongju was paramount to the peninsula as capital of the Silla Dynasty. You'll find its treasures preserved at one of the country's best museums, while royal tombs and historical structures make downtown an open-air exhibition. Just outside the city are two of Korea's most important Buddhist sites.

> 🔍 HIDDEN GEM
> **Hwangnidan-gil**
> Centered on Poseok-ro just west of the Daereungwon royal tombs is the trendy Hwangnidan-gil neighborhood, which is filled with quirky stores, cafés, indie bookshops, and a retro photo studio.

①
Daereungwon Ancient Tomb Complex
대릉원 일원

📍 262 Hwangnam-dong ⏰ 9am-10pm daily

Emerging in Gyeongju in 57 BCE, the Silla Dynasty would conquer the Baekje and Goguryeo kingdoms in the 7th century, uniting the peninsula and ruling it until 935 CE. The dynasty's latter centuries in particular were a period of remarkable blossoming.

Nearly two dozen tumuli containing the tombs of Silla royals dot the grounds of Daereungwon. Most of them, and the most important, are south of Taejong-ro. Of these, the highlight is Cheonmacheong (Horse of Heaven Tomb), thought to date to at least the early 6th century CE. Cheonmacheong is the only tomb you can enter. Inside its surprisingly spacious interior is an exhibition about its 1973 excavation, which unearthed thousands of precious artifacts, most of which now reside at the Gyeongju National Museum (*p226*). Another tomb of interest is Hwangnamdaechong, a double tumulus thought to belong to a married couple.

②
Gyeongju Historic Site Wolseong District
경주역사유적지구월성지구

🚌 ⏰ **Wolseong Fortress & Cheomseongdae: 24hrs**

This district, just south of downtown, preserves several major historical sites. It was where Wolseong Fortress (월성) was built in 101 CE, though some crescent-shaped earthworks are all that remain of the Silla royal residence. Still, shady paths make it an enjoyable place to poke around.

North of the palace site is Cheomseongdae (첨성대). Its name meaning "star-gazing platform," this is the oldest astronomical observatory in Asia, built in the mid-7th century CE. Just 30 ft (9 m) tall, it might not look like much to modern eyes, but it was a significant building in the Silla era, the observations of Cheomseongdae astronomers could determine everything from the timing of rice planting to royal court decisions. The cylindrical tower is constructed from 365 stones – one for each day of the year.

East of Wonhwa-ro is the former site of **Donggung** (동궁), a secondary palace where the prince lived and where banquets were held, and **Wolji Pond** (월지), a lovely artificial pond with three islands that was built by King Munmu in 674 CE. Try to visit after dark, when the surrounding pavilions are illuminated and reflected in the water.

Donggung Palace and Wolji Pond

 102 Wonhwa-ro
9am-10pm daily

---

③
Seokguram Grotto
석굴암

238 Seokgul-ro
9am-5pm daily
seokguram.org

Seokguram Grotto was built from 742 to 774 CE by the Silla chief minister Kim Dae-seong, supposedly to honor his parents from a previous life. After passing through an antechamber and a short corridor, visitors reach the main chamber, where a 12-ft (3.5-m) stone statue of the historical Buddha sits surrounded by disciples and bodhisattvas beneath a 23-ft (7-m-) tall dome. Surely Kim's former parents would have been suitably impressed.

The grotto can be reached from Bulguksa Temple by hopping on the local bus or hiking along a pleasant 1.2-km (0.7-mile) trail.

---

④
Bulguksa Temple
불국사

 385 Bulguk-ro 9am-6pm daily bulguksa.or.kr

A 30-minute bus ride from central Gyeongju, Bulguksa is among Korea's most majestic temples. Construction began in 528 CE and lasted until the late 700s, though the complex had to be almost entirely rebuilt after the Japanese invasions of the 1590s. Further restoration work was done from 1963 to 1973. The temple is home to six registered National Treasures, the most impressive of which are the Seokgatap and Dabotap pagodas in the main courtyard. Though both were built around 750, they exhibit strikingly different styles. Other National Treasures are the two stone staircases leading up to Bulguksa's prayer halls. Note the lotus petal carvings on the western stairs.

Must See

Did You Know?

A sutra inside Seokgatap Pagoda is thought to be the world's oldest woodblock print.

↑ A Buddha statue in Bulguksa Temple

GYEONGJU NATIONAL MUSEUM

국립경주박물관

186 Iljeong-ro ⏰ 10am-6pm daily (closes 7pm Sat, Sun & public hols) 🚫 Jan 1, Seollal, Chuseok 🌐 gyeongju.museum.go.kr

After the National Museum of Korea *(p94)*, the Gyeongju National Museum is the finest museum in the country. Its massive collection of Silla artifacts is spread across several buildings and outdoor areas, and merits a full day of exploration on its own.

The museum's Silla History Exhibition Hall traces the kingdom's rise and expansion, exploring things like its conquest of Baekje and Goguryeo and the *hwarang* (flower youths) – elite warriors who were highly trained in Buddhism and the arts. This is supplemented by the Wolji Exhibition Hall, which displays just a small selection of the more than 30,000 objects unearthed during a 1970s excavation of Donggung Palace and Wolji Pond, including roof tiles, utensils, and Chinese porcelain. The cultural heights that Silla reached, particularly in the realm of Buddhist sculpture, are on display in the Silla Art Exhibition Hall, while the museum grounds hold hundreds of pagodas, statues, and the like.

> **INSIDER TIP**
> **Nights at the Museum**
>
> The museum stays open until 9pm on the last Wednesday of each month and every Saturday between March and December.

> **Did You Know?**
>
> The Divine Bell of King Seongdeok is the largest bell in Korea and weighs a hefty 18.9 tons.

↑ Pottery and other Silla artifacts on display at the Gyeongju National Museum

↑ Memorial stone supports in the museum's outdoor exhibition

↑ Resplendent gold earrings unearthed from one of Gyeongu's royal tombs

Museum Highlights

Must See

Divine Bell of King Seongdeok

▶ King Gyeongdeok began crafting this massive bell *(right)* to honor his father, King Seongdeok, but didn't live to see its completion, in 771 CE. Featuring floral medallions, arabesques, and an intricately detailed dragon at its crown, the bell is considered an artistic masterpiece and is displayed in its own outdoor pavilion.

The Silla Smile Roof Tile

This humble roof tile is decorated with a face whose smile is every bit as enigmatic as the Mona Lisa's. Found in the early 20th century, it was bought at an antique shop by a Japanese collector and only returned to Korea in 1972.

Gold Crown from Cheonmachong Tomb

▼ The rulers of the Silla kingdom used gold as a symbol of authority. This 13-inch (33-cm) crown *(left)* was one of the most impressive objects discovered during the 1973 excavation of Cheonmachong Tomb. Five branches embellished with cashew-shaped pieces of jade extend upward, while delicate chains dangle from the frame.

Maitreya Triad Buddha

▶ The baby faces on these Buddhist figures have made them a favorite with museum-goers, but they're also important for the uniqueness of the central Buddha *(right)*, the only one from the Three Kingdoms period depicted seated on a chair. The bodhisattvas to the Buddha's left and right, each wearing a jeweled crown, hold lotus flowers.

A SHORT WALK
ANCIENT GYEONGJU

Distance 1.5 miles (2.4 km) **Time** 40 minutes
Nearest bus stop Donggung Palace and Wolji Pond

Locator Map
For more detail see p225

It's a bit of a cliché to call a place an outdoor museum, but that's exactly what Gyeongju is. You'll stumble across tombs, temples, and other remnants of the Silla Dynasty all over the city – though with the exception of Bulguksa and Seokguram, the most important sites lie downtown and can easily be explored on foot (or bike, if you prefer). The area is especially beautiful in spring, when cherry blossoms and fields of yellow rapeseed provide bursts of color.

Cheonmacheong Tomb is named for a mudguard featuring a painting of a heavenly horse (cheonma) found in a 1973 excavation.

Hwagnamdaechong Tomb is believed to be the burial site of a husband and wife.

Visit **Choi Young Hwa Bakery** for Hwangnam bbang, a Gyeongju specialty: pastries filled with a sweet red-bean paste.

The **Daereungwon Ancient Tomb Complex** is the site of 23 tumuli that contain the graves of Silla royals.

The 40.7-ft- (12.4-m-) high and 186-ft- (56.7-m-) wide **Tomb of King Michu** is the resting place of Silla's 13th king, who ruled from 264 to 284 CE.

WOLJI OR ANAPJI?

You might sometimes see Wolji Pond referred to as Anapji. After Silla rule collapsed, the pond fell into ruin and people began calling it Anapji, meaning, roughly, "pond where only wild geese and ducks go." The name Wolji wasn't "rediscovered" until the 1980s, when it was found inscribed on pottery fragments. It's a much prettier and, nowadays, more fitting name: "pond that reflects the moon."

→ Pavilions on Wolji Pond, formerly known as Anapji

Cheomseongdae Observatory was constructed during the reign of Queen Seondeok (r. 632–647).

Pink muhly grass, sunflowers, and other colorful plants fill the **decorative garden** just east of Cheomseongdae Observatory.

Silla royals once kept a menagerie of exotic birds and animals in the grounds of **Donggung Palace and Wolji Pond.**

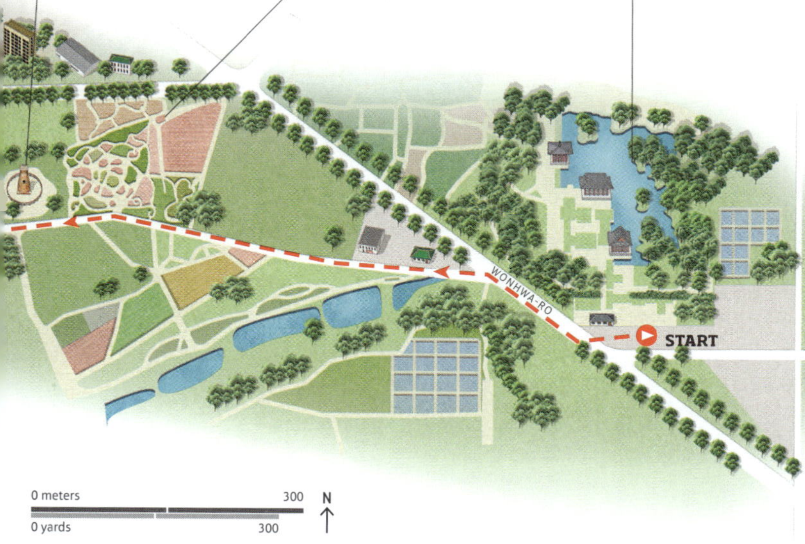

❷
HAEINSA TEMPLE

⬛ D5 **📍 122 Haeinsa-gil** **🚌 From Daegu to Haeinsa, then 1.2-mile (2-km) walk** **🕐 8:30am–6pm daily (winter: to 5pm)** **🌐 haeinsa.or.kr**

Remote and beautiful, Haeinsa is one of Korean Buddhism's "Three Jewels." For 600 years, the temple has safeguarded the Tripitaka Koreana, a 13th-century collection of woodblock carvings.

Founded in 802 CE, Haeinsa possesses one of the most scenic settings of all Korean temples, ascending Mount Gayasan in a series of terraces, while the surrounding ridges of Gayasan National Park recede into the distance. At its highest and most sacred point is the Janggyeong Panjeon, a rectangular assemblage of buildings that store the Tripitaka Koreana, Korean Buddhism's greatest treasure. Meaning "Three Baskets" in Sanskrit, the Tripitaka is a collection of Buddhist scriptures, and the one stored at Haeinsa is the most complete version in mainland Asia: 81,258 printing blocks filled with Chinese characters.

Hoping to bolster its resistance to Mongol invaders by appealing to the power of the Buddha, in 1236 the Goryeo kingdom initiated a project to compile a complete version of the Tripitaka. They were finished in 1251 and moved to Haeinsa Temple for safekeeping in the 1390s.

The Janggyeong Panjeon was built around 1488 to house the Tripitaka Koreana. Its materials and design regulate humidity and ventilation, preserving the woodblocks.

The Jeokmukdang serves as the monks' living quarters.

Buddhists believe that ringing the temple bell eases the suffering of beings in hell. Sounding the unpan gong and the mogeo drum has a similar effect on creatures in the air and water.

BUILDING BLOCKS

How was a Tripitaka Koreana woodblock made? First, birchwood from Jeju, Geojedo, or Wando island was soaked in seawater for three years to strengthen it and prevent it from rotting. Next, the wood was shaped into a board, boiled in salt water, dried, and planed. Only then did an engraver begin the painstaking work of carving more than 300 characters into relief on each side. Finally, brackets were attached to the ends of the board, lacquer was applied, and copper plates were added to the corners for decoration. One down, 81,257 to go.

Must See

↑ Lanterns decorating Haeinsa's main hall, Daejeokgwangjeon

The Daejeokgwangjeon is Haeinsa's main hall. It was rebuilt in 1818 and enshrines a statue of the Vairocana Buddha.

The granite Jeongjungtap Pagoad is thought to date to the 9th century. In 1926, nine Buddha statues were discovered in its upper pedestal.

The Gwaneumjeon is part of Haeinsa's Buddhist school. Monks study sutras here.

In the past, only great monks were allowed in the main temple, so the Gugwangnu was built as a place for laypeople to worship.

↑ Illustration of Haeinsa Temple

> 💬 **INSIDER TIP**
> **Tripitaka Tour**
>
> To view the Tripitaka Koreana, you must reserve a spot on a tour (10am Sun) at least two weeks in advance. If you're unable to use the form on the temple's website (Korean only), call 055 934 3006.

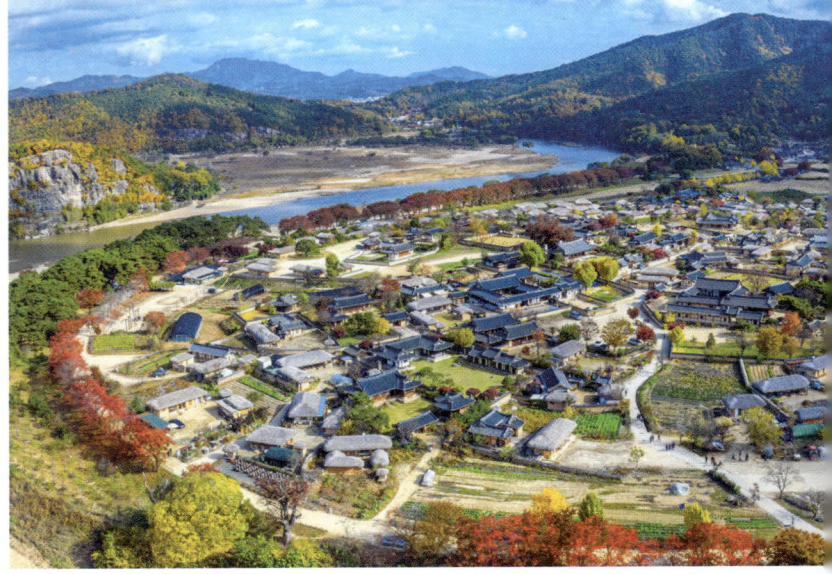

③

ANDONG
안동

E4 63 miles (102 km) N of Daegu From Seoul, Busan, Daegu From Seoul, Busan, Daegu, Daejeon 122-16, Gyeongdong-ro; www.tourandong.com

The past feels just a bit more present in Andong. In the Joseon era, the region was home to the country's most important Confucian academies; today, it still offers a taste of life as it was lived centuries ago. Although the city itself is pleasant enough, its real attractions are scattered across the surrounding countryside.

> **GREAT VIEW**
> **Buyongdae Cliff**
>
> In Hahoe, take a ferry across the river and then a short, steep trail to the top of Buyongdae Cliff, where you'll have unimpeded views of the village nestled in the river bend.

①

Andong Hahoe Folk Village
안동 하회마을

15.5 miles (25 km) W of Andong Summer: 9am-6pm daily; winter: 9am-5pm daily hahoe.or.kr

Andong Hahoe Folk Village is Korea's most well-known traditional settlement and, since the 16th century, has been the home of the Pungsan Ryu family. Clay-walled alleys wind between thatch- or tile-roofed *hanok* homes, many built over a century ago, and a 600-year-old zelkova stands at the village center, while trees line the bank of the Nakdonggang River. Though many homes have been converted to guesthouses or restaurants, Hahoe remains a functioning community, and spending a day here (or, better yet, staying overnight) is an encounter that's hard to replicate. Village experience centers let you try calligraphy and tea ceremonies, and you can sometimes watch craftspeople at work or reenactments of traditional weddings. Don't miss the Hahoe Mask Dance (*p29*), one of Korea's most beloved folk performances. Learn more about it at the **Hahoe Mask Museum** (하회세계탈박물관), outside the village entrance.

Hahoe Mask Museum

 9:30am-6pm daily Jan 1, Seollal, Chuseok mask.kr

→ Folklore mask on display at Hahoe Mask Museum

↑ View of Hahoe Folk Village, nestled below hills west of the city

② Dosan Seowon
도산서원

🏠 154 Dosanseowon-gil 🕘 9am-6pm daily (Nov-Jan to 5pm) 🌐 andong.go.kr/dosanseowon

This was Joseon Korea's most important *seowon*, or Confucian school. The revered scholar Yi Hwang (the face on the 1,000-won note) established a small academy here in 1561; after his death, his students expanded the compound. Between the beautiful surroundings and the grace of its classrooms and courtyards, it's hard to conceive of a more ideal learning environment.

③ Bongjeongsa Temple
석굴암

🏠 222 Bongjeongsa-gil 🚌 🕘 Summer: 7am-7pm daily; winter: 8am-6pm daily 🌐 bongjeongsa.org

Founded in the 670s, Bongjeongsa has been especially well preserved. Original murals are still visible in the main hall, and Geungnakjeon Hall is one of Korea's oldest wooden buildings, dating to the 13th century. A pavilion near the temple's entrance was built by some of Yi's students, revealing how Buddhism and Confucianism intermingled.

Must See

EAT

Andong Jjimdak Golmok
안동찜닭골목

One of a number of restaurants serving *andong jjimdalk* (braised chicken with potatoes and glass noodles) in Andong Gu Market.

🏠 E4 📍 Intersection of Beonyeong-gil and Beonyeong-1-gil

ⓦ ⓦ ⓦ

Iljik Sikdang
일직식당

Right next to Andong Station, this restaurant is renowned for its grilled salted mackerel, a local specialty.

🏠 E4 📍 676 Gyeongdong-ro
📞 054 859 6012

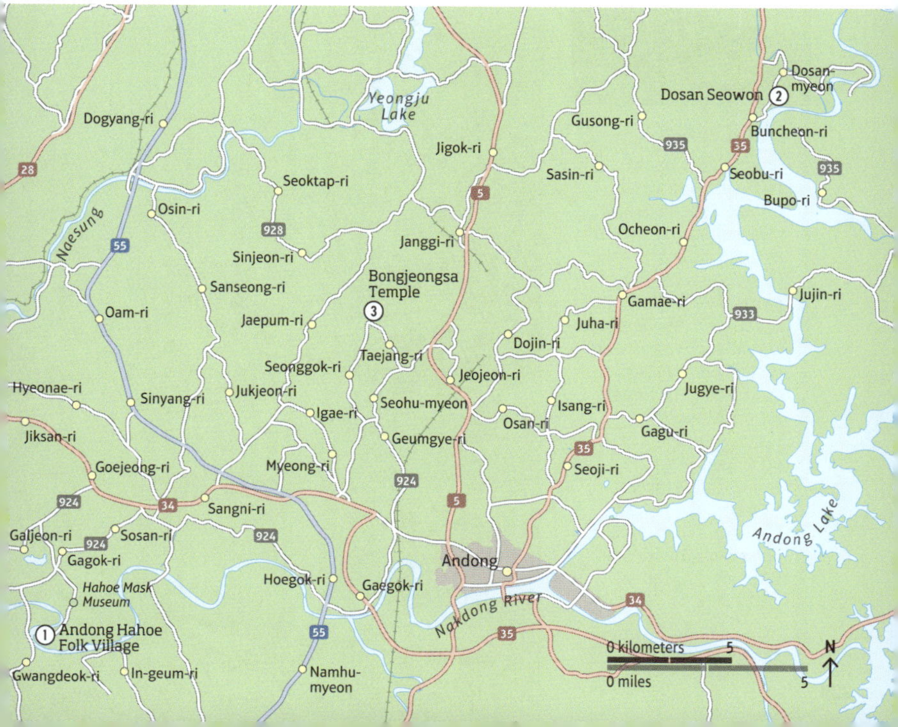

ⓦ ⓦ ⓦ

4
JIRISAN NATIONAL PARK
지리산국립공원

▲D5 ⏱64 miles (103 km) E of Gwangju 🚌 From Jinju, Hamyang, Hadong, Gurye, Namwon 🌐knps.or.kr

For centuries, Jirisan has attracted seekers and ascetics. Make your own pilgrimage here and you'll discover one of Korea's last truly wild places – and maybe even a bit of enlightenment.

Jirisan, the "Mountain of the Wise Man," was Korea's first national park, established in 1967. Marking the southern terminus of the Baekdudaegan range, the preserve is an untamed collection of soaring peaks, thick forests, and stream-laced valleys that provides sanctuary to some of the country's most elusive creatures, including the Asiatic black bear. It is also the country's largest national park (excluding marine parks), sprawling across 186 sq miles (483 sq km) and three provinces, and you can't see it all in a single visit. Base yourself in Hamyang, Jinju *(p242)*, or Hadong in Gyeongsangnam-do Province if you want to explore Jirisan's eastern half. Its western half is best reached from Namwon, in Jeollabuk-do, or Gurye, in Jeollanam-do.

In the park's east, you'll find mainland South Korea's tallest peak, the 6,283-ft (1,915-m) Cheonwangbong (천왕봉). In shamanistic tradition, it's also among the most sacred. Ascents begin from Jungsan-ri Village, in the park's southeast, or the

MOON BEARS

One of Korea's most recognizable animals is the Asiatic black bear, more commonly known as the moon bear thanks to the crescent-shaped patch of white on its chest. With numbers in Korea dwindling to near extinction, in 2004 the government launched an ambitious restoration program, introducing six bears from Russia's far east to Jirisan. The program has been a considerable success, and more than 80 bears now call the park home.

↑ The bronze entry gate to Hwaeomsa, Jirisan's most important temple

> *Must See*

TOP 3 HIKES IN JIRISAN

Jungsan-ri (Kalbawi) Course
중산리 (칼바위) 코스
Bag South Korea's highest mainland peak on this all-day out-and-back 7-mile (11-km) hike to Cheonwangbong.

Mount Jirisan Traverse
지리산 종주
Following Jirisan's ridgeline the 20-mile (31-km) length of the park, this tough trek from Gurye is truly epic.

Piagol Course
피아골코스
The first half of this 10-mile (16-km) valley trail is fairly flat – ideal for a casual stroll.

Baekmudong Visitor Center, in the north. Also on this side of the park is the Chilseon Gyegok Valley (칠선계곡). With a rushing stream, seven waterfalls, and Jirisan's only primeval forest, it's remarkably beautiful. Its rough terrain also makes it somewhat dangerous, with access limited to Fri–Sun in May, June, September, and October; hikers must apply for a permit *(reservation.knps. or.kr)* and complete a safety course before setting out.

In Jirisan's west, the Baemsagol Gyegok (뱀사골계곡) and Piagol Gyegok (피아골계곡) valleys are more accessible and nearly as pretty, especially in fall, when their maples turn a brilliant crimson. Here too is Hwaeomsa Temple (화엄사), where registered National Treasures include an unusual stone pagoda that balances atop the heads of four seated lions. Baemsagol is most easily reached from Namwon; Piagol and Hwaeomsa from Gurye.

↑ Jirisan National Park bursting into spring flower

EXPERIENCE MORE

5

Daegu
대구

 E5 ■ 68 miles (110 km) NW of Busan ■ From Seoul, Busan, Daejeon, Pohang ■ From Seoul, Busan, Ulsan, Pohang ℹ Dongdaegu Station; tour.daegu.go.kr

Known for sweltering summers, conservative politics, and fried chicken, Daegu is a lively college town and a good base for exploring northern Gyeongsang-do Province.

Centered on Namseong-ro downtown, the 350-year-old **Daegu Yangnyeongsi** (대구약령시) was long Korea's most important herbal medicine market, supplying doctors across East Asia. Though more modern businesses have moved in, anise-scented herbal medicine shops stocked with dried roots still predominate. The **Daegu Yangnyeongsi Oriental Medicine Museum** (대구약령시한의약박물관) explores the market's history and traditional medical techniques.

North of the market, shady Gyeongsanggamyeong Park (경상감영공원) is where the provincial government was headquartered during the late Joseon Dynasty; two buildings from that era survive amid the fountains and bamboo. Just off the park's southwest corner, the **Daegu Modern History Museum** (대구근대역사관) recounts the city's 20th-century history, including the founding of Samsung here in 1938.

On Daegu's west side, **83 Tower** (83타워) provides elevated views from atop Duryusan Mountain. Just below, the rides and shows of **Eworld** (이월드) amusement park make for a great family excursion.

Across town, Kim Kwang-seok Road (김광석 다시 그리기 길) commemorates a beloved folk rock singer born in the area. Lined with many boutiques, craft ateliers, galleries, cafés, and murals, it's a magnet for buskers and hosts occasional music festivals and record fairs.

83 Tower and Eworld

○ ○ ○ ○ ■ 200 Duryu-gongwon-ro ■ Duryu, Nae-dang ○ 83 Tower: 11am–8:30pm daily; Eworld: hours vary, check website ⓦ eworld.kr

Daegu Modern History Museum

■ 67 Gyeongsang-gamyeong-gil ■ Jungangno ○ 9am–6pm Tue–Sun ■ Jan 1, Seollal, Chuseok ⓦ daeguartscenter.or.kr/dmhm

Daegu Yangnyeongsi Oriental Medicine Museum

○ ■ 49 Dalgubeoldae-ro 415-gil ■ Banwoldang ○ 9am–6pm Tue–Sun ■ Jan 1, Seollal, Chuseok ⓦ daegu.go.kr/dgom/index.do

6

Palgongsan National Park
팔공산국립공원

 E4 ■ Palgongsan-ro 185-gil, Daegu; 175 Palgongsan-ro, Chilgok ■ From Daegu ⓦ knps.or.kr

Just north of Daegu, Palgongsan is Korea's newest national park, having been upgraded from provincial park status in 2023. Its 49 sq miles (126 sq km) stretch east to west along a granite ridgeline that tops out at the 3,914-ft (1,193-m) Birobong Peak, which is flanked by the only slightly shorter Dongbong and Seobong peaks.

Buddhists have regarded Palgongsan as sacred for centuries. There are

---

TOP 3 DAEGU FRIED CHICKEN RESTAURANTS

Dongmun Chicken
동문치킨
■ 29 51-1 Jong-ro
☎ 053 254 8872
Tiny place with graffiti-covered walls and old-school flavors.

The Big Bonbu
더큰본부
■ 8 Ayang-ro 9-gil
☎ 0507-1378-7458
Try the fried *dalk-ddong-jip* (chicken gizzards) with octopus here.

Ttang Ttang Chicken
땅땅치킨
ⓦ codd.co.kr
Popular local chain that also operates a fried chicken theme park.

→ Statue of legendary folk rock singer Kim Kwang-seok, born in Daegu in 1964

Hiking the rocky ridges of lush Palgongsan, an easy day trip from Daegu

two impressive religious sites in the park's more accessible eastern section. Founded in 493 CE, **Donghwasa Temple** (동화사) is one of the oldest in Korea, though most of its buildings date from the 17th century, including the lovely main hall. To the southeast, Gatbawi (팔공산갓바위) is a large 9th-century Buddha carving that's something of a pilgrimage site. The unusual flat rock atop the Buddha's head is thought to resemble traditional hats called *gat*, giving the statue its name. In Palgongsan's west is the Gunwi Buddhist Triad Grotto (군위삼존석굴), a trio of Buddha statues in a cliffside cave. Also on that side of the park is Gasansanseong Fortress (가산산성), which was built between the mid-1600s and mid-1700s and has a unique three-wall structure. Centuries later, it was the site of a Korean War battle.

Did You Know?

On the day of Korea's university entrance exam, Daegu parents visit Gatbawi to pray for high scores.

Donghwasa Temple
⌂ 1 Donghwasa-1-gil, Daegu
⏱ 24hr 🌐 donghwasa.net

Pohang
포항

🗺 F4 ⌂ 70 miles (112 km) N of Busan 🚆 Train from Seoul, Busan, Daegu, Ulsan, Daejeon 🚌 From Seoul, Busan, Daegu, Ulsan ℹ Pohang Station; www.pohang.go.kr

Life in the blue-collar city of Pohang revolves around two things: steel and the sea. The international steel manufacturing giant POSCO has its headquarters and a massive plant here, and while you can't visit, you can tour the adjacent **POSCO Museum** (포스코역사박물관), which combines cool machinery and mind-boggling statistics with some truly championship-level PR-speak ("the precious tears of joy that flowed were just as hot as the molten iron").

Many of the fruits of Pohang's other major industry end up at **Jukdo Market** (죽도시장). After docking in the city's inner harbor, fishing boats offload crabs, squid, shrimp, and everything else oceanic to be sold by Jukdo's Wellington-booted denizens.

Pohang's other top sights lie on a peninsula east of the city. In the atmospheric fishing village of Guryongpo is Guryongpo Japanese Houses Street, a road of refurbished colonial-era homes that now accommodate shops and restaurants. You can see what they looked like on the inside at the **Guryongpo Modern History Museum** (구룡포 근대역사관) which runs tours (in Korean only). At the peninsula's tip is scenic Homigot Cape (호미곶), mainland Korea's easternmost point. It's the site of the endlessly photographed Hands of Coexistence (상생의손), a pair of enormous statues of hands, with one rising from a plaza and the other poking up out of the ocean.

POSCO Museum
⌂ 14 Donghaean-ro 6213-beon-gil ⏱ 9am-6pm Mon-Fri, 10am-5pm Sat 🚫 National hols 🌐 museum.posco.co.kr

Jukdo Market
⌂ 13-1 Jukdosijang 13-gil
⏱ 8am-10pm daily

Guryongpo Modern History Museum
🎫 ⌂ 153-1 Guryongpo-gil
⏱ 10am-5:30pm Tue-Sun

The thatch roofs of Yangdong Folk Village and *(inset)* a traditional house

8
Yangdong Folk Village
양동마을

F4 **7 miles (11 km) W of Pohang** **From Pohang, Gyeongju** **Apr–Sep: 9am–7pm daily; Oct–Mar: 9am–6pm daily** **yangdongvillage.or.kr**

Together, Yangdong Folk Village and Andong Hahoe Folk Village *(p232)* make up a UNESCO World Heritage Site, with both recognized as outstanding examples of Joseon-era clan villages. While Andong gets all the crowds, travelers often overlook Yangdong. Don't tell anyone, but it might actually be the more appealing of the two. It's bigger, for one thing – the biggest traditional village in Korea – and its relative lack of visitors makes it easier to appreciate its throwback atmosphere.

Yangdong was founded in the 1400s by two aristocratic clans, the Sons of Gyeongju and the Lees of Yeogang. It gained renown as the source of several major Confucian scholars, "Hojae" Lee Eon-jeok (1491–1553) being the most famous. There are around 600 traditional homes in the village, some of which are more than 500 years old. Homes with tile roofs belonged to members of the aristocracy; those with thatch roofs were the residences of tenant farmers. Of particular note is Hyangdan, a huge manor house that King Jungjong built for Lee's mother when he was named the provincial governor.

Today, several homes have been converted to restaurants and guesthouses. Staying in the village overnight is a fantastic way to immerse yourself in the spirit of Korea's past. Village tours are conducted in Korean.

9
Mungyeongsaejae Provincial Park
문경새재도립공원

D3 **932 Saejae-ro, Mungyeong** **From Mungyeong** **00507 1321 0709**

For centuries, Mungyeong-saejae Pass was one of the only routes through the Sobaeksan Mountains, and thus one of the only links between the southeastern Gyeongsang region and Seoul. After Japanese forces

---

CONFUCIANISM

Confucianism is a belief system based on the writings of the Chinese philosopher Kong Qui (551–479 BCE), known in the West as Confucius. Its central concern is the development of good moral character. To that end, it emphasizes education, filial piety, and clear relations between social classes. Confucianism took hold in Korea with the establishment of the Joseon Dynasty, which adopted it as a guiding philosophy. While its days as a state ideology are long over, its influence remains embedded in society.

used the pass to reach the capital in the early stages of the Imjin War (1592–1598), Korea's rulers set about fortifying the strategic point, building a series of three gates across the narrow pass. The gates still stand, and the hiking trail connecting them is one of the most pleasant in central Korea, winding through forests and along mountain streams. Since it follows the pass, it's also relatively flat. It's about 4 miles (6.5 km) from the first gate to the third, which marks the border between Gyeongsangbuk-do and Chungcheongbuk-do provinces; plan on five hours to hike out and back.

Just beyond the first gate is the **Mungyeongsaejae Open Set** (문경새재 오픈세트장), an enormous film set of more than 100 "historic" buildings, including replicas of Seoul's Gwanghwamun Gate and Gyeongbokgung Palace *(p68)*. *Kingdom*, *The Red Sleeve*, and many other period dramas have been shot here. The film set is open to the public when not in use, so visitors can use the set to recreate their favorite scenes.

Mungyeongsaejae Open Set

9am–6pm daily (Nov–Feb: to 5pm)
Jan 1, Chuseok, Seollal

Buseoksa Temple
부석사

E3 345 Buseoksa-ro From Yeongju pusoksa.org

Buseoksa is exactly what a Korean temple should be. It's ancient, established in 676 CE; remote, high up in

→

Hiking along a spectacular canyon in Juwangsan National Park in fall

GREAT VIEW
Sobaeksan Range Ridges

From the terrace in front of Buseoksa's Muryangsujeong Hall, nearby tiled temple roofs give way to the beautiful Sobaeksan ridgelines that recede in endless waves to the horizon.

the Sobaeksan Mountains, miles from the nearest city; and beautiful, with some of the loveliest Buddhist architecture anywhere in the country.

Any visit begins with a symbolically purifying hike up 108 stairs to the temple entrance – with each step you rid yourself of one of the 108 earthly imperfections. Once inside, you're rewarded with gorgeous sight lines and five registered National Treasures, including Muryangsujeong Hall, one of the oldest wooden buildings in Korea.

Buseoksa is best reached from the small city of Yeongju.

Juwangsan National Park
주왕산국립공원

F4 69-7 Gongwon-gil, Cheongsong From Juwangsan knps.or.kr

This remote national park is known throughout the country for its brilliant fall foliage, though its rocky peaks, scenic valleys, and clear streams make it appealing any time of year.

The park's most popular hiking course begins near the main entrance and follows a stream through the Juwang Valley, passing waterfalls and interesting rock formations. In the south of the park is Jusanji Pond (주산지). Tightly encircled by forested mountains and with partly submerged willow trees rising from its surface, it's a beguiling sight, especially at dawn when the scene is often wrapped in fog. Acclaimed director Kim Ki-duk chose the pond as the setting for his classic 2003 movie *Spring, Summer, Fall, Winter…and Spring*.

12

Ulleungdo Island
울릉도

G2 98 miles (158 km) E of Donghae From Pohang, Gangneung, Donghae, Hupo-myeon 5-3 Dodong-1-gil, 785-25 Ulleungsunhwan-ro, 171 Ulleungsunhwan-ro; www.ulleung.go.kr

Some 81 miles (130 km) east of the mainland and reachable only by ferry, Ulleungdo is a real bragging-rights destination. Get them while you can, as a new airport is scheduled to open here in a few years.

The island is the tip of an extinct volcanic cone and has appropriately dramatic topography. Most folks live in small coastal villages, and the economy largely revolves around fishing. At night, the surrounding waters are illuminated by fleets of squid boats.

Ulleungdo's main settlement is at Dodonghang Port. Here you'll find most places to stay, restaurants, and the start of the thrilling, 2.2-mile (3.6-km) Haengnam Coastal Walking Path (행남해안산책로), parts of which are bolted into cliffsides above the waves. In the island's northeast corner are Gwaneumdo (관음도), an islet with a walking trail and large populations of streaked shearwaters; the Samseonam Rocks (삼선암), three towering formations that stick out of the water like fins; and Cheonbu Underwater Observatory (천부해중전망대), from which you can view local sealife from 16 ft (5 m) beneath the surface. On the island's remote west side, Ulleungdo Lighthouse (울릉도등대) provides amazing views over the rugged coast. Hike up to it or take a monorail from Taehahang Port.

13

Ulsan
울산

F5 32 miles (51 km) NE of Busan From Seoul, Busan, Pohang, Daegu 646 Saneop-ro; www.tour.ulsan.go.kr

Ulsan is the machine that makes Korea go. It's home to the world's largest shipyard, two giant oil refineries, and a huge automotive plant. Fortunately for travelers, it also has a few decent sights.

Lining both banks of the Taehwagang River for several kilometers is Taehwagang National Garden (태화강 국가정원), a delightful collection of themed gardens, artificial ponds, and walking paths. Be sure to stroll through the enchanting Simni Bamboo Grove and gaze out at the river from the Osan Manhoejeong Pavilion.

At the river mouth and surrounded by Ulsan's factories, Jangsaengpo Port (장생포항) was the center of Korea's whaling industry before the international ban. It's now the site of the **Jangsaengpo Whale Museum** (장생포고래박물관), which has minimal English but neat displays. Whale-watching cruises depart from here on weekends between April and November (2pm, with an additional 10am sailing in summer).

Also in Ulsan is Korea's most mysterious prehistoric site. On cliffs along a stream west of the city are the Bangudae Petroglyphs (반구대암각화), Neolithic or Bronze Age engravings that depict hunting and whaling scenes. Unfortunately, they're submerged most of the year and can only be seen from mid-fall to late winter. Check with the local tourism authorities before setting out.

> **INSIDER TIP**
> **Ulleungdo Ferries**
>
> Ferries to Ulleungdo take at least 2 hours 30 minutes. Travel is dependent on favorable weather, so if you visit the island, budget an extra day or two into your itinerary.

← A fisherman poling along a mist-shrouded waterway in the Upo Wetland

Jangsaengpo Whale Museum

 244 Jangsaengpogorae-ro ⏱ 9am–6pm Tue-Sun 🚫 Seollal, Chuseok 🌐 whalecity.kr

---

14

Tongdosa Temple
통도사

📍 E5 📌 108 Tongdosa-ro, Yangsan 🚌 Tongdosa Jeongmun 🌐 tongdosa.or.kr

Founded in the 640s, Tongdosa is regarded as one of the Three Jewels of Korean Buddhism, together with Haeinsa (p230) and Songgwangsa (p196). It's one of the country's largest temples, with more than 60 buildings whose faded paint and rustic wood give them an appealingly trapped-in-time feel. Tongdosa's main hall was in fact a rare survivor of the 16th-century Japanese invasions. It looks out over the Geumgang Gyedan, an altar and stupa said to house relics of the Buddha. A museum near Tongdosa's entrance has displays on these and other temple treasures.

15

Upo Wetland
우포늪

📍 E5 📌 220 Uponeup-gil, Changnyeong 🚌 Uponeup, Jumae ⏱ 24hr 🌐 cng.go.kr/tour/upo.web

Upo is the largest riverine wetland in Korea, covering a square mile (2.5 sq km). Formed by the Topyeong-cheon Stream and flooding of the Nakdonggang River, the Ramsar-listed preserve is an important habitat for Eurasian spoonbills, Baikal teals, whooper swans, and other birds. It's also the site of a program working to reintroduce crested ibises to the area. Visitors can walk more than 6 miles (10 km) of trails through the wetland; some of these are open to bikes, which can be rented from a stall near Upo's south entrance.

STAY

Ashton Hotel
애쉬튼호텔

Centrally located hotel, offering good rates, cozy rooms, and Ulsan's only rooftop pool.

📍 F5 📌 8 Jungang-ro 213-beon-gil, Ulsan 🌐 ashtonhotel.co.kr

Bukchondaek
북촌댁

Sleep like an aristocrat in one of Hahoe Folk Village's noblest houses, dating from 1797.

📍 E4 📌 7 Bukchon-gil, Andong 🌐 bukchondaek.com

EXPERIENCE Gyeongsang-do Province

16
Jinhae
진해

▲ E6 ⌂ 27 miles (43 km) W of Busan 🚌 From Busan, Ulsan, Daegu, Gwangju 📍 142 Jinhoe-ro; www.culture.changwon.go.kr

This district of Changwon City is home to Korea's naval academy, but it's less associated with cruisers than with cherry blossoms. The pops of pink and white can be seen across Korea each spring, but nowhere puts on a show quite like Jinhae, whose Jinhae Gunhangjae (진해군항제) is the country's biggest cherry blossom festival. Check its website (*jgfestival.or.kr*) for dates; peak blossom is usually in late March.

TOP 3 JINHAE SPOTS FOR BLOSSOM

Anmin Maru
안민마루
From this rest stop on the cherry tree-lined Anmingogae-gil you can take a panorama of Jinhae and the port through the blossoms.

Gyeonghwa Station
경화역 간이역
Bright white petals rain down over an old locomotive and passenger cars parked on disused tracks.

Yeojwacheon Stream
여좌천
Face north from where Yeojwanam-ro crosses the stream to capture a fairy-tale cherry tree canopy over the water.

17
Jinju
진주

 D6 ⌂ 65 miles (105 km) W of Busan 🚌 From Busan, Daegu, Gwangju 🚆 From Seoul, Busan, Daegu, Gwangju 📍 626 Namgang-ro; www.inju.go.kr

Jinju is a top destination for anyone interested in the Imjin War, the series of 16th-century invasions launched by Japanese daimyo Toyotomi Hideyoshi. His forces twice laid siege to riverside **Jinjuseong Fortress** (진주성), which became the setting for one of the war's most famous stories. As the invaders celebrated their 1593 victory, a *gisaeng* (female entertainer) named Nongae lured a Japanese general away from the party, embraced him, and threw herself into the river, killing them both. Within the fortress grounds is the striking **Jinju National Museum** (국립진주박물관), designed by renowned architect Kim Swoo-geun. Displays cover the war and local history and culture.

Jinjuseong Fortress and Jinju National Museum
 📍 626 Namgang-ro ⏰ Fortress: 5am–11pm daily (Nov–Feb: to 10pm); museum: 9am–6pm Tue–Sun 🌐 jinju.museum.go.kr

---

18
Geojedo Island
거제도

 E6 ⌂ 44 miles (71 km) SW of Busan 🚌 From Seoul, Busan, Daegu, Tongyeong 📍 Gohyeon Bus Terminal; www.tour.geoje.go.kr

During the Korean War, this large island was the site of UN forces' largest POW camp. More than 170,000 captured soldiers were held at what's now the **Historic Park of Geoje POW Camp** (거제포로수용소유적공원), a museum and collection of exhibition halls. Off Geoje's southeast coast is Haegeumgang (해금강), a stunning islet of sheer gray cliffs that plunge into the sea and are pocked with narrow inlets and sea caves. Tour boats depart from several island locations.

Cherry blossoms in bloom during the colorful Jinhae Gunhangjae festival

Historic Park of Geoje POW Camp

◉ ⌂ 61 Gyeryong-ro ⏰ 9am-6pm ✕ Tue, Seollal, Chuseok 🌐 gmdc.co.kr/_pow

19

Oedo Botania
외도 보타니아

🅰 E6 ⌂ 3 miles (5 km) S of Geojedo Island 🚢 From Geojedo Island ⏰ Summer: 8am-7pm daily; winter: 8:30am-5pm daily 🌐 oedobotania.com

There are passion projects, and then there's Oedo Botania. After riding out a storm on the small, windswept Oedo Island, local fisherman Lee Chan-ho decided he liked it enough to buy it, purchasing it with his wife, Choi Ho-sook, in 1974. After trying and failing to raise pigs and grow tangerines, they spent the next two decades turning the entire island into an enormous, Mediterranean-style botanical garden, complete with marble statues, Roman columns, and plants sourced from across the globe. The result is a remarkable, uncanny mash-up of coastal Korea and Italian Riviera. Numerous Geoje cruise companies sail to the island.

> **INSIDER TIP**
> **Combo Cruises**
>
> Haegeumgang Cruise (hggtour.net), Jangseungpo Oedo Cruises (bluecitygeoje.com), and Jisepo Oedo Cruises (geojecruise.com) all offer trips that visit both Haegeumgang and Oedo Island.

20

Tongyeong
통영

🅰 E6 ⌂ 58 miles (93 km) SW of Busan 🚌 From Seoul, Busan, Daegu, Gwangju ℹ 267 Tongyeonghaean-ro; www.tongyeong.go.kr

The south coast town of Tongyeong has one of the most beautiful settings in Korea, perched on a mountainous peninsula that's encroached upon by countless bays. Here, land and sea hardly seem like separate entities. Naturally, the city has a storied maritime history. Both the Joseon navy's and the legendary Admiral Yi Sun-sin's *(p55)* command posts were here. The early 17th-century Sebyeonggwan Hall (세병관) still stands at the former, the **Samdo Sugun Tongjeyeong** (삼도수군통제영). The other buildings are reconstructions. Downtown, replicas of Yi's *geobukseon*, or "turtle ships," are moored in Gangguan Port (강구안).

The Tongyeong Canal, dug through the peninsula's narrowest point in the 1930s, separates the city center from what's now Mireukdo Island. To reach it, either take a bus across the Chungmugyo Bridge or walk through the Tongyeong Undersea Tunnel. On the island, the **Jeon Hyuk Lim Museum of Art** (전혁림 미술관) celebrates the influential 20th-century painter and Tongyeong native. Just east of the museum is the **Tongyeong Cable Car** (통영케이블카), which runs to the summit of Mount Mireuksan (미륵산). There may be no better view in Korea: dark green mountains sloping into the sea and islands running to the horizon in every direction.

Samdo Sugun Tongjeyeong
◉ ⌂ 27 Sebyeong-ro ⏰ 9am-6pm daily 📞 055 645 3805

Jeon Hyuk Lim Museum of Art
⌂ 10 Bongsu-1-gil ⏰ 10am-5pm Wed-Sun 📞 055 645 7349

Tongyeong Cable Car
◉ ⌂ 205 Balgae-ro ⏰ 10am-4:30pm daily; extended hours in May, Aug, Oct ✕ 2nd & 4th Wed of the month and in inclement weather 🌐 cablecar.ttdc.kr

Tongyeong's cable car, with gorgeous views of the city across a sea of green slopes

The cascading Cheonjeyeon waterfall

JEJU ISLAND

Civilization on Jeju Island developed under the Tamna kingdom but in place of a record of its origins, there's only legend that states its three divine founders emerged out of three holes in the ground thousands of years ago. Tamna conducted maritime trade with nations from Japan down to South Asia, and during the Three Kingdoms period (57 BCE–668 CE), it entered into tributary relationships with Baekje and Silla. In 1105, Goryeo annexed the island and changed its name to Jeju. The island maintained some degree of autonomy until 1404, when the Joseon Dynasty brought it fully under its control, recognizing that Jeju's remoteness made it an ideal place to exile criminals and officials.

During the Japanese colonial period, Jeju suffered further, especially when Japan turned it into a military base and conscripted islanders to build facilities or work as comfort women. Among the country's notable pro-independence protests was an early 1930s demonstration led by Jeju's *haenyeo* (female divers) that drew 17,000 people. Sadly, independence brought little relief and the Jeju Uprising in 1948 was met with an overwhelming campaign of repression.

Yet since this time, Jeju's history has been more tranquil. Fishing and citrus farming have aided the economy, and the pleasant climate, beautiful beaches, and stunning volcanic formations here have seen it grow into a major tourist destination.

JEJU ISLAND

Must Sees
1. Seongsan Ilchulbong
2. Manjanggul Lava Tube
3. Hallasan National Park
4. Jeju Olle Trail

Experience More
5. Jeju City
6. Jeju Museum of Art
7. Jeju 4.3 Peace Park
8. Jeju World Natural Heritage Center and Geomunoreum
9. Sangumburi Crater
10. Haenyeo Museum
11. Udo Island
12. Seopjikoji
13. Seongeup Folk Village
14. Seogwipo
15. Jungmun Tourist Complex
16. Water Wind Stone Museum
17. Jeju Museum of Contemporary Art
18. Osulloc Tea Museum
19. Gapado Island

Did You Know?

Seongsan Ilchulbong attracted around 1.55 million visitors in 2023.

①
SEONGSAN ILCHULBONG
성산일출봉

🅰 G1 🚙 284-12 Ilchul-ro 🚌 From Jeju City & Seogwipo ⏰ Mar, Apr, Sep & Oct: 5am–7pm daily; May–Aug: 4:30am–8pm daily; Nov–Feb: 6am–6pm daily 🚫 Summit Trail: 1st Mon of the month

Few sights in Korea can compare to the majesty of Seongsan Ilchulbong at sunrise. As first light falls, this enormous tuff cone emerges from the darkness, the perfect summation of the island's strange beauty.

Even by Jeju's lofty standards, Seongsan Ilchulbong is an impressive sight, dwarfing everything around it. Its citadel-like qualities have long been apparent – Seongsan means "Fortress Mountain" – and during the Joseon Dynasty it served as a military base. Today, though, the focus is on its beauty and dramatic location at Jeju's easternmost point, summed up in the second half of its name, Ilchulbong, which means "Sunrise Peak."

Seongsan Ilchulbong is a parasitic volcanic cone – or *oreum* in the Jeju dialect – that formed roughly 50,000 to 120,000 years ago through an undersea volcanic eruption. It's free to take a short trail down to the black-sand beach beneath it, where you can gaze up at the massif and feel rather small. A small *haenyeo* (p259) restaurant sells freshly caught abalone and sea urchin here, too. For a small fee, you can hike the trail up to the cone's rim, which reaches 591 ft (180 m). A large observation deck provides amazing views of the grass-filled crater and the coastline. It's especially captivating at dawn, but any time of day is stunning.

PICTURE PERFECT
Seongsan Ilchulbong Sunrise

One of the best places to photograph Seongsan Ilchulbong at sunrise, or any time really, is Gwangchigi Beach (광치기해변), at the start of the peninsula connecting the cone with mainland Jeju.

Must See

↑ Sunrise over Seongsan Ilchulbong – one of Korea's most magical sights

1 From the air, Seongsan Ilchulbong looks like a gigantic satellite dish. It's connected to mainland Jeju by road, but was an island for much of its history.

2 The near-vertical shape of the cone's walls formed over centuries as they were carved away by waves and currents.

3 Stairs lead up to the cone's rim, about a 50-minute hike there and back.

MANJANGGUL LAVA TUBE

만장굴

F1 ◊ 182 Manjanggul-gil ◊ From Jeju City & Seogwipo (via Gimnyeong) ◊ 9am–6pm daily ◊ 1st Wed of the month

Descend into the island's depths to spelunk Manjanggul, one of the largest lava tubes in the world. Cavernous ceilings, lava flowlines, and fantastical formations hint at the powerful forces that shaped the island thousands of years ago.

Manjanggul Lava Tube formed via a lava flow from the Geomunoreum parasitic cone (p258) between 100,000 and 300,000 years ago. At some point, the surface of the flow cooled enough to solidify, trap, and insulate the lava beneath it, and the now-superheated lava cut a path through the subterranean rock as it made its way toward the sea. Eventually, the eruption stopped and the lava drained out, leaving a hollow tube behind.

That tube is immense. Manjanggul is one of the largest known lava tubes in the world, measuring 4.6 miles (7.4 km) long and reaching 75 ft (23 m) high and 59 ft (18 m) wide. Just a short section of the tube is open to visitors, but within it, you can make out lava flow lines on the walls and encounter a number of strange lava formations. Among these are a lava raft, a rock that floated atop the lava flow before solidifying in place, and a giant lava column that formed when liquid rock running from the ceiling to the floor hardened.

As you explore, take a moment to remember whose very little footsteps you're following in. In 1946, local teacher Bu Jong-hyu and his elementary school students began exploring Manjanggul, and in the course of a year, they managed to not only discover a new entrance but also measure the tube's entire length using a 6.6-ft (2-m) rope.

↑ The entrance to the tube, where bizarre underground lava formations await

↑ A lava column at Manjanggul, at 25 ft (7.6 m) it's the tallest known in the world

GEOMUNOREUM LAVA TUBE SYSTEM

Manjanggul is only the largest part of the greater Geomunoreum Lava Tube System, which consists of eight tubes that run northeast from the Geomunoreum parasitic cone for a combined 8 miles (13 km). According to UNESCO, the Geomunoreum system is the best-preserved lava tube system on the planet, making it a globally important site for scientists researching Earth's history, features, and processes. At present, Manjanggul is the only lava tube open to the public.

Must See

Did You Know?

Manjanggul is just one of more than 200 known lava tubes on Jeju Island.

↑ The vast lava tube, at 4.6 miles (7.4 km), one of the largest in the world

HALLASAN NATIONAL PARK

🅵1 🏛 Eorimok Visitor Center: 2070-61 1100-ro;
Seongpanak Visitor Center: 1865 516-ro, Jeju City
🚌 From Jeju City 🌐 jeju.go.kr/hallasan/index.htm

Mount Hallasan dominates and defines Jeju. Rising from the very center of the island, its lofty presence is inescapable, while its volcanic activity has shaped Jeju's terrain for millennia. Naturally, it's also a magnet for hikers lured by the challenge of Korea's ultimate ascent.

At 6,398 ft (1,950 m), Mount Hallasan is South Korea's tallest mountain, as well as one of its most sacred. A shield volcano, Hallasan formed through eruptions of highly fluid lava, the last occurring in 1007. At its summit is a 1,969-ft- (600-m-) wide caldera called Baeknokdam, which is partly filled by a shallow crater lake at certain times of the year, while the slopes are defined by parasitic cones, thick forests, valleys, and alpine wetlands. Hallasan's upper reaches were made a national park in 1970.

Despite its height, Hallasan's gentle slopes mean that hikes here aren't particularly difficult so long as you're prepared. Two trails reach the summit at Baeknokdam. The easier of the two, the Seongpanak Trail, is a 6-mile (9.6-km) route up the eastern flank that begins at the Seongpanak Visitor Center. It runs mostly through forest, and partway up there's a short spur to the Saraoreum parasitic cone. Slightly shorter but much more challenging is the Gwaneumsa Trail, which begins at Gwaneumsa Temple and ascends Hallasan's north flank. Many hikers go up Seongpanak and descend via Gwaneumsa. There are also three

Did You Know?

Mount Hallasan has more than 360 parasitic cones, or *oreum*, scattered across the island.

↑ A roe deer scuttling through the undergrowth along the Yeongsil Trail

> **INSIDER TIP**
> **Hiking Mount Hallasan**
>
> To hike Seongpanak or Gwaneumsa trail you need to make a reservation *(visithalla.jeju.go.kr)*. On all trails, you must also begin your hike by a certain time; check the park website for details.

trails up Hallasan's western and southern sides that terminate at the South Wall Junction, just below the summit. Of these, the 3.6-mile (5.8-km) Yeongsil and 4.2-mile (6.8-km) Eorimok trails are the most popular, both relatively gentle hikes. Keep an eye out for Hallasan's roe deer as you go.

Weather on Hallasan can change rapidly, and the mountain is prone to fog, high winds, and, as you approach the summit, cold temperatures, even in summer. If you hike the mountain, make sure you're dressed properly and are prepared for any condition.

→ The rain-filled Baeknokdam caldera atop Hallasan, a worthy reward for hikers

← Hikers soaking up epic views from Hallasan's Yeongsil Trail

253

Did You Know?

The name of Jeju Olle's mascot, Ganse, comes from *ganse-dari*, meaning "slow idler" in local dialect.

Scenic ocean views from the coastal trail near Songaksan Mountain

Network Highlights

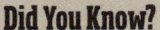

Route 5

▽ One of the Olle network's prettiest walks, this south coast route runs across 66-ft- (20-m-) high cliffs and through the Wimi-ri Camellia Habitat, where flowers bloom bright red in winter. It wraps up at Soesok- kak, an estuary pool popular with canoeists.

Route 1

▲ This route starts with treks up two *oreum* that treat hikers to east coast panoramas. It ends by passing Seong- san Ilchulbong (p248), a port where horses were once shipped to the main- land, and Gwangchigi Beach. In the middle, a long section hugs the coast.

Route 8

▲ Among Jeju Olle's longest, this 12-mile (20-km) trail mixes fish- ing villages with the large Jung- mun Tourist Complex, passing Yakcheonsa Temple, the columnar joints of Jusangjeolli Cliffs, and Jungmun Saekdal Beach en route.

Must See

④
JEJU OLLE TRAIL
제주올레길

🅐 F1-G1 🌐 jejuolle.org

Twenty-seven routes, 272 miles (437 km), and limitless possibilities: the Jeju Olle Trail system traces the perimeter of Jeju, running past beaches, tuff cones, orange groves, fishing villages, among other areas of natural beauty. Pick a path and lace up your walking shoes – there's no better way to experience the island.

The Jeju Olle Trail is a network of 21 interlinked hiking paths encircling Jeju, plus two spurs and four routes on outlying islands. Most are between 9 and 12 miles (15–20 km). Run by a local nonprofit, the trails provide a great opportunity to experience Jeju's unique culture and topography up close.

The Jeju Olle website and stone markers at the beginning of each trail provide maps and detailed info for each route, and paths are clearly marked by arrows, ribbons, or the Jeju Olle horse mascot. Start and end points are generally close to bus stops. Hikers can pick up trail info at the Jeju Olle Tourist Center, in Seogwipo, or the information centers found on 14 of the trails. Centers also sell Jeju Olle Passports that you can stamp as you complete sections. These fun souvenirs also provide discounts at many Jeju businesses.

HIKING PRACTICALITIES

Jeju Olle Trail routes are generally not too difficult and can be hiked year-round. Good walking shoes are a must, and it's a good idea to dress in layers, as the weather can change quickly. Trails close at 6pm in summer and 5pm in winter; most take 5 to 6 hours to complete, so plan accordingly. For extra peace of mind, you can rent a Jeju Safety Tracking Device for free at Jeju International Airport, which will notify the police of your location in an emergency.

Route 15

▼ This trail has two routes: A, a hilly inland path of forests and zinnia fields, and B, a flat coastal stroll that passes a *haenyeo* school and Aewol, a town of hip seaside cafés and gorgeous sunsets.

Route 10

▲ Starting at Hwasun Golden Sand Beach, Route 10 passes in front of Sanbangsan, a towering lava dome, before taking hikers up to Songaksan Viewpoint, which looks across the strait to Gapado Island. There's also a Joseon-era signal tower to check out.

Route 19

▲ In Jeju's north, this route has a bit of everything: sandy beaches and *gotjawal* forests, fishing ports and farm roads, *oreum* and off-shore islands. There are also memorials to the Jeju April 3 Incident and the anti-colonial struggle.

EXPERIENCE MORE

STAY

Chuidasun Resort
취다선 리조트
Stays at this serene wellness resort include meditation, yoga, and tea classes.

🅰F1 🏠2688 Haemajihaean-ro, Seogwipo 🌐chuidasun.com

Hotel WhistleLark
호텔 휘슬락
Comfortable hotel a block from the shore in central Jeju City. All rooms have terraces.

🅰F1 🏠26 Seobudu-2-gil, Jeju City 🌐whistlelark.co.kr

Playce Camp
플레이스 캠프
This hip, artsy stay offers organized activities and good food and drink options. Some rooms have views of Seongsan Ilchulbong.

🅰F1 🏠20 Dongyuam-ro, Seogwipo 🌐phoenixhnr.co.kr/page/main/playcecamp

Podo Hotel
포도호텔
All rooms at this beautiful, Jun Itami-designed property have tubs fed by hot springs.

🅰F1 🏠863 Salloknam-ro, Seogwipo 🌐podo.thepinx.co.kr

Jeju City
제주시

🅰F1 🏠North-central Jeju Island ✈From most Korean airports 🚢From Mokpo, Jindo Island, Nokdong (Goheung), Wando, Sacheon ℹ15 Yongduam-gil; www.visitjeju.net

Jeju City may be the island's capital and gateway, but it tends to be overlooked in favor of the isle's rural charms and natural wonders. Before you head for the hinterlands, though, it's worth spending a day or two here to learn some Jeju 101 and check out the local art scene.

> **Did You Know?**
>
> Seoul Gimpo to Jeju City is the world's busiest air route, with more than 14 million passengers per year.

The city's signature sight is Yongduam (용두암), a volcanic rock said to resemble a dragon's head. It's underwhelming but the waterfront park is a nice place to watch the crashing waves. Jeju's history, culture, and dialect are distinct from the mainland's, and both the **Jeju National Museum** (국립제주박물관) and the **Jeju Folklore and Natural History Museum** (제주특별자치도 민속자연사박물관) provide good introductions to its geology, ecology, and lifestyles as well as to the Tamna kingdom, which ruled the island between the 2nd and early 15th centuries.

Downtown, at 25 Gwandeok-ro, the **Jeju-mok Gwana Government Office** (제주목 관아) served as the center of island government in both the Tamna and Joseon eras. The original complex was destroyed by fire in 1434, but several buildings have been reconstructed.

Nearby, the lively Tap-dong neighborhood is home to the **Arario Museum** (아라리오뮤지엄), whose collection, spread

↑ The memorial hall at Jeju 4.3 Peace Park, commemorating victims of the Jeju Uprising

across three separate buildings (a former motel and cinema), includes work by Damien Hirst, Gu Bon-ju, Andy Warhol, and other art world luminaries. The Dongmun Motel I branch, where edgy pieces occupy gutted but still intact motel rooms, is especially thrilling.

Jeju National Museum

17 Iljudong-ro ⊙ 9am-6pm Tue-Sun ⊗ Jan 1, Seollal, Chuseok ⊕ jeju.museum.go.kr

Jeju Folklore and Natural History Museum

40 Samseong-ro ⊙ 9am-6pm Tue-Sun ⊗ Jan 1, Seollal, Chuseok ⊕ jeju.go.kr/museum

Jeju-mok Gwana Government Office

25 Gwandeok-ro ⊙ 9am-6pm daily ⊕ jeju.go.kr/mokkwana/index.htm

Arario Museum

Dongmun Motel I: 37-5 Sanji-ro; Dongmun Motel II: 23 Sanji-ro; Tapdong Cinema: 14 Tapdong-ro ⊙ 10am-7pm Tue-Sun ⊕ arariomuseum.org

The reconstructed, Joseon-period Jeju-mok Gwana Government Office

⑥
Jeju Museum of Art
제주도립미술관

F1 2894-78 1100-ro ⊞ From Jeju City ⊙ 9am-8pm Tue-Sun (Oct-Jun: to 6pm) ⊗ Jan 1, Seollal, Chuseok ⊕ jeju.go.kr/jmoa

This museum's permanent collection centers on Jeju artists and works inspired by the island. Its temporary exhibitions cover a wider remit, as does the Jeju Biennale, organized by the museum every other winter. A sculpture garden occupies the grounds outside. As intriguing as the art is the building itself. Partway up Hallasan Mountain, the museum is housed in an austere concrete and glass box that seems to float on a reflecting pond. A rooftop garden provides views of the volcano.

⑦
Jeju 4.3 Peace Park
제주4·3평화공원

F1 430 Myeongnim-ro ⊞ From Jeju City ⊙ 9am-6pm daily ⊗ 1st & 3rd Mon of the month ⊕ jeju43peace.or.kr

These peaceful grounds commemorate the Jeju Uprising, known among Koreans as the Jeju April 3 Incident. On that date in 1948, leftist guerillas attacked 12 police stations on the island. They were responding to years of police abuse and a UN plan to hold elections that would cement the peninsula's division, but the South Korean and U.S. military authorities saw a communist plot and responded with a heavy-handed campaign of repression, arresting thousands. After Jejuites largely boycotted the election, President Syngman Rhee declared martial law on the island in November. For the next four months, the military, under U.S. supervision, carried out a scorched-earth campaign, burning 40,000 homes across the island and deeming anyone caught more than 3 miles (5 km) from the coast a suspected insurgent to be shot on sight. Civilian resistance groups committed their own atrocities, forcibly conscripting young men and murdering residents of villages considered pro-government. By the time restrictions were lifted, in 1954, as many as 30,000 people had been killed, one-tenth of Jeju's population.

Monuments in the park pay tribute to the victims, and a memorial hall explores these events, whose memory was officially suppressed until the early 1990s.

↑ Sangumburi Crater, one of Jeju's many natural wonders

8
Jeju World Natural Heritage Center and Geomunoreum
제주세계자연유산센터
거문오름 우도

🅰 G1 🏠 569-36 Seongyo-ro 🚌 From Jeju City ⏰ 9am-5:50pm daily 🚫 1st Tue of the month, Seollal, Chuseok 🌐 jeju.go.kr/wnhcenter/index.htm

Jeju is a recipient of the so-called UNESCO Triple Crown, with the entire island or parts of it having been designated a World Natural Heritage, Biosphere Reserve, and Global Geopark.

The Jeju World Natural Heritage Center digs into the island's many natural wonders, from its tuff cones and soft corals to its eerie *gotjawal* forests. A fair bit of the center's space is dedicated to Geomunoreum, a parasitic cone that gave birth to a lava tube system that includes Manjanggul (p250).

Guided hikes around the cone depart from the center every half hour between 9am and 1pm. Visitor numbers are limited to 450 per day, so it is best to reserve a spot in advance on the center's website. Independent hiking is not permitted.

9
Sangumburi Crater
산굼부리

🅰 G1 🏠 768 Bijarim-ro 🚌 From Jeju City ⏰ Mar-Jun, Sep & Oct: 9am-6:40pm daily; Jul & Aug, Nov-Feb: 9am-5:40pm daily 🌐 sangumburi.net

Sangumburi is Jeju's largest and deepest parasitic crater, some 330 ft (100 m) deep and 1.7 miles (2.7 km) in circumference. It's also the only maar crater in Korea, having formed when subterranean magma came into contact with groundwater. The crater is its own microhabitat, with vegetation significantly different from that found elsewhere on Hallasan. You can't enter the crater itself, but you can view it from paths on one side.

10
Haenyeo Museum
해녀박물관

🅰 G1 🏠 26 Haenyeobang-mulgwan-gil, Hado-ri 🚌 From Jeju City & Seogwipo ⏰ 9am-6pm Tue-Sun 🚫 Jan 1, Seollal, Chuseok 🌐 jeju.go.kr/haenyeo/index.htm

This small museum near Jeju's northeast coast is devoted to the island's *haenyeo*, female divers who descend to depths of up 65 ft (20 m) to collect seaweed, abalone, sea cucumber, octopuses, and other marine products in the coastal waters. You'll find display cases holding traditional tools and diving suits as well as exhibits that cover everything from *bulteok*, stone-walled enclosures where *haenyeo* rest and exchange tips on the best spots to dive, to *sumbi-sori*, the unique whistling sound divers make when they surface before disappearing into the deep again. Other displays expound on the lives of Jeju women in past eras more generally. Hado-ri, the village where the museum is located, has one of Jeju's largest populations of *haenyeo*.

> **HIDDEN GEM**
> **Sehwa Beach**
>
> Just up the street from the Haenyeo Museum, this beach is one of the prettiest on the island, with turquoise waters lapping over bright white sand and black basalt rocks.

HAENYEO

It's one of Jeju's most striking scenes: a group of elderly women in black wetsuits slowly emerging from the sea, nets heavy with abalone, clams, and seaweed. Though not unique to Jeju, the island is now the only place in Korea where these *haenyeo*, or female divers, exist in significant numbers.

Records of women diving for abalone in Jeju go back to at least 1629, but the practice likely began centuries earlier. It is heavily communal, with *haenyeo* working in groups, the most skilled heading out first, followed by novices and elderly divers into calmer waters. The *haenyeo*'s work has had a major impact on Jeju culture. In contrast to the mainland's patriarchal society, their economic power resulted in more equal arrangements on the island. Historically, it wasn't unusual for *haenyeo* to be their family's primary breadwinner.

The physical, unglamorous nature of the work means that, predictably, there's been a precipitous drop in the number of Jeju's *haenyeo*, with numbers plunging from around 24,000 to roughly 3,000 in the past half-century. Climate change has also affected the profession, as warming waters have brought about a decline in sealife. Still, the famously hardy divers aren't prepared to disappear just yet. The addition of Jeju's *haenyeo* culture to UNESCO's list of Intangible Cultural Heritage helped breath a bit of life into the practice, and recent years have seen the establishment of *haenyeo* schools and more younger women opting for a life lived among the waves.

↑ A *haenyeo* diver at work without any oxygen tanks

↑ A basket of fresh conch being unloaded after a dive

Haenyeo divers bringing in the day's catch off Jeju ↑

THE FORMATION OF JEJU ISLAND

The geology and topography of Jeju are noticeably different from those of the mainland, a result of the island's starkly different birth and evolution. Jeju was formed through four bursts of volcanic activity that occurred between roughly 2 million and 250,000 years ago. At the center of it all was Mount Hallasan, which makes up much of the island and gave rise to many of its unique features, from parasitic cones and lava tubes to craters and eerie *gotjawal* forests.

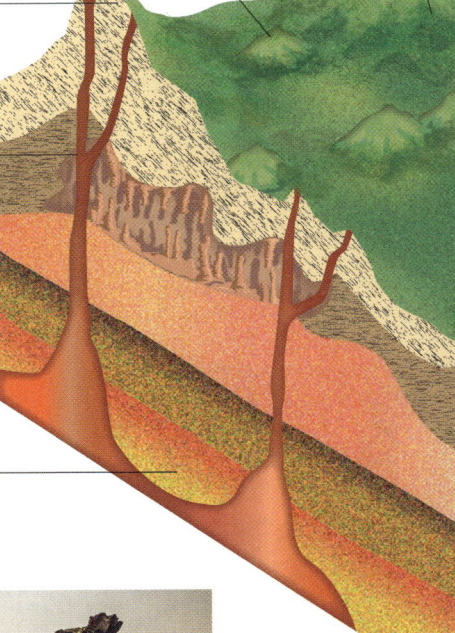

Tuff rings, like Jeju's Songaksan (p255), are formed by powerful explosions that occurr when magma comes into contact with water. Within Songaksan's ring are a crater and cinder cone.

Jeju is home to several gotjawal forests, where trees growing on basalt are unable to take deep root and so lean on one another. Hwansangsup Forest is a fine example of this dense tangle.

Dominating Jeju, Mount Hallasan (p252) is a giant shield volcano, akin to Hawaii's Mauna Loa. Most of the mountain was formed by lava from its vent, though more viscous lava shaped its mounded summit.

Lava tubes are created when the surface of a lava flow cools and solidifies, leaving the hot lava beneath to cut through the subterranean rock. When the lava drains out, large tubes like the one found at Manjanggul Lava Tube (p250) are left behind.

Jeju's bedrock is primarily the result of volcanic activity and includes basalt, silicic volcanic rocks, pyroclastic rocks, volcanic ash, and volcaniclastic sediments.

← Yongduam Rock, a basalt rock formation eroded by wind and waves

↑ Walking in Sangumburi Crater, one of several maar craters on Jeju

Maar craters, such as Sangumburi (p258), are created when magma comes into contact with groundwater and the ensuing steam explosion leaves a huge hole in the ground.

Like most of Jeju's oreum (parasitic cones), Geomunoreum (p258) is a cinder cone, formed when ash, cinders, and other material emitted in an explosive eruption accumulated around its vent.

Columnar jointing can be seen along Jeju's coast, but nowhere as dramatic as the Jusangjeolli Cliffs (p264). Jointing occurs when lava cools, contracts, and forms vertical cracks that split the rock into pillars.

Jeju is pocked by lava domes, such as Sanbangsan (p255), in the island's southwest. Unable to travel very far, highly viscous lava solidified soon after being emitted, forming a tall rounded structure.

↑ Illustration showing the major geological features of Jeju Island

Did You Know?

Mount Hallasan has more parasitic cones than any other volcano in the world.

↑ Dramatic Someorioreum, Udo's highest point, capped by a lighthouse

⓫ Udo Island
우도

▲ G1 📍 1.5 miles (2.4 km) NE of Jeju Island 🚢 From Seongsan Port, Dumun Port 📍 70 Udohaean-gil; visitjeju.net

Just off Jeju's northeast coast, Udo Island makes for a great getaway if your Jeju getaway isn't getaway enough. Its southeast corner is dominated by Someorioreum (소머리오름), or Cow Head Tuff Cone. The rest of Udo is largely a flat lava plateau. Just northeast of Someorioreum are the Huhaeseokbyeok (후해석벽) black lava cliffs and a black-sand beach. On the east coast, you'll find Seobinbaeksa (서빈백사해수욕장), also known as Sanho (산호해수욕장), a white coral-sand beach seemingly stolen from Thailand. Across the island, Hagosudong Beach (하고수동해수욕장), on a snug bay, is almost as nice. Bikes and scooters are great ways to get around Udo and can be rented at the ports.

⓬ Seopjikoji
섭지코지

▲ G1 📍 30 miles (49 km) SE of Jeju City 🚌 From Jeju City

In the Jeju dialect, *seopji* refers to a narrow piece of land, and *koji* means "promontory." This narrow promontory south of Seongsan Ilchulbong is one of the best places on the island to view the tuff cone, delivering handsome views of its profile from across the water.

The Phoenix Island resort complex takes up most of Seopjikoji, but an excellent public trail runs above the cliffs along its eastern face, providing views of the ocean and the black and deep red volcanic rocks that make up its coastline. It starts at the promontory's southernmost point. If you're driving, or making the long walk from the nearest bus stop, keep right as you approach Phoenix Island and follow Seopjikoji-ro. From the parking lot at the road's end, the trail takes you past a Joseon-era signal fire beacon, a candlestick-shaped rock jutting out of the ocean, and the Bangdupo Lighthouse.

Near the end of the trail are the Phoenix-owned **Yumin Art Nouveau Museum** (유민 아르누보 뮤지엄), home to a collection of French Art Nouveau glass, and the eye-catching Glass House (글라스하우스). The latter houses a restaurant and café and has two protruding glass wings set at a 90-degree angle. Both buildings were designed by Pritzker-winning Japanese architect Ando Tadao.

Yumin Art Nouveau Museum
🔗 📍 107 Seopjikoji-ro ⏰ 9am–6pm daily 🚫 1st Tue of the month 🌐 phoenixhnr.co.kr/en/page/main/jeju

⓭ Seongeup Folk Village
성읍마을

▲ G1 📍 30 Seongeup-jeonguihyeon-ro 🚌 From Seogwipo ⏰ 24 hr 🌐 jeju.go.kr/seongeup/index.htm

This time-capsule place is the best-preserved Joseon village in Jeju and, between 1423

Did You Know?

Udo is famous for its peanuts, and you'll find places selling peanut ice cream across the island.

> ### DOL HAREUBANG
>
> Today, *dol hareubang* (돌하르방) – volcanic stone statues of men with bulging eyes in rounded hats – are beloved symbols of Jeju, and its hardest-working ambassadors. For centuries, though, they served as totems, placed at village entrances to ward off misfortune. Roughly 45 premodern *dol hareubang* still exist on Jeju. Twelve of these, dating to 1754, can be found at Seongeup Folk Village.

and 1914, was the administrative center of a large swath of the island. Within its 0.75-mile (1.2-km) walls are more than 100 structures, including old government buildings, a guesthouse for visiting officials, and a Confucian school.

Really, however, its greatest attraction are its modest homes, many of them still private residences. Built of volcanic rock and mud, they're covered in thatched roofs tied down with crosshatched ropes to protect against wind. Kimchi pots fill the yards, and bright orange persimmons dangle from tree branches.

Visitors to the village can join traditional craft programs and stay overnight in comfortable guesthouses.

Seogwipo
서귀포

F1 30 miles (49 km) S of Jeju City From Jeju City 2-13 Namseongjung-ro; visitjeju.net

Seogwipo is Jeju's second-largest city and its main south coast settlement. Like Jeju City, it's often seen more as a base for exploring other parts of the island than a destination in its own right, but it has several sights that merit a visit.

This part of Jeju is studded with waterfalls, and there are two absolute stunners on either side of Seogwipo. On the eastern edge of the city, **Jeongbang Waterfall** (정방폭포) is the only one on the continent that empties directly into the ocean, pouring over a 75-ft (23-m) cliff and into a pool linked to the sea. Across town, **Cheonjiyeon Waterfall** (천지연폭포) is a beautiful 72-ft (22-m) cascade that's surrounded by chestnut trees, camellias, and orchids. The deep pool at its base is home to a population of eels.

Seogwipo's best urban attraction is the **Lee Jung-seop Art Gallery** (이중섭미술관), dedicated to one of 20th-century Korea's most important painters. Born in what's now North Korea, Lee fled south at the start of the Korean War, settling in Seogwipo for 11 productive months. He's most famous for his landscapes and paintings of bulls, while his human figures seem to presage the work of Keith Haring.

Jeongbang Waterfall

37 Chilsimni-ro 214-beon-gil 9am–5:20pm daily

Cheonjiyeon Waterfall

2-15 Namseongjung-ro 9am–10pm daily

Lee Jung-seop Art Gallery

33 Lee Jung-seop-ro 9am–6pm Tue–Sun Jan 1, Seollal, Chuseo culture.seogwipo.go.kr/jslee

↑ The paradisical Cheonjiyeon Waterfall, surrounded by forest

15

Jungmun Tourist Complex
중문관광단지

F1 9 miles (15 km) W of Seogwipo From Jeju City 38 Jumungwangwang-ro, visitjeju.net

This complex on Jeju's southwest coast is the island's answer to Waikiki, a sprawling collection of luxury hotels, restaurants, shops, a casino, a golf course, and no shortage of kitschy attractions. If you're after sun, sand, sea, and zero intrusions from the outside world, look no further.

The complex surrounds Jungmun Saekdal Beach (중문색달해수욕장), a beautiful strip of white sand with flecks of red, black, and gray that's bookended by volcanic cliffs. It's one of the country's top spots for surfing, parasailing, and windsurfing. Unsurprisingly, it can get crowded in summer.

Southeast of the beach are the **Jusangjeolli Cliffs** (주상절리대), whose dramatic columnar jointing was created by the cracking and contracting of rapidly cooling lava some 200,000 years ago.

North of the beach is **Cheonjeyeon Waterfall** (천제연폭포) – not to be confused with Seogwipo's Cheonjiyeon Waterfall – which pours over three tiers in a narrow gorge. Nearby, the **Yeomiji Botanic Garden** (여미지식물원) has a 125-ft (38-m) observatory and sprawling indoor and outdoor gardens. Families, or anyone who's ever longed to see Seurat's *A Sunday on La Grande Jatte* re-created with stuffed animals, should be sure to check out the **Teddy Bear Museum** (테디베어뮤지엄) located nearby.

Jusangjeolli Cliffs
36-30 Ieodo-ro, Seogwipo 9am-5:30pm daily

Cheonjeyeon Waterfall
132 Cheonjeyeon-ro, Seogwipo 9am-5:50pm daily

Yeomiji Botanic Garden
93 Jungmung-wangwang-ro, Seogwipo 9am-6pm daily yeomiji.or.kr

Teddy Bear Museum
31 Jungmun-gwangwang-ro 110-beon-gil, Seogwipo 9am-6pm daily teddybearmuseum.com

---

16

Wind Water Stone Museum
수풍석뮤지엄

F1 71 Sanroknam-ro 762-beon-gil From Donggwang Yukgeori Tours: Jul & Aug: 10:30am, 3pm; Sep-Jun: 1:30pm, 3pm waterwindstonemuseum.co.kr

Located within a hotel and housing development on Hallasan's southwest slopes, this "musuem" is a collection of three buildings by the late Korean-Japanese architect Jun

← The rugged basalt rock columns of Jusangjeolli Cliffs

A tea bush teacup in the gardens of the Osulloc Tea Museum

Itami. Each is a poetic meditation on a particular element, nature interpreted through human construction. To visit them, you must join one of the twice-daily guided tours. They're conducted in Korean, though when you encounter the buildings and artworks, language feels beside the point. Book well in advance in summer: the online reservation form only accepts Korean credit cards, but you can reserve by phone on the number listed on the museum website.

Jeju Museum of Contemporary Art
제주현대미술관

F1 35 Jeoji-14-gil From Jeju City Jul-Sep: 9am-7pm Tue-Sun; Oct-Jun: 9am-6pm Tue-Sun Jan 1, Seollal, Chuseok jeju.go.kr/jejumuseum/index.htm

Opened in 2007, the Jeju Museum of Contemporary Art is located amid the Jeoji Culture and Artists' Village. Nearly all pieces in both the permanent collection and rotating exhibits are by Korean artists. Highlights include Park Gwang-jin's Jeju landscapes, which depict subjects such fields of yellow rapeseed flowers running down to black volcanic rocks or Hallasan wrapped in moody fall fog. A sculpture park and performance hall can be found outside.

Osulloc Tea Museum
오설록 티뮤지엄

F1 15 Shinhwayeoksa-ro From Jeju City Summer: 9am-7pm daily; rest of year: 9am-6pm daily us.osulloc.com/osulloc-tea-museum

Osulloc is Korea's most well-known tea company and has three fields in southern Jeju. Its Seogwang fields, where the tea museum is located, have a foggy climate, which helps produce leaves with a vivid color. The word "museum" is doing some heavy lifting here. Essentially, this is a shop, roastery, and tearoom with a few information panels on the walls. Nevertheless, it's a great place to purchase some of Osulloc's excellent tea or to enjoy a freshly prepared cup. Just don't expect peace and quiet: the complex is enormously popular. Across the street from the museum, you can wander between rows of green tea bushes, savoring their lovely aroma.

Gapado Island
오설록 티뮤지엄

F2 2.5 miles (4 km) S of Jeju Island From Unjinhang Port

This little island off Jeju's southern coast is reachable via a 20-minute ferry ride. When you disembark, you'll be greeted by a round stone shrine where islanders still conduct traditional rites. Gapado's flat terrain makes it an easy place to walk or cycle. You can hike the entire island on an S-shaped Olle Trail in just a couple of hours, rambling through tiny villages and fields of barley and breaking for a warm bowl of abalone porridge. To really savor the solitude, though, opt to spend a night in a local guesthouse.

DRINK

Dorrell
도렐

Terrific coffee near Seongsan Ilchulbong. Try the Nutty Cloud.

G1 20 Dongnyuam-ro 0507 1437 3011

Haejigae
해지개

Café with stylish trad-contemporary design and glorious sunsets.

F1 52 Aewolbukseo-gil 0507 1358 8586

In's Mill
인스밀

A sleek café in a renovated barley granary inspired by Jeju's agricultural past.

F1 22 Ilgwadaesu-ro 27-beon-gil insmill.com

NEED TO KNOW

Entrance of Gangnam Subway station

Before You Go 268

Getting Around 270

Practical Information 274

BEFORE YOU GO

Things change, so plan ahead to make the most of your trip. Be prepared for all eventualities by considering the following points before you travel.

AT A GLANCE

CURRENCY
South Korean Won (KRW)

AVERAGE DAILY SPEND

SAVE	SPEND	SPLURGE
₩80,000	₩150,000	₩350,000

BOTTLED WATER	COFFEE	BEER	DINNER FOR TWO
₩1,500	₩6,000	₩7,000	₩50,000

CLIMATE

Temperatures average 79°F (26°C) in summer and drop below 32°F (0°C) in winter.

South Korea has a summer rainy season, with July and August seeing the most precipitation.

Air pollution can reach unhealthy levels, especially around Seoul. Conditions are worst from March to April.

ELECTRICITY SUPPLY

Power sockets are type C and F, fitting two-pronged plugs. Standard voltage is 220v.

Passports and Visas

For entry requirements, including visas, consult your nearest South Korean embassy or check the South Korean **Ministry of Foreign Affairs** website. Citizens of the UK, US, Australia, and New Zealand do not need a visa for stays of up to 90 days. Citizens of Canada do not need a visa for stays of up to six months. Visitors from other countries may require a visa and visitors from other countries may require a visa, and certain travelers from visa-exempt countries must apply in advance for a **Korea Electronic Travel Authorization** (K-ETA). At present, travelers from visa-exempt countries between the ages of 17 and 65 do not need a K-ETA.

Korea Electronic Travel Authorization
w k-eta.go.kr
Ministry of Foreign Affairs
w mofa.go.kr

Government Advice

Now more than ever, it is important to consult both your and the South Korean government's advice before travelling. The **UK Foreign, Commonwealth and Development Office (FCDO)**, the **US State Department**, the **Australian Department of Foreign Affairs and Trade**, and the South Korean Ministry of Foreign Affairs offer the latest information on security, health, and local regulations.

Australian Department of Foreign Affairs and Trade
w smartraveller.gov.au
UK Foreign, Commonwealth and Development Office (FCDO)
w gov.uk/foreign-travel-advice
US State Department
w travel.state.gov

Customs Information

You can find information on laws relating to goods and currency taken in or out of South Korea on the **Korea Customs Service** website.
Korea Customs Service
w customs.go.kr

Insurance

We recommend taking out a comprehensive insurance policy covering medical care, theft, loss of belongings, cancelations and delays. Read the small print carefully.

Vaccinations

No inoculations are required to visit South Korea. You may wish to be vaccinated against Japanese encephalitis if you are planning to spend an extended period of time in rural areas.

Booking Accommodations

South Korea offers a wide range of accommodations, from five-star hotels to campsites. *Hanok* inns and guesthouses are great for experiencing traditional lodging. **Visit Korea** provides detailed accommodations information.
Visit Korea
w visitkorea.or.kr

Money

Major credit and debit cards are accepted by most businesses, including taxis, though some websites do not accept foreign cards. Contactless payments are common, but it's always a good idea to carry cash for markets. Cash machines (ATMs) can be found at banks and convenience stores. Tipping is not part of the culture in South Korea.

Travelers With Specific Requirements

Broadly speaking, it's easiest to get around in Seoul and other urban areas, where nearly all metro stations are accessible, low-floor buses are common, and many streets and metro stations have tactile paving. In the capital, the **Visit Seoul Accessibility Guide** details the facilities available at key tourist locations, while the Seoul Tourism Organization operates **Danurim**, a tourism service specifically for travelers with specific requirements. Danurim provides complimentary airport transfers for wheelchair users, and can assist with booking wheelchair-accessible taxis. It also offers free rentals of wheelchairs, ramps, and other devices.

Rural areas can present challenges, as older infrastructure means that many building are not accessible. Some popular tourist locations endeavor to accommodate all, however. The Jeju Olle Trail, for example, has clearly marked wheelchair-accessible sections.
Danurim
w seouldanurim.net
Visit Seoul Accessibility Guide
w english.visitseoul.net/accessible-seoul

Language

The official language is Korean. Most younger Koreans can communicate in English, especially in urban areas. English signage is common throughout the country.

> Situations can change quickly and unexpectedly. Always check before visiting attractions and hospitality venues for up-to-date opening hours and booking requirements.

Opening Hours

Saturdays and Sundays: Banks, post offices, and government offices are closed.
Mondays: Many museums and tourist attractions are closed; if Monday is a holiday, they often close on Tuesday instead.
Public holidays: Schools, post offices, and banks are closed.

PUBLIC HOLIDAYS

Jan 1	New Year's Day
Jan/Feb	Seollal (Lunar New Year)
Mar 1	Independence Movement Day
May 5	Children's Day
May	Buddha's Birthday
Jun 6	Memorial Day
Aug 15	Liberation Day
Oct 3	National Foundation Day
Sep/Oct	Chuseok
Oct 9	Hangeul Day
Dec 25	Christmas Day

GETTING AROUND

Whether you're spending time in Seoul or traveling around the country, discover how best to reach your destination and travel like a pro.

AT A GLANCE

PUBLIC TRANSPORT COSTS

SEOUL
₩1,500
Single journey by bus or metro

SEOUL TO BUSAN
₩59,800
Single journey by high-speed train

BUSAN
₩1,700
Single journey by bus or metro

TOP TIP
Buy a reloadable T-Money card to use on buses and the metro across the country.

SPEED LIMIT

EXPRESSWAYS
100 km/h (62 mph)

NATIONAL AND PROVINCIAL ROADS
80 km/h (50 mph)

URBAN AREAS
50 km/h (31 mph)

SCHOOL ZONES
30 km/h (19 mph)

Arriving by Air

Nearly all international flights to South Korea arrive at **Incheon Airport**, 57 km (35 miles) west of Seoul. Some flights from China, Japan, and Southeast Asia are handled by Gimpo International Airport, on Seoul's western edge; Gimhae International Airport, 18 km (11 miles) west of Busan; and Jeju International Airport, 5 km (3 miles) west of Jeju City.
Incheon Airport
w airport.kr
Other airports:
w airport.co.kr

Internal Flights

Frequent flights linking the mainland with Jeju Island depart from airports across the country. A network of domestic routes connects cities around the peninsula, but intercity travel by train or bus is usually more convenient.

Train Travel

South Korea's rail system provides an efficient, and inexpensive way to travel the country. (There are no trains on Jeju Island.) **Korail**, the national railway company, operates several types of trains: high-speed KTX trains that travel on major routes, express ITX-Saemaeul trains, and local Mugunghwa trains. Free Wi-Fi is available on all. Tickets can be purchased at stations, on the Korail website, or through the KORAILTALK app. Foreign travelers also have the option of buying a Korail Pass, which offers unlimited rail travel for three or five consecutive days, or on any two or four days within a 10-day period. Pass carriers must still reserve a seat in advance.

When traveling, keep in mind that some cities, like Seoul, have multiple stations and that trains may only depart from one of them. For instance, if there doesn't appear to be a train to your destination from Seoul Station, check the schedules at Yongsan and Cheongnyangni, the capital's other train stations.
Korail
w korail.com

GETTING TO AND FROM INCHEON AIRPORT

Distance to city	Transportation	Journey time	Fare
57 km (35 miles)	Airport Railroad Express Train	45 mins	₩13,000
	Airport Railroad All Stop Train	1 hr	₩4,450
	Airport Limousine Bus	1 hr 10 mins	₩17,000
	Taxi	45 mins	₩65,000

RAIL JOURNEY PLANNER

Plotting South Korea's main rail routes, this map is a handy reference for traveling between cities by train. Journey times are for the fastest available service.

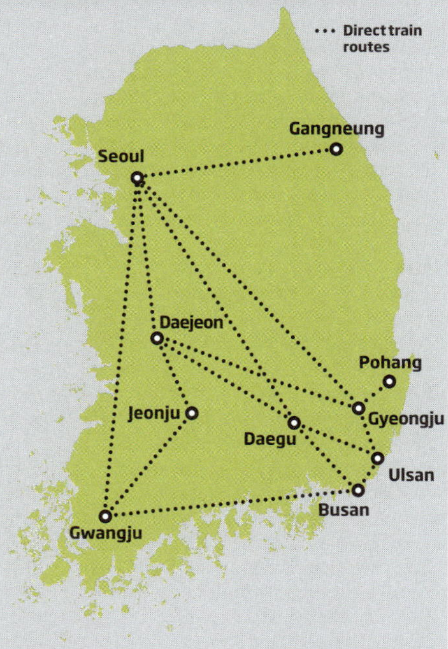

··· Direct train routes

Seoul to Busan	2 hrs 45 mins
Seoul to Daegu	1 hr 50 mins
Seoul to Daejeon	1 hr 10 mins
Seoul to Gangneung	2 hrs
Seoul to Gwangju	2 hrs 10 mins
Seoul to Gyeongju	2 hrs 15 mins
Seoul to Jeonju	1 hr 50 mins
Seoul to Pohang	2 hrs 30 mins
Seoul to Ulsan	2 hrs 20 mins
Busan to Daegu	1 hr 40 mins
Busan to Daejeon	1 hr 40 mins
Busan to Gyeongju	35 mins
Busan to Ulsan	20 mins
Daejeon to Daegu	1 hr 40 mins
Daejeon to Gwangju	2 hrs
Daejeon to Gyeongju	1 hr
Daejeon to Jeonju	1 hr 15 mins
Daejeon to Ulsan	1 hr 15 mins
Daejeon to Pohang	1 hr 20 mins

Public Transportation

It's easy to get around using public transportation in South Korea, as several cities have metro systems and even rural villages have local bus networks. Timetables, transportation maps, and other info can be obtained at stations and tourist information centers.

Google Maps can be used to plan routes when traveling via public transport, but South Korea's **Naver Maps** is more accurate and provides more detailed information. Unfortunately, English names in Naver Maps are sometimes inaccurate, so travelers may find they need to use a combination of the two. Subway Korea is also a useful app for plotting routes on the country's metro systems.

Naver Maps
w map.naver.com

Tickets

Single-ride tickets for buses can be purchased with cash upon boarding; single-ride tickets for the metro can be purchased with cash from kiosks in stations. A much more efficient, and cheaper, way to travel, however, is to use a reloadable T-Money transit card. These can be purchased and reloaded at convenience stores and kiosks in metro stations, including at the entrance to the Airport Railroad at Incheon Airport. Note that station kiosks only accept cash. Using a T-Money card gets you slightly discounted fares and enables free transfers between buses or between bus and metro.

Metro

Seoul, Busan, Daejeon, Daegu, and Gwangju have metros. The Seoul metro connects much of Gyeonggi-do Province with the capital. Fares are based on distance. If purchasing a single ticket from a kiosk, select your destination and pay the appropriate amount. If using a T-Money transit card (p270), tap your card when entering and exiting the turnstiles, and the fare will automatically be deducted. Fare adjustment machines are located inside turnstiles if your single-ride ticket or card has insufficient funds.

Signs and announcements in stations and on trains are provided in both Korean and English. All cars have priority seating for the elderly and disabled, and some cars have designated spaces for wheelchair users. Metros in Seoul, Busan, Daejeon, and Daegu operate from approximately 5am to midnight; the Gwangju metro operates from 5:50am to 10:40pm.

Bus

Local buses operate more or less the same throughout the country, whether you're in Seoul or a small village. Board through the front door and exit through the rear door. If purchasing a single ride, deposit cash in the box next to the driver when boarding. Change is given. If using a T-Money transit card, tap your card on the scanner next to the driver when boarding. Tap again on the scanner next to the rear door when getting off; doing so will permit you to transfer to another bus or the metro for free.

Long-Distance Bus Travel

South Korea's long-distance bus network reaches just about every corner of the country, making it a good option both for traveling city-to-city and for getting off the beaten path. Express buses travel longer, direct routes. Intercity buses cover shorter distances and may make stops en route. Many cities have separate express and intercity bus terminals. Both express and intercity buses come in three classes: economy, excellent, and premium. Excellent- and premium-class buses are more expensive but offer more comfortable seats and more legroom. Tickets can be purchased at bus terminals or online through **Kobus**, **Bustago**, or **TxBus**. Many transportation companies operate buses, but there's little to differentiate them. Buses do not have on-board restrooms; on longer routes, they'll stop at rest stations where passengers can use the restroom and purchase snacks.

Bustago
w bustago.or.kr
Kobus
w kobus.co.kr
TxBus
w intercitybus.tmoney.co.kr

Boats and Ferries

Ferries run to many islands off the west and south coasts. **Incheon** and **Mokpo** are the primary points of departure. Neither city's ferry terminal website has an English-language ticketing page, but travelers should have little trouble purchasing a ticket when they want to depart. Ferries to Ulleungdo Island (p240) depart from Pohang, Hupohang, Mukhohang (Donghae), and Gangneung. Travel is weather-dependent, so travelers to the island should allow for an extra day in their itinerary in case ferry service is suspended.

Incheon Coastal Passenger Terminal
w ipfc.or.kr
Mokpo Ferry Passenger Terminal
w mokpo.ferry.or.kr

Taxis

There are two types of taxis in Korea. Regular cabs are white, silver, or, in Seoul, orange.

Mobeom taxis are black and provide a more luxurious ride for a higher price. A light on the vehicle's roof indicates that a taxi is available. To hail a cab on the street, extend your arm, palm face down. You can also reserve or summon a taxi using the Kakao T app (p274).

Securing a taxi in popular nightlife areas late at night can be difficult. Taxis are metered and have uniform fares that are clearly displayed. You can pay in cash or by card; many taxis also accept T-Money. There's no need to tip. **Uber** does not operate a direct ride-sharing service in Korea, but you can use the app to book a taxi.
Uber
uber.com

Driving

South Korea has a well-maintained road network, and road signs include both Korean and English. That said, most travelers are better off foregoing a car. Traffic congestion in urban areas, aggressive drivers, and high rental car costs mean that driving is rarely the best way to get around, especially given the country's extensive and affordable public transportation network.

The main exception to this is Jeju Island (p244). The lack of a rail system and a less extensive bus network mean that driving is the most convenient way of getting around there. And since so many travelers rent cars on the island and competition for their business is fierce, rental costs are far lower than they are on the mainland. To drive in Korea, you will need both a valid license from your own country and an International Driving Permit. Google Maps does not work for driving in Korea and travelers are better off using Naver Maps (p272) instead.

Car Rental

To rent a car in South Korea you must be at least 21 years of age and have at least one year of driving experience. Vehicles can be rented at airports and rental company offices in cities. You're more likely to find English-speaking staff at airports. Major rental companies include **Lotte Rent-a-Car** (which partners with Hertz), **SK Rent-a-Car** (which partners with Avis), and, on Jeju Island, **Jeju One Car**.
Jeju One Car
jejuonecar.net
Lotte Rent-a-Car
www.lotterentacar.net
SK Rent-a-Car
homepage.skcarrental.com

Rules of the Road

Koreans drive on the right side of the road. Traffic enforcement cameras to monitor speeding are common. Punishments for speeding and other violations are strictly enforced in school zones. At intersections with traffic lights, you may only turn left when a green left-turn arrow is displayed unless a visible blue sign reading "비보호" (unprotected left turn) is present. Motorcycles are not permitted on expressways. The blood alcohol content limit for drivers is 0.03 per cent and is strictly enforced. Hitchhiking in South Korea is not common.

Cycling

Cycling is gradually growing in popularity in South Korea. The **Rivers Guide** website provides information on long-distance bike routes in the country. Several cities have bike-sharing systems. Seoul's is called **Ttareungi (Seoul Bike)** and has docking stations all over the city. Cyclists should use designated bike lanes when available and travel on the right side of the road when there is no bike lane. When biking on roads, cyclists are not allowed to make left turns when traveling through intersections.

Wearing helmets was made mandatory in 2018 for two-wheeled vehicles, including bikes and e-scooters, though some residents have called for the law to be repealed. It is strictly prohibited to ride a bike while under the influence of drink or drugs.
Rivers Guide
riverguide.go.kr
Ttareungi (Seoul Bike)
bikeseoul.com

Walking

Dense cities and a national obsession with hiking make South Korea a terrific place to walk. In urban areas, major sights are often within walking distance of one another, and the blocks between them are typically a captivating mix of markets, shops, cafés, and street vendors. For travelers for whom a simple stroll isn't enough, Korea offers ample opportunities for truly epic rambles – especially given that over 70 per cent of the country is mountainous. The popular **Jeju Olle Trail** (p255) consists of 27 routes that run for 272 miles (437 km), around Jeju Island's perimeter, some of which are accessible for travelers with specific requirements (p269), and several outlying islets. Meanwhile, the impressive **Korea Dulle Trail** runs for 2,796 miles (4,500 km) along the country's coastline and northern border.
Jeju Olle Trail
jejuolle.org
Korea Dulle Trail
durunubi.kr

PRACTICAL INFORMATION

A little local know-how goes a long way in South Korea. Here you can find all the essential advice and information you will need during your stay.

AT A GLANCE

EMERGENCY NUMBERS

POLICE
112

TRAVEL HELPLINE
1330

FIRE, AMBULANCE
119

INFECTIOUS DISEASES
1339

TIME ZONE
South Korea follows Korean Standard Time. It is 9 hours ahead of UTC. It does not observe daylight saving time.

TAP WATER
Unless otherwise stated, tap water in South Korea is safe to drink.

WEBSITES

Visit Korea
South Korea's official tourism website (visitkorea.or.kr)

Visit Seoul
Seoul's official tourism website (visitseoul.net)

Kakao T app
A useful app for calling or booking a taxi. Set up an account before departing your home country.

Personal Security

South Korea is a safe country and most visits are trouble-free. However, use common sense to ensure personal safety: keep valuables out of sight and exercise caution at night. If you have something stolen, report the crime to the police as soon as possible, and get a copy of the crime report to make an insurance claim. Contact your embassy or consulate if your passport is stolen, you suffer a serious crime or accident.

Attitudes toward LGBTQ+ individuals in South Korea are improving, but acceptance lags behind what travelers from Europe and North America might expect. Seoul has South Korea's largest LGBTQ+ scene, centered on the Itaewon, Hongdae, and Jongno neighborhoods. Organizations such as Haengseongin, Chungusai, and the **Korean Sexual-Minority Culture and Rights Center** provide support for the Korean LGBTQ+ community and are places LGBTQ+ individuals can contact for assistance.
Korean Sexual-Minority Culture and Rights Center
w kscrc.org

Health

Healthcare in South Korea is of high quality. Travel health insurance is recommended, but even without it, basic care is fairly affordable. Several large hospitals in Seoul have international clinics with English-speaking staff or interpretation services, including **Seoul National University Hospital**. For minor ailments, pharmacies (yakguk) can provide over-the-counter medication. Most pharmacists can understand explanations of symptoms in English. Look for signs reading "약국" (pharmacy) or "약" (medicine).
Seoul National University Hospital:
w snuh.org

Smoking, Alcohol, and Drugs

Smoking and vaping are prohibited in nearly all indoor public spaces, including bars, cafés, and restaurants, though some buildings have

designated smoking areas. Many localities also ban smoking in certain outdoor spaces, such as plazas and parks. Individuals may purchase and consume tobacco products and alcohol from January 1 of the year they turn 19, regardless of their date of birth. South Korea enforces a 0.03 per cent blood alcohol content limit for drivers and takes a zero-tolerance approach to drunk driving. Punishments can range from fines to imprisonment. The country also has one of the world's strictest drug policies. All drugs are illegal, and possession of even a small amount incurs harsh penalties, from heavy fines to lengthy prison sentences.

ID

Visitors to South Korea are required to carry ID on them. A photocopy or digital photo of your passport photo page (and visa if applicable) should suffice.

Local Customs

Koreans traditionally greet others by bowing, though this is often little more than a head nod. Shoes should be removed when entering a home. Some businesses also require visitors to remove their shoes; a shoe rack at the entrance should make this obvious. When giving something to, or receiving something from, a person older than you, it's polite to use two hands; gently touching the fingertips of one hand to the opposite forearm is sufficient.

Visiting Places of Worship

Dress modestly when visiting a temple or other place of worship. Wear knee-length shorts or skirts and a shirt that covers your shoulders and torso. Remove your shoes if required.

Responsible Tourism

The climate crisis is having an impact on South Korea, with rising temperatures and extreme weather becoming more frequent. Do your bit by carrying a refillable water bottle, taking quick showers, and using public transportation. If you rent a car on Jeju Island (p244), opt for an electric vehicle (EV). Wildfires are increasingly a threat, so dispose of cigarette butts carefully, completely extinguish campfires, and follow all posted fire-prevention guidelines.

Cell Phones and Wi-Fi

Free Wi-Fi is available in many public spaces and on buses, and cafés will often share their Wi-Fi password with customers. Foreign cell phones may not work in South Korea, so check before traveling. Local SIM cards and portable Wi-Fi hotspots can be rented from **Korea Telecom**, **LG U+**, or **SK Telecom** at Incheon International Airport (p270). A SIM card provides a local phone number, ideal for joining restaurant waiting lists.

Korea Telecom
w roaming.kt.com
LG U+
w lguplus.com/ib-roaming/pc/eng
SK Telecom
w skroaming.com

Post

Korea Post operates the country's postal service. Post offices are typically open 9am–6pm Monday to Friday. International airmail can take up to two weeks to reach North America, Europe, or Australia.
Korea Post
w koreapost.go.kr

Taxes and Refunds

South Korea's VAT rate is 10 per cent. Non-Korean citizens can receive VAT tax refunds on purchases made at stores that display a tax refund sign. Upon purchase, present your passport and state that you would like a tax refund. Refunds can be claimed at major airports or tax refund booths in large cities.

Discount Cards

Seoul offers the **Discover Seoul Pass**, which provides entry to major tourist attractions and grants discounts on other activities. It can be purchased for 48-, 72-, or 120-hour durations and is available on an app or a physical card (the latter also functions as a transportation card).
Discover Seoul Pass
w discoverseoulpass.com

INDEX

Page numbers in **bold** refer to main entries

1-cha, 2-cha, 3-cha **97**
40-Step Culture & Tourism Theme Street (Busan) **211**, 219

A

ACC Magic Mountain (Gwangju) 185
Accommodation: booking 269
  Templestays **165**
  see also Hotels
Air travel 270, 271
Alcohol 274-5
Ambulances 274
Amusement parks: Baekje Cultural Land (Buyeo) **157**
  Everland **124**
  Eworld (Daegu) 236
  Jindo Dog Theme Park 196
  LEGOLAND® Korea Resort (Chuncheon) 141
  SeoulLand (Seoul Grand Park) 126
Andong 221, **232-3**
Andong Hahoe Folk Village 177, **232**
Ando Tadeo 262
Aquariums 102, 132
Arario Museum (Seoul) **73**
Archaeological sites: Gochang **194**
  Songsan-ri (Gongju) 164
  see also Temples; Tombs
Architecture **30-31**
  hanok **74-5**
  Incheon Open Port Modern Architecture Museum 112-13, 115
Arii Hills (Jeongseon) 146
Arirang **146**
Art 49
  Gwangju art walk 184-5
  Heyri Art Valley **123**
  see also Crafts; Museums and galleries
Asia Culture Center (Gwangju) **182**

B

Baekdamsa Temple (Seoraksan National Park) 138
Baekje Cultural Land and Baekje Historical Museum (Buyeo) **157**
Baekje Kingdom 52, 53, 103, 156, 164
Balloons, hot-air 120
Barbecues 11, 33
Bars *see* Drinks
Baseball: Sajik Baseball Stadium (Busan) **216**
Beaches: Byeonsan 180
  Daecheon **167**
  Gijipo **155**
  Gosapo 180
  Gwangalli (Busan) **215**
  Gyeokpo 180
  Gyeongpo (Gangneung) **132**
  Haeundae (Busan) 208
  Jeongdongjin **143**, 149
  Kkotji **155**
  Mallipo **154-5**
  Mohang 180
  Sehwa 258
  Sokcho 135
  Yangyang 142
Bears **234**

Beauty products 37
Beer 13, 43
Beomeosa Temple (Busan) **216-17**
Beopjeong 99
Beyond the Center (Seoul) **91-105**
  drinks 97
  hotels 102
  map 92-3
  restaurants 101
  walk 104-5
Bicycles *see* Cycling
BIFF Square (Busan) **210**, 218
Birds: Eulsukdo Ecological Park (Busan) 212, 213
  Heuksando Island 196
  Suncheonman Wetland **188-9**
  Upo Wetland **241**
Biryong Falls (Seoraksan National Park) 139
Blossom photo spots (Jinhae) 242
Boats: ferries 272
  Mokpo National Maritime Museum 195
Bongeunsa Temple (Seoul) **100**
Bonghwangru Pavilion (Juknokwon) 187
Bongjeongsa Temple (Andong) **233**
Books: Bosu Book Street (Busan) **212**, 218
  Paju Book City **123**
Boseong **198**
Bosu Book Street (Busan) **212**, 218
Breweries 13, 43
BTS 35, 57, 99, 148
Buddhism **79**
  art 48
  see also Temples
Bukchon Hanok Village (Seoul) **72-7**
Bukchon Traditional Culture Center (Seoul) **72-3**, 77
Bukhansan National Park **98**
Bulguksa Temple (Gyeongju) **225**
Bupyeong Kkangtong Market (Busan) **211**, 218
Busan 18, 114, **203-19**
  drinks 208
  hotels 214
  map 204-5
  restaurants 233
  shopping 211
  walk **218-19**
Busan Cinema Center **217**
Busan Modern and Contemporary History Museum **210-11**, 219
Busan Museum of Contemporary Art **212-13**
Busan Tower 210, 219
Buseoksa Temple **239**
Buses 272
Busosanseong Fortress (Buyeo) **157**
Buyeo 151, **156-7**
Buyeo National Museum **156**
Buyongdae Cliff 232
Byeonsanbando National Park **178-81**
Byeonsan Beach 180

C

Cafés 42
  see also Drinks
Carpenter's revenge **123**
Cars 270, 273
  see also Driving tours

Cathedrals: Jeondong (Jeonju) 174
  Myeong-dong (Seoul) 84
Caves: Gosu (Danyang) 161
  Hwanseongul **146-7**
Central Buddhist Museum (Seoul) 78
Central Seoul 62, **65-89**
  drinks 85
  hotels 73
  map 66-7
  restaurants 82
  shopping 80
Ceramics: Gyeonggi Museum of Contemporary Ceramic Art **126-7**
Chaebol (family-run conglomerates) 89
Chaeseokgang Cliffs 180-81
Changdeokgung Palace (Seoul) **81**
Changgyeonggung Palace (Seoul) **81**
Changnyongmun Gate (Suwon Hwaseong Fortress) **119**
Cheomseongdae Observatory (Gyeongju) 229
Cheonbuldong Valley (Seoraksan National Park) 139
Cheondogyo religion 79, 221
Cheonggyecheon Stream (Seoul) **80-81**
Cheongju 151, **158**
Cheongpung Cable Car 169
Cheongpung Cultural Heritage Complex 169
Cheonmachong Tomb (Gyeongju) 227, 228
Cheonwangbong 1 Course 41
Cheorwon 129, **141**
Cheorwon Peace Observatory 141
Chiaksan National Park **141**
Chinatown (Incheon) **112**, 114
Christianity **79**, 166
Chuncheon **140-41**
Chun Doo-hwan, General 57, 137, 182
Chungcheong-do Province 17, **151-69**
  restaurants 157
  shopping 167
Chungju Coffee Museum 168
Chungjuho Lake **158-9**
  driving tour **168-9**
Churches *see* Cathedrals
Cinema 34
  Busan Cinema Center **217**
  Mungyeongsaejae Open Set 239
Clearing After Rain on Mount Inwang (Jeong Seon) 95
Climate 268
Confucianism 54, 174, 221, **238**
Cosmetics 37
Crafts 36
Credit cards 269
Crime 274
Culture *see* Pop culture; Traditional culture
Culture Station Seoul 284 104
Currency 268, 269
Customs information 268
Cycling 39, 273

D

Daecheon Beach **167**
Daecheongbong (Seoraksan National Park) 41, 139

Daecheongho Lake **158**
Daegu 221, **236**
Daegwallyeong Yangtte Ranch **145**
Daehan Empire History Museum (Seoul) 83
Daehwa Corporation office (Incheon) 115
Daejeon 151, **160-61**
Daemisan Akeobong Peak 168
Daereungwon Ancient Tomb Complex (Gyeongju) **224**, 228
Daeseung Falls (Seoraksan National Park) 138
Dance 47
Dance with Two Swords (Sin Yun-bok) 48
Dangun 52, 122-3
Danyang **161**, 169
Deogyusan National Park **190-91**
Deoksugung Palace (Seoul) **83**
Disabled travelers 269
Discount cards 275
Diving: *haenyeo* **259**
  Haenyeo Museum **258**
DMZ (Demilitarized Zone) **116-17**
DMZ Museum **142**
Doctors 274
Dogs: Jindo Dog Theme Park 196
Dol hareubang (statues) **263**
Dongdaemun (Seoul) **70-71**
Dongdaemun Design Plaza **71**
Donggung (Gyeongju) **225**, 229
Donggureung **127**
Dorasan Peace Park (The DMZ) **116-17**
Dosan Seowon (Andong) **233**
Drinks **42-3**
  breweries 13, 43
  Busan 208
  Chungju Coffee Museum 168
  Jeju Island 265
  Jeolla-do Province 191
  Jeonju Korean Liquor Museum 174, 175
  Sool Gallery (Seoul) **73**
  Seoul 46, 85, 97
  see also Food and drink; Tea
Driving tours: Chungjuho Lake **168-9**
  Gangwon Nature Road Course 6 **148-9**
Drugs 274-5

E

Electricity supply 268
Emergency numbers 274
Entertainment **46-7**
Eoulmadang-ro (Seoul) **96**
Etiquette 42, 275
Euljiro (Seoul) **85**
Events *see* Festivals and events
Everland **124**

F

F1963 **214-15**
Farms: Daegwallyeong Yangtte Ranch **145**
Fashion 36, 71
Fermented food 32
Ferries 272
  Ulleungdo Island 240
Festivals and events **50-51**
Film *see* Cinema
Fire services 274

Flow Control (Gwangju) 184
Folk villages: Andong Hahoe **232**
  Bukchon Hanok (Seoul) **72-7**
  Jeonju Hanok **174-5**
  Naganeupseong **198-9**
  Seongeup **262-3**
  Yangdong **238**
Food and drink **32-3**
  Kimchi Academy (Seoul) 77
  Korean barbecue 11, 33
  street food 218
  temple food **33**
  see also Drinks; Restaurants
Fortresses 31
  Busosanseong (Buyeo) **157**
  Geumjeongsanseong (Busan) **217**
  Gochangeupseong (Gochang) 194
  Gongsanseong (Gongju) 164
  Gwangseongbo (Ganghwado Island) 122, 123
  Haemieupseong **166**
  Jinjuseong 242
  Namhansanseong **127**
  Sangdansaneong (Cheongju) 158
  Suwon Hwaseong **118-21**
Freedom Park (Incheon) 115

G

Gaeamsa Temple 181
Galleries *see* Museums and galleries
Gamcheon Culture Village (Busan) **213**
Ganghwado Island **122-3**
Ganghwa Peace Observatory (Ganghwado Island) 122, 123
Gangnam (Seoul) 91, **100**
Gangneung **132-3**, 149
Gangneung Coffee Street **132**
Gangwon-do Province 17, **129-49**
  map 130-31
  restaurants 135
Gangwon Nature Road Course 6 **148-9**
Gapado Island **265**
Garden of Morning Calm **126**
Gardens *see* Parks and gardens
Gaya confederacy 52, 203
Geology: Jeju Island **260**
Geomunoreum (Jeju Island) **258**, 261
Geomunoreum Lava Tube System **250**
Geumjeongsanseong Fortress (Busan) **217**
Geumsansa Temple **191**
Gijipo Beach **155**
Gilsanga Temple (Seoul) **99**
Gochang **194**
Goguryeo kingdom 52, 53, 129
Gojedo Island **242-3**
Gojong, King 69, 83, 122
Gongju 151, **164**
Goryeogung Palace Site (Ganghwado Island) 122, 123
Goryeo kingdom 54, 230
Gosapo Beach 180
Goso 1004 Mural Village (Yeosu) 201
Government advice 268
Gudambong 169
Gukdong Port (Yeosu) 201
Gukje Market (Busan) **211**

Guksadang (Seoul) 104
Gungnamji Pond (Buyeo) **157**
Gunsan **190**
Gwangaeto 53
Gwangalli Beach (Busan) **215**
Gwanghulmun (Seoul) 105
Gwanghwamun Square (Seoul) **78**
Gwangjang Market (Seoul) **84**
Gwangju 171, **182-5**
Gwangju Art Street 185
Gwangju National Museum **183**
Gwangju Swarms (Terahni) 185
Gwangju Uprising (1980) 56, **182**
Gyeokpo Beach 180
Gyeokpo Port 180
Gyeongbokgung Palace (Seoul) **68-9**
Gyeonggi-do Province 16, **109-27**
  hotels 127
  map 110-11
Gyeonggi Museum of Contemporary Ceramic Art **126-7**
Gyeonghuigung Palace (Seoul) **82**
Gyeongju **224-9**
Gyeongju Historic Site Wolseong District **224-5**
Gyeongju National Museum **226-7**
Gyeongpo Beach (Gangneung) **132**
Gyeongpoho Lake (Gangneung) **132**
Gyeongsang-do Province 19, **221-43**
  hotels 241
  map 222-3
  restaurants 233, 236
Gyeongui Line Forest Park (Seoul) **96-7**
Gyeon Hwan 53
Gyeryongsan National Park **166**

H

Hadid, Zaha 71
Haedong Yonggungsa Temple (Busan) **216**
Haeinsa Temple **230-31**
Haemieupseong Fortress **166**
Haenyeo **259**
Haenyeo Museum **258**
Haesindang Park **143**
Haeundae (Busan) **208-9**
Hallasan National Park **252-3**
Hamel, Hendrick **200**
Hanbit Tower (Daejeon) 160
Han dynasty 52
Hangang River 91, 122, 125, 140-41
Hangeul script 95
Han Kang 183
Hanok **74-5**
  Bukchon Hanok Village (Seoul) **72-7**
  Jeonju Hanok Village **174-5**
  Namsangol Hanok Village (Seoul) 88
Han Yong-un ("Manhae") 137
Healthcare 274
Heuksando Island **196-7**
Heunginjimun Gate (Seoul) **70**
Heyri Art Valley **123**
High1 Resort **147**
Hiking 10, 38, **40-41**, 273
  Bukhansan National Park 98
  Jeju Olle Trail **254-5**
  Jirisan National Park 234

Index

Hiking (cont.)
  Mount Hallasan 253
  Seoraksan National Park 137
  Seoul Hiking Tourism Center 98
Historic buildings 30
  Cheongnamdae 158
  Gwanghulmun (Seoul) 105
  Gyeongpodae Pavilion (Gangneung) 132
  Heunginjimun Gate (Seoul) **70**
  Hyangiram Hermitage (Yeosu) 199
  Imyeonggwan Sammun (Gangneung) **133**
  Jeju-mok Gwana Government Office (Jeju City) 256, 257
  Jinnamgwan (Yeosu) 199
  Namdaemun (Seoul) **84-5**
  Ojukheon (Gangneung) **133**
  Pungnammun Gate (Jeonju) **175**
  Samdo Sugun Tongjeong (Tongyeong) 243
  Sinheung-dong Japanese House (Gunsan) 190
  Workers' Party of Korea Building (Cheorwon) 141
  see also Cathedrals; Folk villages; Fortresses; Palaces; Temples
History **44-5**, **52-7**
Hongdae (Seoul) 91, **96-7**
Hongdae Playground (Seoul) **97**
Hongdo Island **197**
Hospitals 274
Hotels: booking 269
  Busan 214
  Gyeonggi-do Province 127
  Gyeongsang-do Province 241
  Jeju Island 256
  Seoul 73, 102
Hot springs 11, 135
Hun Kyu, Kim 49
Hwahongmun Gate (Suwon Hwaseong Fortress) **119**
Hwangnamdaechong Tomb (Gyeongju) 95, 228
Hwangnidan-gil (Gyeongju) 224
Hwangsangsup Forest 260
Hwanseongul Cave **146-7**
Hwaseomun Gate (Suwon Hwaseong Fortress) **119**
Hwaseong Haenggung Palace (Suwon Hwaseong Fortress) **119**

I

ID 275
Imjingak Tourist Area (The DMZ) **116**
Imjin War (1592-98) 55, 78, 239, 242
Imyeonggwan Sammun (Gangneung) **133**
Incheon **112-15**
Incheon, Battle of (1950) **112**
Incheon Art Platform 113
Incheon Open Port **112-13**
Independence Hall of Korea **161**
Independence movement 56, 79, 80, **161**
Insa-dong (Seoul) **80**
Insurance 269
Internet access 275
Itaewon (Seoul) **89**
Itami, Jun 264-5
Itineraries: 3 Days in Jeju Island 23
  3 Days in Seoul 21
  5 Days in the Southern Provinces 24-5
  10 Days in South Korea 27-9

J

Jagalchi Market (Busan) **206-7**, 218
Janganmun Gate (Suwon Hwaseong Fortress) **120**
Jangdo Island (Yeosu) 200
January 21 Incident Pine Tree (Seoul) 104
Japanese 58th Bank building (Incheon) 115
Jeju 4.3 Peace Park **257**
Jeju City **256-7**
Jeju Island 19, **245-65**
  drinks 265
  geology **260**
  hotels 256
  itinerary 23
  map 246-7
Jeju Museum of Art **257**
Jeju Museum of Contemporary Art **265**
Jeju Olle Trail 40, **254-5**
Jeju Uprising (1948) 245, 257
Jeju World Natural Heritage Center **258**
Jeokbyeokgang Cliffs 180
Jeolla-do Province 18, **171-201**
  drinks 191
  map 172-3
  restaurants 175
Jeongak (traditional music) 176
jeongdongjin Beach **143**, 149
Jeonghyeon, Queen 102
Jeongjo, King 118-20
Jeongneung Royal Tomb (Seoul) **102**
Jeongnimsa Temple Site and Museum (Buyeo) **156-7**
Jeong Seon (painter) 89, 95
Jeongseon 129, **146**
Jeonju **174-5**
Jeonju Hanok Village **174**
Jeonju Hyanggyo 174
Jikso Falls 181
Jindo Island **196**
Jinhae **242**
Jinju **242**
Jirisan National Park **234-5**
Jjimjilbang (public bathhouses) **135**
Jogyesa Temple (Seoul) **78**
Joint Security Area (The DMZ) **117**
Jongmyo Shrine (Seoul) **80**
Jongpo Marine Park (Yeosu) 201
Joseon Dynasty 44, 45, **54-5**
  art 48
  Gyeongbokgung Palace (Seoul) **68-9**
  Jongmyo Shrine (Seoul) **80**
  Korean Folk Village **125**
  Seolleung and Jeongneung Royal Tombs (Seoul) **102**
  Suwon Hwaseong Fortress **118-19**
Juknokwon **186-7**
Jultagi (tightrope walking) 177
Jungjong, King 102, 238
Jungmun Tourist Complex **264**
Jungoe Park (Gwangju) **183**
Jusangjeolli Cliffs 261, 264
Juwangsan National Park **239**

K

Kangkangee Arts Village (Busan) **212**
K-drama 10, 34
Kim Bu-seong 117
Kim Bu-sik 54
Kimchi Academy (Seoul) 77
Kim Dae-seong 225
Kim Il Sung 117

Kim Jae Kyu 56
Kim Kwang-seok 236
Kim Swoo-geun **31**, 242
Kkotji Beach **155**
Kong Qui (Confucius) 238
Korea Dulle Trail 40
Korean Empire (1897-1910) 55, 83
Korean Folk Village **125**
Korean War (1950-53) 45, 56
  40-Step Culture & Tourism Theme Street (Busan) **211**, 219
  Battle of Incheon **112**
  Cheorwon **141**
  DMZ (Demilitarized Zone) **116-17**
  DMZ Museum **142**
  Historic Park of Geoje POW Camp (Gojedo Island) 242, 243
  War Memorial of Korea (Seoul) **88-9**
K-pop 10, 35, 57, **99**, 148
KT&G Sangsangmadang (Seoul) **96**
Kukje Gallery (Seoul) **73**

L

Language 269
Lava tubes *see* Volcanoes
Lee, Heejoon 49
Lee Bul 49
Lee Byung-chul 89, 124
Lee Eon-jeok ("Hojae") 238
Lee Jinju 49
Lee Jung-seop 263
Leeum Museum of Art (Seoul) **89**, 124
LEGOLAND® Korea Resort (Chuncheon) 141
LGBTQ+ community 47, 89, 274
Libraries: Forest of Wisdom (Paju Book City) 123
Local customs 275
Lotte World Tower (Seoul) **102**

M

MacArthur, General Douglas 115
Magoksa Temple **165**
Mahan Confederacy 109, 151
Maisan Provincial Park **191**
Makgeolli (rice wine) 42
Mallipo Beach **154-5**
Mancheonha Skywalk 169
Manjanggul Lava Tube **250-51**, 260
Maps: Andong 233
  Asia 15
  Bukchon Hanok Village (Seoul) 76-7
  Busan 204-5, 218-19
  Buyeo 157
  Byeonsanbando National Park 180-81
  Central Seoul 66-7
  Chungcheong-do Province 152-3
  Chungjuho Lake driving tour 168-9
  DMZ (Demilitarized Zone) 117
  Dongdaemun 71
  Gangwon-do Province 130-31
  Gangwon Nature Road Course 6 148-9
  Gwangju 183, 184-5
  Gyeonggi-do Province 110-11
  Gyeongju 225, 228-9
  Gyeongsang-do Province 222-3
  hiking 40-41

278

Maps (cont.)
　Hongdae (Seoul) 97
　Incheon 113, 114-15
　Jeju Island 246-7
　Jeolla-do Province 172-3
　Jeonju 175
　rail journey planner 271
　Seoraksan National Park 138-9
　Seoul 60-61
　Seoul: Beyond the Center 92-3
　Seoul: Central Seoul 73
　Seoul: Hanyangdoseong 104-5
　South Korea 14-15, 61
　Suwon Hwaseong Fortress 119
　Taeanhaean National Park 155
　Ulleungdo Island 222
　Yeosu: Namparang-gil Course 55 200-201
Markets: Bupyeong Kkangtong (Busan) **211**, 218
　Dongdaemun **71**
　Gukje (Busan) **211**
　Gwangjang (Seoul) **84**
　Jagalchi (Busan) **206-7**, 218
　Jeongseon Arirang 146
　Jukdo (Pohang) 237
　Namdaemun (Seoul) 85
　Noryangjin Fisheries Wholesale Market (Seoul) **101**
　Yeosu Seafood 201
May 18 Democracy Square (Gwangju) **182**
Memorials: War Memorial of Korea (Seoul) **88-9**
Michu, King 228
"Miracle on the Han" 57
Mobile phones 275
Mohang Beach 180
Mokpo **195**
Monasteries *see* Temples
Mona Yongpyong Ski Resort **144-5**
Money 268, 269
Mongols 54, 122
Moon bears **234**
Moon villages **213**
Mount Hallasan 40, 252-3, 260-61
Mount Jirisan Traverse 41
Mu, King 157
Mudeungsan National Park **183**
Muju Deogyusan Resort 190, 191
Mungyeongsaejae Provincial Park **238-9**
Mureung Valley **145**
Muryeong, King 164
Museums and galleries 12, **48-9**
　Arario Museum (Jeju City) 256-7
　Arario Museum (Seoul) **73**
　Asia Culture Center (Gwangju) **182**
　Baekje Historical Museum (Buyeo) **157**
　Book City Letterpress Museum (Paju Book City) 123
　Bukchon Traditional Culture Center (Seoul) **72-3**, 77
　Busan Modern and Contemporary History Museum **210-11**, 219
　Busan Museum of Contemporary Art **212-13**
　Buyeo National Museum **156**
　Central Buddhist Museum (Seoul) 78
　Cheonggyecheon Museum (Seoul) 80-81
　Cheongju Early Printing Museum 158
　Cheongju National Museum 158
　Cheongpung Cultural Heritage Complex 169

Museums and galleries (cont.)
　Chungju Coffee Museum 168
　Culture Station Seoul 284 104
　Daebul Hotel Exhibition Hall (Incheon) 113, 114
　Daegu Modern History Museum 236
　Daegu Yangnyeongsi Oriental Medicine Museum 236
　Daehan Empire History Museum (Seoul) 83
　DMZ Museum **142**
　Ganghwa History Museum (Ganghwado Island) 122, 123
　Gochang Dolmen Museum 194
　Gongju National Museum 164
　Gunsan Modern History Museum 190
　Guryongpo Modern History Museum (Pohang) 237
　Gwangju Biennale Exhibition Hall 183
　Gwangju History & Folk Museum 183
　Gwangju Museum of Art 183
　Gwangju National Museum **183**
　Gyeonggi Museum of Contemporary Ceramic Art **126-7**
　Gyeongju National Museum **226-7**
　Haenyeo Museum **258**
　Hahoe Mask Museum (Andong) 232
　Hoam Museum of Art (Everland) 124
　Incheon Open Port Modern Architecture Museum 112-13, 115
　Incheon Open Port Museum 113, 115
　Jangsaengpo Whale Museum 240, 241
　Jeju Folklore and Natural History Museum 256, 257
　Jeju Museum of Art **257**
　Jeju Museum of Contemporary Art **265**
　Jeju National Museum 256, 257
　Jeju World Natural Heritage Center **258**
　Jeongnimsa Temple Site and Museum (Buyeo) **156-7**
　Jeon Hyuk Lim Museum of Art (Tongyeong) 243
　Jeonju Hanok Village History Hall 174
　Jeonju Korean Liquor Museum 174, 175
　Jinju National Museum 242
　Jjajangmeon Museum (Incheon) 112, 114
　Kangkangee Village Museum (Busan) 212
　Kansong Art Museum (Seoul) 48
　Korean Folk Village **125**
　Korea Tea Museum (Boseong) 198
　Kukje Gallery (Busan) 214, 215
　Kukje Gallery (Seoul) **73**
　Lee Jung-seop Art Gallery (Seogwipo) 263
　Leeum Museum of Art (Seoul) **89**, 124
　Lotte Museum of Art (Seoul) 102
　Mokpojin History Park 195
　Mokpo Modern History Museum 195

Museums and galleries (cont.)
　Mokpo National Maritime Museum 195
　Munui Cultural Heritage Complex 158
　Museum of Korean Emigration History (Incheon) 113
　Museum of Korean Traditional Music (Seoul) **103**
　Nam June Paik Art Center **124**
　National Hangeul Museum (Seoul) 95
　National Intangible Heritage Center (Jeonju) **175**, 177
　National Museum of Korea (Seoul) **94-5**
　National Museum of Korean Contemporary History (Seoul) 78
　National Museum of Modern and Contemporary Art (Seoul) **82**
　National Science Museum (Daejeon) 160, 161
　Osulloc Tea Museum **265**
　POSCO Museum (Pohang) 237
　Provisional Capital Memorial Hall (Busan) **212**
　Seodaemun Prison History Hall (Seoul) **99**
　Seoul Baekje Museum 103
　Seoul City Wall Museum **70-71**
　Seoul Museum of Art (SEMA) 83
　Seoul Museum of Craft **72**
　Seoul Museum of History **82-3**
　Seoul Olympic Museum of Art (SOMA) 103
　Seoul Urban Life Museum **98**
　Sool Gallery (Seoul) **73**
　Suwon Hwaseong Museum **119**
　Taebaek Coal Museum 147
　Teddy Bear Museum (Jungmun) 264
　Uam Historical Park (Daejeon) 160, 161
　War and Women's Human Rights Museum (Seoul) **100-101**
　War Memorial of Korea (Seoul) **88-9**
　Wind Water Stone Museum **264-5**
　Yumin Art Nouveau Museum (Seopjikoji) 262
Music 35
　Arirang **146**
　Jindo National Gugak Center 196
　K-pop 35, 57
　live-music venues 35
　Museum of Korean Traditional Music (Seoul) **103**
　Sejong Center for the Performing Arts (Seoul) 78
　Seoul Arts Center **103**
　traditional culture **176**
Myeong-dong (Seoul) **84**
Myeong-dong Cathedral (Seoul) 84
Myeongnyang, Battle of (1597) 55, 88, **196**
Myeongseong, Empress 55, 69

N

Naejangsan National Park **194**
Naesosa Temple 181
Naganeupseong Folk Village **198-9**
Naksan Park (Seoul) 105
Namdaemun (Seoul) **84-5**
Namdaemun Market (Seoul) 85
Namhansanseong Fortress **127**

Nami Island **140**
Nam June Paik Art Center **124**
Namparang-gil Course 55 (Yeosu) **200-201**
Namparang Trail 41
Namsan Cable Car (Seoul) 88
Namsangol Hanok Village (Seoul) 88
Namsan Mountain (Seoul) **88**
National Gugak Center 177
National Hangeul Museum (Seoul) 95
National Intangible Heritage Center (Jeonju) **175**, 177
National Museum of Korea (Seoul) **94-5**
National Museum of Korean Contemporary History (Seoul) 78
National Museum of Modern and Contemporary Art (Seoul) **82**
National parks: Bukhansan **98**
  Byeonsanbando **178-81**
  Chiaksan **141**
  Deogyusan **190-91**
  Gyeryongsan **166**
  Hallasan **252-3**
  Jirisan **234-5**
  Juwangsan **239**
  Mudeungsan **183**
  Naejangsan **194**
  Odaesan **144**, 148
  Palgongsan **236-7**
  Seoraksan **136-9**
  Songnisan **159**
  Taeanhaean **154-5**
  Taebaeksan **147**
  Woraksan **160**, 169
Natural wonders 13
Neolithic see Archaeological sites
Nightlife 12, 46
  1-cha, 2-cha, 3-cha **97**
  Hongdae (Seoul) **96-7**
  see also Music; Theater
Nongak (traditional music) 177
North Korea: DMZ (Demilitarized Zone) **116-17**, 142
Noryangjin Fisheries Wholesale Market (Seoul) **101**
N Seoul Tower 88, 105

O

Odaesan National Park **144**, 148
Odongdo Island 199
Oedo Botania **243**
Ojukheon (Gangneung) **133**
Oksunbong 169
Oksun Bridge Observatory 169
Olympic Games (1988) 57, 102
Olympic Park (Seoul) **102-3**
Oncheon-ri Village 168
Osaek-ri Village (Seoraksan National Park) 139
Osulloc Tea Museum **265**
Outdoor activities see Sports and outdoor activities

P

Paik Nam June **124**
Paju Book City 109, **123**
Palaces 13
  Changdeokgung (Seoul) **81**
  Changgyeonggung (Seoul) **81**
  Deoksugung (Seoul) **83**
  Donggung (Gyeongju) 225, 229
  Gyeongbokgung (Seoul) **68-9**
  Gyeonghuigung (Seoul) **82**
  Hwaseong Haenggung (Suwon Hwaseong Fortress) **119**

Paldalmun Gate (Suwon Hwaseong Fortress) **118**
Palgongsan National Park **236-7**
Park Chung-hee, General 56-7, 104
Park Geun-hye 57
Parks and gardens:
  Changdeokgung Palace (Seoul) **81**
  Cheonggyecheon Stream (Seoul) **80-81**
  Dorasan Peace Park (The DMZ) **116-17**
  Freedom Park (Incheon) 115
  Garden of Morning Calm **126**
  Gyeongui Line Forest Park (Seoul) **96-7**
  Haesindang Park **143**
  Heewon Garden (Everland) 124
  Imjingak Tourist Area (The DMZ) **116**
  Jeju 4.3 Peace Park **257**
  Jungoe Park (Gwangju) **183**
  Maisan Provincial Park **191**
  Mungyeongsaejae Provincial Park **238-9**
  Naksan Park (Seoul) 105
  Namsan Mountain (Seoul) **88**
  Oedo Botania **243**
  Olympic Park (Seoul) **102-3**
  Sejong National Arboretum 164-5
  Semiwon (Yangsu-ri) 125
  Seonyudo Park (Seoul) **101**
  Seoul Grand Park (Gwacheon) **126**
  Taejongdae Resort Park (Busan) **215**
  Yeomiji Botanic Garden (Jungmun) 264
Passports 268, 275
Personal security 274
Pharmacies 274
Phones 275
Pohang **237**
Police 274
Pop culture **34-5**, 100
Postal services 275
Prisons: Seodaemun Prison History Hall (Seoul) **99**
Provisional Capital Memorial Hall (Busan) **212**
Public art 49
Public holidays 269
Public Room (Gwangju) 185
Public transport 270, 272
Pungnammun Gate (Jeonju) **175**
Pyeongchang 129, 148

R

Railways see Train travel
Religion **79**
  see also Shrines; Temples
Responsible tourism 275
Restaurants: Busan 233
  Chungcheong-do Province 157
  Gangwon-do Province 135
  Gyeongsang-do Province 233, 236
  Jeolla-do Province 175
  Seoul 82, 101
  see also Food and drink
Rhee, Syngman 56, 212, 257
Rice wine 42
Rules of the road 273
Ryu, Sungsil 49

S

Sado, Crown Prince 118
Saemaul Undong campaign 56

Safety: government advice 268
  hiking 41
  personal security 274
Sajik Baseball Stadium (Busan) **216**
Samakasan Mountain Lake Cable Car (Chuncheon) 140-41
Samcheon-dong Makgeolli Alley (Jeonju) **175**
Samdo Sugun Tongjeong (Tongyeong) 243
Samsung 55, 89
  Everland **124**
  Leeum Museum of Art (Seoul) 89, 124
Sangbang-ri Mural Village 169
Sangbansan 261
Sangumburi Crater **258**, 261
Sculpture: Haesindang Park 143
Seafood: Jagalchi Market (Busan) **206-7**, 218
  Noryangjin Fisheries Wholesale Market (Seoul) **101**
Sehwa Beach 258
Sejong 151, **164-5**
Sejong Center for the Performing Arts (Seoul) 78
Sejong the Great, King 54, **55**, 78, 95
Seodaemun Prison History Hall (Seoul) **99**
Seogwipo **263**
Seokguram Grotto (Gyeongju) **225**
Seolleung Royal Tomb (Seoul) **102**
Seongdeok, King 227
Seongeup Folk Village **262-3**
Seongjong, King 81, 102
Seongsan Ilchulbong **248-9**
Seongsu (Seoul) 91, **99**
Seongyojang (Gangneung) **132-3**
Seonso Village (Yeosu) 200
Seonyudo Park (Seoul) **101**
Seopdari bridges **144**
Seopjikoji **262**
Seoraksan National Park **136-9**
Seoul 16, **58-105**
  Beyond the center 63, **91-105**
  Central Seoul 62, **65-89**
  cycling 39
  history 54
  itinerary 21
  map 60-61
Seoul Arts Center **103**
Seoul City Wall Museum **70-71**
Seoul Grand Park (Gwacheon) **126**
Seoul Museum of Art (SEMA) 83
Seoul Museum of Craft Art **72**
Seoul Museum of History **82-3**
Seoul Sky 102
Seoul Urban Life Museum **98**
Seungmu (traditional music) 177
Shamanism 79, 104
Shin Salmdang 133
Shopping 11, **36-7**
  Busan 211
  Chungcheong-do Province 167
  Dongdaemun **71**
  Ssamziegil (Seoul) 80
  taxes and refunds 275
Shrines: Guksadang (Seoul) 104
  Jongmyo Shrine (Seoul) **80**
Silla Kingdom 53-4, 224, 226-7
Sinduri Coastal Sand Dune **154**
Sinheungsa Temple (Seoraksan National Park) 139
Sin Yun-bok 48
Skiing see Winter sports
Sky Tower (Yeosu) 199
Smoking 274-5
Sobaeksan Mountains 239
Sogdo (Incheon) **113**

280

Soho Dongdong Bridge (Yeosu) 200
Soju 43
Sokcho **134-5**
Songaksan 260
Songgwangsa Temple **198**
Songnisan National Park **159**
Song Si-yeol 160
Sool Gallery (Seoul) **73**
Southern Provinces, itinerary 24-5
Specific needs, travelers with 269
Speed limits 270
Sports and outdoor activities **38-9**, 46
    Sajik Baseball Stadium (Busan) **216**
    see also Winter sports
Ssamziegil (Seoul) 80
Ssanggyeru Pavilion 194
Station of the 14th Regiment (Yeosu) 201
Street food: Busan 218
Subways 272
Sudeoksa Temple **165**
Suncheonman Wetland **188-9**
Surfing 39
    Yangyang 142, 143
Suwon Hwaseong Fortress **118-21**
Suwon Hwaseong Museum **119**
Suyeon Sanbang (Seoul) 105

T

Taeanhaean National Park **154-5**
Taebaeksan National Park **147**
Taejo, King 54, 65, 127
Taejongdae Resort Park (Busan) **215**
Talchum (masked performances) 177
Tap water 274
Taxes 275
Taxis 272-3
Tea 43
    Daehan Dawon Boseong Green Tea Field 198
    Korea Tea Museum (Boseong) 198
    Osulloc Tea Museum **265**
Technology 12
Temples 44, 275
    food in **33**
    staying in **165**
    Baegyangsa 194
    Baekdamsa (Seraksan National Park) 138
    Beomeosa (Busan) **216-17**
    Beopjusa (Songnisan National Park) 159
    Bongeunsa (Seoul) **100**
    Bongjeongsa (Andong) **233**
    Bulguksa (Gyeongju) **225**
    Buseoksa **239**
    Cheongpyeongsa (Chuncheon) 141
    Dongguksa (Gunsan) 190
    Donghaksa 166
    Donghwasa 237
    Gaeamsa 181
    Gapsa 166
    Geumsansa **191**
    Gilsanga (Seoul) **99**
    Haedong Yonggungsa (Busan) **216**
    Haeinsa **230-31**
    Jeondeungsa (Ganghwado Island) 122, 123
    Jeongnimsa Temple Site and Museum (Buyeo) **156-7**
    Jogyesa (Seoul) **78**

Temples (cont.)
    Magoksa **165**
    Naejangsa 194
    Naesosa 181
    Naksansa (Yangyang) 142
    Sangwongsa (Odaesan National Park) 144
    Sinheungsa (Seoraksan National Park) 139
    Songgwangsa **198**
    Sudeoksa **165**
    Tapsa 191
    Tongdosa **241**
    Ulseondang (Incheon) 112, 114
    Unjusa **195**
    Woljeongsa (Odaesan National Park) 144, 148
    see also Buddhism
Terahni, Nader 185
Theater 47
    Incheon Art Platform 113
    Seoul Arts Center **103**
Theme parks *see* Amusement parks
Third Tunnel (The DMZ) **117**
Three Kingdoms Period (57 BC-668 CE) 53, 91
Time zone 274
Tipping 269
Tombs: Cheonmachong (Gyeongju) 227, 228
    Daereungwon Ancient Tomb Complex (Gyeongju) **224**, 228
    Donggureung **127**
    Hwagnamdaechong (Gyeongju) 228
    Seolleung and Jeongneung Royal Tombs (Seoul) **102**
    Songsan-ri (Gongju) 164
    Tomb of King Michu (Gyeongju) 228
Tongdosa Temple **241**
Tongyeong **243**
Towangseong Falls (Seoraksan National Park) 139
Traditional culture 10
    performances **176-7**
    see also Folk villages
Train travel 270, 271
Travel **270-73**
Tripitaka Koreana woodblocks 54, **230**, 231
Ttangkkeut Village **197**

U

Udo Island **262**
Ulleungdo Island 222, **240**
Ulsan **240**
Ulsanbawi (Seoraksan National Park) 139
United Nations (UN) 112, 116, 242
Unjusa Temple **195**
Upo Wetland **241**

V

Vaccinations 269
View Folly (Gwangju) 185
Visas 268
Volcanoes, Jeju Island **248-61**

W

Walks 273
    Bukchon Hanok Village (Seoul) **76-7**
    Busan **218-19**
    Gwangju 184-5
    Gyeongju **228-9**

Walks (cont.)
    Hanyangdoseong (Seoul) **104-5**
    Incheon **114-15**
    Yeosu: Namparang-gil Course 55, **200-201**
    see also Hiking
Wang Geon, General 54
War and Women's Human Rights Museum (Seoul) **100-101**
War Memorial of Korea (Seoul) **88-9**
Water, drinking 274
Water sports 39
Weather 268
Websites 274
Wetlands: Suncheonman **188-9**
    Upo **241**
Wi-Fi 275
Wildlife: Jangsaengpo Whale Museum 240, 241
    moon bears **234**
    see also Aquariums; Birds; National parks
Wind Water Stone Museum **264-5**
Winter Olympics (2018) 38, 129, 132, 144
Winter sports 38
    High1 Resort **147**
    Mona Yongpyong Ski Resort **144-5**
    Muju Deogyusan Resort 190, 191
Wolji Pond (Gyeongju) 225, 229
Wolmido Island (Incheon) **113**
Woraksan National Park **160**, 169
World War II 55, 56, 101, 161

Y

Yangdong Folk Village **238**
Yangsu-ri **125**
Yangyang **142-3**
Yeosu **199**
    Namparang-gil Course 55 (Yeosu) **200-201**
Yeosu Seafood Market 201
Yi Hwang 221, 233
Yi I 133
Yi Seong-gye 54, 174
Yi Sun-sin, Admiral 55, 78, 88, 243
Yi Sun-sin Square (Yeosu) 201
Yongdusan Mountain (Busan) **210**
Yongsan Observatory 189
Yoon Suk-yeol **57**
Yuan dynasty 54
Yuri, King 52

PHRASE BOOK

Korean uses its own alphabet, called Hangeul. Pronouncing Korean words is a tough task – some sounds simply do not have English-language equivalents. For example, there's only one character for "l" and "r," with the pronunciation somewhere between the two. Additionally, several Korean consonants have relaxed, aspirated, and tensed forms, where different letters represent the sounds "b," "p," and "bb," for instance. See the Guidelines for Pronunciation for explanations of how to pronounce the alphabet's letters and diphthongs (British English readings offer the closest equivalents).

In written Korean, words are divided into syllable blocks, each of which must begin with a consonant and include at least one vowel. Letters retain their same basic shape but may stretch or condense to fit the block. Today, Korean is typically written as English is: left to right and top to bottom. This phrase book gives the English word or phrase, followed by the Korean script, then the romanization.

GUIDELINES FOR PRONUNCIATION

Consonants
Some consonants are pronounced differently depending upon whether they start or finish a syllable. In these cases, the terminal readings have been given in parentheses.

ㄱ	g	ㄴ	n
ㄷ	d (t)	ㄹ	r/l
ㅁ	m	ㅂ	b
ㅅ	s (t)	ㅇ	silent at the start of syllables (ng)
ㅈ	j (t)		

Aspirated consonants
ㅊ	ch (t)	ㅋ	k (g)
ㅌ	t	ㅍ	p (b)
ㅎ	h (t)		

Tensed consonants
ㄲ	gg	ㄸ	dd
ㅃ	bb	ㅆ	ss
ㅉ	jj		

Vowels
ㅏ	a as in "car"
ㅑ	ya as in "yard"
ㅓ	eo as in "uh"
ㅕ	yeo as in "yob"
ㅗ	o as in "ore"
ㅛ	yo as in "yoga"
ㅜ	u as in "boo"
ㅠ	yu as in "you"
ㅡ	eu no English equivalent; similar to "pull"
ㅣ	i as in "pea"
ㅐ	ae as in "hat"
ㅒ	yae as in "yam"
ㅔ	e as in "ten"
ㅖ	ye as in "yes"
ㅘ	wa as in "waffle"
ㅙ	wae as in "wax"
ㅚ	oe as in "way"
ㅝ	wo as in "won"
ㅞ	we as in "wet"
ㅟ	wi as in "we"
ㅢ	ui pronounced as ㅡ + ㅣ at start of syllable; pronounced as ㅣ at end of syllable

TRANSLITERATION OF ENGLISH WORDS

Korean does not have some sounds that are present in English, notably "f," "th," "v," and "z." This can sometimes be a source of confusion with English loan words that have entered the Korean vocabulary. The following are typical pronunciation changes when English words are transliterated into Hangeul:

"f" becomes "p" or "hw," so "fighting" is pronounced "pighting" or "hwiting"
"th" becomes "s" or "d," so "thread" is pronounced "sread" and "smoothie" is pronounced "smoodie"
"v" becomes "b" so "live," is pronounced "libe"
"z" becomes "j" so "zombie," is pronounced "jombie"

DIALECTS

Standard Korean (Seoul dialect) pronounces all syllables with equal stress and even intonation. Many regions – most notably Gyeongsang-do Province, Jeolla-do Province, and Jeju Island–have their own dialects, with their own pronunciations and vocabularies. Pronunciations given in this phrase book follow standard Korean and will be understood throughout the country.

POLITE WORDS AND PHRASES

Social relations are built into the Korean language, with verb conjugations and, occasionally, vocabulary changing based on the relative statuses of the speaker and listener. Fortunately, Koreans don't expect foreigners to grasp the nuance and always use the correct conjugation, so even if you use an informal conjugation with, say, a senior citizen you've just met, your efforts will be appreciated. Complete sentences provided in this phrase book are given in the most common polite form.

COMMUNICATION ESSENTIALS

Yes	예/네	ye/ne
No	아니요	aniyo
Hello	안녕하세요	annyeonghaseyo
Goodbye (to person leaving)	안녕히 가세요	annyeong higaseyo
Goodbye (to person staying)	안녕히 계세요	annyeong higyeseyo
Please (when asking for something)	…주세요	…juseyo
Thank you	감사합니다	Gamsahamnida
No, thank you	괜찮아요	Gwaenchanayo
You're welcome	괜찮아요	Gwaenchanayo
Excuse me	실례합니다	Shillyehamnida
I'm sorry	미안합니다	Mianhamnida
Do you speak English?	영어 할 수 있어요?	Yeong-eo hal su isseoyo?
Is there someone who can speak English?	영어를 할 줄 아는 분 있어요?	Yeongeo-reul hal jul a-neun bun isseoyo?

English	Korean	Romanization
I can't speak Korean	저는 한국어를 못 해요	Jeo-neun hangugeo-reul mot haeyo
I don't understand	이해가 안가요/모르겠어요	Ihae-ga anga-yo/Moreugesseoyo
Please help me	도와주세요	Dowa-juseyo

USEFUL PHRASES

What's your name?	이름이 뭐예요?	Ireum-i mweoyeyo?
My name is...	제 이름은 …이에요	Je ireum-eun …ieyo
I'm from...	저는 …에서 왔어요	Jeo-neun …eseo wasseoyo
Pleased to meet you	만나서 반가워요	Mannaseo ban-gaweoyo
How are you?	잘 지냈어요?	Jal jinaesseoyo?
I'm fine	잘 지냈어요/좋아요	Jal jinaesseoyo/Jo-ayo
Where is...?	…이 어디 있어요?	…eodi isseoyo?
Where is the restroom?	화장실이 어디 있어요?	Hwajangsil-i eodi isseoyo?
Where can I buy...?	…어디에서 살 수 있어요?	…eodieseo sal su isseoyo?
What time is it?	지금 몇 시예요?	Jigeum myeossiyeyo?
What is this/that?	이게/저게 뭐예요?	I-ge/Jeo-ge mweoyeyo?
How do you use this?	어떻게 사용해요?	Eoddeoke sayonghaeyo?
Could I please have...?	…좀 주시겠어요?	…jom jusigesseoyo?
Is there...here?	여기에 …있어요?	Yeogi-e …isseoyo?

IN AN EMERGENCY

Call a doctor!	의사 불러주세요!	Uisa bulleo-juseyo!
Call an ambulance!	구급차 불러주세요!	Gugeupcha bulleo-juseyo!
Call 119! (Korean emergency number)	119 불러주세요!	Il-il-gu bulleo-juseyo!
Call the police!	경찰 불러주세요!	Gyeongchal bulleo-juseyo!
Help!	도와주세요!	Dowa-juseyo!
Fire!	불이야!	Bul-iya!
Stop!	멈춰!	Meomcheo!
Where is the hospital?	병원이 어디예요?	Byeongwon-i eodiyeyo?
Where is the police station?	경찰서가 어디예요?	Gyeongchalseoga eodiyeyo?

MONEY

English	Korean	Romanization
Do you take credit cards/cash?	신용카드/현금 받아요?	Sinyong-kadeu/Hyeon-geum badayo?
Could you change this into won please?	원화로 바꿔주실 수 있어요?	Wonhwa-ro baggweo-jul su isseoyo?
ATM	에이티엠(기)/자동 현금 인출기	ATM(gi)/jadong hyeon-geum inchulgi
Bank	은행	eunhaeng
Cash	현금	hyeon-geum
Credit card	신용카드	sinyong-kadeu
Currency exchange	환전소	hwanjeonso
Dollars	달러	dalleo
Pounds	파운드	paundeu
Won	원	won

SHOPPING

English	Korean	Romanization
Where can I buy...?	…어디에서 사요?	…eodi-eseo sayo?
Do you have...?	…있어요?	…isseoyo?
I'm just looking	그냥 볼게요	Geu-nyang bolgeyo
May I try this on?	이것 입어볼 수 있어요?	Igeot ibeobol su isseoyo?
How much does this cost?	얼마예요?	Eolma-yeyo?
Can you give me a discount?	할인해 줄 수 있어요?	Harinhae jul su isseoyo?
It's cheap/expensive	싸요/비싸요	Ssayo/Bissayo
Bookstore	서점	seojeom
Boutique	부티크	butikeu
Clothes	옷	ot
Convenience store	편의점	pyeonuijeom
Department store	백화점	baekhwajeom
Market	시장	sijang
Sale	세일/할인	saeil/harin
Souvenir shop	기념품 가게	gi-nyeompum ga-ge
Supermarket	슈퍼마켓/마트	syupeomaket/ma-teu

ACCOMMODATION

Do you have any vacancies?	방 있어요?	Bang isseoyo?
I'd like a room	방 하나 주세요	Bang hana juseyo
I have a reservation	저는 예약했어요	Jeo-neun yeyakhaesseoyo
I don't have a reservation	저는 예약 안 했어요	Jeo-neun yeyak an haesseoyo
How much is the room?	방이 얼마예요?	Bang-i eolma-yeyo?
Does that include breakfast?	가격에 아침식사 포함돼 있어요?	Gagyeok-e achim-shiksa pohamdwae isseoyo?
What time is checkout?	체크아웃은 몇 시예요?	Chekauseun myeossiyeyo?
Can I leave my luggage here for a while?	여기에 짐을 맡길 수 있어요?	Yeogi-e jim-eul matgil su isseoyo?
Air conditioning	에어컨	ae-eo-keon
Bath	욕조	yokjo
Campground	캠핑장	caemping-jang
Guesthouse	여관	yeogwan
Hotel	호텔	hotel
Key	키/열쇠	ki/yeolsoe
Motel	모텔	motel
Korean-style room	온돌방	ondol-bang
Western-style room	침대방	chimdae-bang
Single room	싱글룸	singgeullum
Double room	더블룸	deobeullum
Twin room	트윈룸	teuwinlum
En-suite room	욕실 딸린 방	yokshil ddallin bang
Shower	샤워	syaweo
Youth hostel	유스호스텔	yuseu hoseutel

GETTING AROUND

English	Korean	Romanization
I'd like to charge my T-Money/transport card	티머니 카드/교통카드를 충전하고 싶어요	T-Money kadeu-reul/Gyotong-kadeu-reul chungjeon-hago shipeoyo
A ticket to...please	…가는 표 주세요	…ga-neun pyo juseyo
How long does it take to get to...?	…까지 얼마나 걸려요?	…ggaji eolmana geollyeoyo?
When does the bus/train for...leave?	…가는 버스/기차 언제 출발해요?	…ga-neun beoseu/gicha eonje chulbalhaeyo?
Which platform for the bus/train to...?	…가는 버스/기차 몇 번 플랫폼에서 타요?	…ga-neun beoseu/gicha myeot beon peullaetpom-eseo tayo?
Is this the bus/train for...?	…가는 버스/기차 맞아요?	…ga-neun beoseu/gicha majayo?

Please take me to...	...가 주세요	...ga-juseyo
Airport	공항	gonghang
Bicycle	자전거	jajeon-geo
Bus	버스	beoseu
Bus station	버스 터미널	beoseu-teomineol
Bus stop	버스 정류장	beoseu jeongnyujang
Car	차/자동차	cha/jadongcha
Ferry	페리/여객선	peri/yeogaekseon
Ferry terminal	여객(선) 터미널	yeogaek(seon) teomineol
Gas station	주유소	juyuso
Motorcycle	오토바이	otobai
Subway	지하철	jihacheol
Subway station	지하철역	jihacheol-yeok
Taxi	택시	taeksi
Ticket office	매표소	maepyoso
Train	기차	gicha
Train station	기차역	gicha-yeok

SIGNS

Open	열림/영업중	yeollim/yeong-eopjung
Closed	닫힘/휴일	dachim/hyu-il
Entrance	입구	ipgu
Exit	출구	chulgu
Emergency exit	비상구	bisanggu
Restroom/toilet	화장실	hwajangsil
Men	남자/남성용	namja/namseongyong
Women	여자/여성용	yeoja/yeoseongyong
Information	정보/안내	jeongbo/annae
Danger	위험	wiheom

DIRECTIONS AND PLACES

Where is...?	...어디예요?	...eodi-eyo?
How do I get to...?	...까지 어떻게 가요?	...ggaji eoddeoke gayo?
What is the address?	주소가 뭐예요?	Juso-ga mweoyeyo?
Straight ahead	직진	jikjin
Left	왼쪽	wen-jjok
Right	오른쪽	oreun-jjok
Behind	뒤에	dwi-ae
In front of	앞에	a-pe
North	북	buk
South	남	nam
East	동	dong
West	서	seo
It's far	멀어요	Meoreoyo
It's close	가까워요	Ga-ggaweoyo

SIGHTSEEING

Art gallery	미술관/갤러리	misulgwan/gaelleori
Church (Catholic)/cathedral	성당	seongdang
Church (Protestant)	교회	gyohoe
City	도시	dosi
Garden	정원	jeongwon
Island	섬	seom
Lake	호수	hosu
Mountain	산	san
Museum	박물관	bangmulgwan
Palace	궁	gung
Park	공원	gong-won
Temple	절/사찰	jeol/sachal
Tourist information office	관광 안내소	gwan-gwang annaeso
Village	마을	maeul

EATING OUT

A table for one/two/three please	한/두/세 명이요	Han/du/se myeong-iyo
Waiter/Waitress (lit. "Here!")	여기요!	Yeogiyo!
How much is that?	얼마예요?	Eolma-yeyo?
Is this spicy?	이거 매워요?	I-geomaeweoyo?
I'd like...	...먹고 싶어요	...meoggo shipeoyo
I'm a vegetarian/vegan	저는 채식주의자예요/비건이에요	Jeo-neun chaeshikju-uija-yeyo/bigeon-ieyo
Cheers!	건배!/위하여!	Geonbae/Wihayeo!
May I have the bill?	계산 해 주세요	Gyesan hae-juseyo
Bar	바/술집/호프	ba/sul-jip/hopeu
Café	카페/커피숍	kape/keopi-syop
Chopsticks	젓가락	jeot-garak
Fork	포크	po-keu
Knife	나이프/칼	nai-peu/kal
Menu	메뉴	menyu
Restaurant	식당/레스토랑	sikdang/reseutorang
Spoon	숟가락	sutgarak
Street food	길거리 음식	gilgeori eumshik

MENU DECODER

Bean sprouts	콩나물	kongnamul
Beef	소고기	so-gogi
Bibimbap	비빔밥	bibimbap
Bread	빵	bbang
Cheese	치즈	chi-jeu
Chicken	닭고기	dak-gogi
Crab	게	gae
Duck meat	오리고기	ori-gogi
Dumplings	만두	mandu
Eel	장어	jang-eo
Eggs	계란	gyeran
Fermented soybean paste	된장	doenjang
Fish/raw fish	생선/회	saengseon/hoe
Fried rice	볶음밥	boggeumbap
Fruit	과일	gwail
Ham	햄	haem
Kimchi	김치	gimchi
Noodles	면/국수	myeon/guksu
Octopus	문어/쭈꾸미	muneo
Orange	오렌지	orenji
Pork	돼지고기	dwaeji-gogi
Potato	감자	gamja
Rice	밥	bap
Salt	소금	sogeum
Soup	국/탕	guk/tang
Soy sauce	간장	ganjang
Squid	오징어	ojing-eo
Tofu	두부	dubu
Tuna	참치	chamchi
Vegetable	채소/야채	chaeso/yachae

DRINKS

Beer	맥주	maekju
Bottled beer	병 맥주	byeong maekju
Draft beer	생맥주	saeng-maekju
Coffee	커피	keopi
Cola	콜라	kolla
Fruit juice	과일 쥬스	gwail jyuseu
Makgeolli	막걸리	makgeolli
Milk	우유	uyu
Soda	탄산음료	tansan-eumryo
Soju	소주	soju

Tea	차	cha
Black tea	홍차	hong-cha
Green tea	녹차	nok-cha
Water	물	mul
(red/white) Wine	(레드/화이트) 와인	(redeu/hwaiteu) wain
Whisky	위스키	wiseuki

NUMBERS

The Korean language uses two number systems: a native Korean system and a Sino-Korean system of Chinese origin. The Korean system goes up to 99 and is used for hours, ages, and counting objects. The Sino-Korean system is used for minutes, dates, months, measurements, money, phone numbers, and more. The Sino-Korean system has been placed on the left and the native Korean system on the right of the below entries. The shortened form of native Korean numbers 1–4 that's used in combination with hours and counting words is given in parentheses.

0	영/공	yeong/gong
1	일/하나 (한)	il/hana (han)
2	이/둘 (두)	i (pronounced "ee")/dul (du)
3	삼/셋 (세)	sam/set (se)
4	사/넷 (네)	sa/net (ne)
5	오/다섯	o/daseot
6	육/여섯	yuk/yeoseot
7	칠/일곱	chil/ilgop
8	팔/여덟	pal/yeodeol
9	구/아홉	gu/ahop
10	십/열	sip/yeol
11	십일/열하나	sip-il/yeol-hana
12	십이/열둘	sip-i/yeol-dul
20	이십/스물	i-sip/seumul
30	삼십/서른	samsip/seoreun
40	사십/마흔	sasip/maheun
50	오십/쉰	osip/swin
60	육십/예순	yugsip/yesun
70	칠십/일흔	chilsip/ilheun
80	팔십/여든	palsip/yeodeun
90	구십/아흔	gusip/aheun
100	백	baek
200	이백	i-baek
1,000	천	cheon
10,000	만	man
100,000	십만	sim-man
1,000,000	백만	baeng-man
100,000,000	억	eok

TIME AND DATES

What time is it?	지금 몇 시예요?	jigeum myeossiyeyo?
When is...?	...언제예요?	...eonjeyeyo?
It's 1:10	한시 십분이에요	Han-shi sip-bun-ieyo
It's 12:30	열두시 삼십분이에요/열두시 반이에요	Yeoldu-shi sam-sip-bun-ieyo/Yeoldu-shi ban-ieyo
Hour	시	shi
Minutes	분	bun
Half past	반	ban
Today	오늘	oneul
Tomorrow	내일	naeil
Yesterday	어제	eoje
This/tomorrow morning	오늘/내일 아침/오전	oneul/naeil achim/ojeon
This/tomorrow afternoon	오늘/내일 낮/오후	oneul/naeil nat/ohu
Tonight/tomorrow night	오늘/내일 저녁/밤	oneul/naeil jeonyeok/bam
Every day	매일	maeil

Sunday	일요일	ilyo-il
Monday	월요일	wolyo-il
Tuesday	화요일	hwayo-il
Wednesday	수요일	suyo-il
Thursday	목요일	mogyo-il
Friday	금요일	geumyo-il
Saturday	토요일	toyo-il

HEALTH

I'm ill	저는 아파요	Jeo-neun apayo
I have (illness/disease)	저는 …에 걸렸어요	Jeo-neun …-e geollyeosseoyo
I have (pain/symptom)	저는 …있어요	Jeo-neun …isseoyo
I'm allergic to...	저는 …에 알레르기가 있어요	Jeo-neun ….-e allereugi-ga isseoyo
Antibiotics	항생제	hangsaengje
Cough	기침	gichim
Congestion	코막힘	komakim
Dentist	치과의사	chigwa-uisa
Diabetes	당뇨(병)	dangnyo(byeong)
Diarrhea	설사	seolsa
Doctor	의사	uisa
Fever	열	yeol
Food poisoning	식중독	shikjungdok
Headache	두통	dutong
Hospital	병원	byeongwon
Medicine	약	yak
Menstrual pad	생리대	saengnidae
Nausea	메스꺼움	meseukkeo-um
Penicillin	페니실린	penishillin
Pharmacy	약국	yakguk
Prescription	처방전	cheobangjeon
Stomach ache	복통	boktong
Tampon	탐폰	tampon
Toothache	치통	chitong

KEEPING IN TOUCH

What's the Wi-Fi password?	와이파이 비밀번호가 뭐예요?	Waipai bimilbeonho-ga mweoyeyo?
What's the phone number?	전화번호가 뭐예요?	Jeonhwa-beonho-ga mweoyeyo?
May I use your phone?	전화 좀 쓸 수 있어요?	Jeonhwa jom sseul su isseoyo?
I would like to call...	…한테 전화하고 싶어요	…hante jeonhwa hago-shipeoyo
I'd like to mail a letter/package to...	우편으로 보내고 싶어요	…u-pyeon-euro bonaego shipeoyo
Airmail	항공 우편	hanggong u-pyeon
Email	이메일	email
Envelope	봉투	bongtu
Letter	편지	pyeonji
Mobile phone	휴대폰/핸드폰	hyudaepon/haendeupon
Package	소포/택배	sopo/taekbae
Post office	우체국	u-che-guk
Postcard	엽서	yeopseo
SIM card	심카드	sim kadeu
Stamp	우표	u-pyo
Telephone	전화기	jeonhwagi
Wi-Fi	와이파이	waipai

ACKNOWLEDGMENTS

Contributor Charles Usher
Senior Editor Keith Drew
Senior Art Editors Laura O'Brien, Stuti Tiwari
Project Editor Sarah Allen
Project Art Editor Ankita Sharma
Editors Edward Aves, Charlie Baker, Catrina Conway, Alex Pathe
Proofreader Kathryn Glendenning
Indexer Hilary Bird
Picture Researcher Marta Bescos
Rights and Permissions Specialist Vagisha Pushp
Deputy Picture Research Manager Virien Chopra
Publishing Assistant Simona Velikova
Illustrators Peter Bull, Mohd. Zishan
Language Consultant Soyi Kim
Jacket Designers Laura O'Brien, Stuti Tiwari
Jacket Picture Researcher Marta Bescos
Project Cartographer Ashif
Senior Cartographer Mohammed Hassan
Cartography Manager Suresh Kumar
Senior DTP Designer Tanveer Zaidi
DTP Designers Jagtar Singh, Ashok Kumar
Pre-production Manager Balwant Singh
Senior Production Controller Samantha Cross
Managing Art Editor Gemma Doyle
Senior Managing Art Editor Priyanka Thakur
Editorial Director Hollie Teague
Art Director Maxine Pedliham
Publishing Director Georgina Dee

The publisher would like to thank the following for their kind permission to reproduce their photographs:

(Key: a-above; b-below/bottom; c-centre; f-far; l-left; r-right; t-top)

Adobe Stock: Michele Burgess 235t; dudlajzov 136-137b, 232, 257; kampwit 260; Kylie 8bl; santi 238t; SiHo 165cr, 231; vadim_ozz 207tr.

Alamy Stock Photo: AF Fotografie 52t; Aflo Co. Ltd. 57bc; Album 52bc; American Photo Archive 56bl; Leonid Andronov 56-57c; Archive Farms Inc / Burton Holmes 55bl; Archive Image 56-57ca; ART Collection 54tl; Matthew Ashmore 211t, 212bl; Menigault Bernard 13t; BFA 259t; Stanley Cabigas 32b; Castle 182; Jui-Chi Chan 116-117tl; Robert Cicchetti 51bl; CMA / BOT 52br; CPA Media Pte Ltd 54bl, 54br; Danita Delimont 250c, 250bl; lionel derimais 36-37tc; Nate Derrick 2-3; Pavel Dudek 115, 224, 256; Efired 26cr; Oscar Espinosa 50cl, 79b, 143cr, 165t; GL Archive 53cla; GRANGER - Historical Picture Archive 55tr; Hemis / GUIZIOU Franck 229; Hemis / MAISANT Ludovic 42t; Hemis / MALLET Jean-François 32t; Hemis / SOULARUE 11cr; John Henshall 45b; imageBROKER / Chris Putnam 74bl; Independent Picture Service 53bl; JIPEN 253t; Jon Arnold Images Ltd 53tr; Jon Arnold Images Ltd / Gavin Hellier 62, 64; Joonae 55bc; Panya Khamtuy 160; NAMHWI KIM 176-177t; Tuomas Lehtinen 63, 90; mauritius images GmbH / Bastian Barenbrock 46t; Thomas McComb 39t, 142-143b, 149, 187cra; Min Won-Ki via ZUMA Wire 50br; Raquel Mogado 40; Newscom / BJ Warnick 39cl, 50cr, 51cr, 79t, 103tr, 156b; Duy Phuong Nguyen 140; NurPhoto SRL / Seung-il Ryu 176bl; Sanga Park 19b, 148, 244; Pictorial Press Ltd 34bl; Frederic REGLAIN 176clb; robertharding 259b; robertharding / Lynn Gail 254crb; Wibowo Rusli 25tr; Thitaporn Santipolvut 12cr; khanh nghia tran 70; SFL Travel 22ca, 77br; Marek Slusarczyk 53tl; Smith Archive 56br; SOPA Images Limited 50tr; Dave Stamboulis 259c; Stockinasia 105; ThamKC 43t; Top Photo Corporation 35b; Ian Trower 12-13bc, 214-215b, 217b, 226bl, 227br; Jorge Tutor 227cla; Jasper van Zandbeek 48-49t; World History Archive 54-55tc, 55cra, 56tl; Xinhua 22crb; Zoonar GmbH / Insung Choi 145.

AWL Images: Danita Delimont Stock 68; Christian Kober 106-107; Jane Sweeney 4, 100cr; Ian Trower 44t, 214t.

Blue Whale Brewhouse: 43br.

Bridgeman Images: Pictures from History 48b.

Chris da Canha: 10tl, 11tr, 12tl, 20cr, 43cl, 46b.

Depositphotos Inc: artyooran.gmail.com 28cl; efired 88; filedimage 26cl; praewa_koreashopping@hotmail.com 38t, 45t; vincentstthomas 216cl.

Dreamstime.com: Aminkorea 262; Leonid Andronov 30-31t, 83cr; Nattanai Chimjanon 100tl, 242t; Kobby Dagan 50bl; Dudlajzov 134-135t, 251, 258; Edwardroom501 96-97tl; Efired 102-103bc; Eurotrip 263t; Augustin Florian 29tr; inter_view 227tl; Kampwit 22cr; Panya Khamtuy 192-193; Mirko Kuzmanovic 30bl, 232br; Ngchiyui 82; Noa80 44b, 198; Thawatchai Onkhambong 51br; Sanga Park 201; Yooran Park 24-25tc, 225; Tawatchai Prakobkit 38b, 190tl; LIAO QIONGNA 265; Stock for you 252-253b; Thejipen 229, Tuomaslehtinen 22bl; Unununius 45cl; Julien Viry 142t; VittoriaChe 57tr; Noppasin Wongchum 248-249t; Zz3701 12bl.

Getty Images: 500px / Reto Fuchs 31cl; 2016 Bloomberg Finance LP 42b; Carl Court 135c; Gamma-Rapho / Bruno PEROUSSE 89; Manfred Gottschalk 159br; Jong-Won Heo 8tl; ImaZinS / coorryd 178-179b; ImaZinS / Purbella 154-155t; ImaZinS / sangpil8989 158b; ImaZinS / SOONMO 144t; ImaZinS / sunyoungyim 166t; Insung Jeon 17b, 150, 209; Robert Koehler 194; Korea Pool 57clb; Maremagnum 16t, 20bl, 58-59, 266-267; NurPhoto 186-187b; Jordan Pix 47t; Plan Shooting 2 / Imazins 10clb; The Washington Post 47cl.

Getty Images / iStock: 35007 206-207br; AaronChoi 196-197t; Subodh Agnihotri 207c; aomam 127; artran 28-29ca, 78, 227tr; colinhui 33cl; csm07 254clb; Oscar Espinosa 207tl; estherpoon 97tc; f11photo 6-7, 72-73; fotoVoyager 8-9c; GWMB 36bl; JBencivenga 181; jikgoe 213tr; july7th 99, 210; Sanghwan Kim 188-189t; Lyn Lai 254bc; inho Lee 20crb; orpheus26 264; pangjee_9 249bl; Sanga Park 18t, 51tl, 83tr, 170, 254t, 255clb; Sean3810 216t; snowtigerman 12br; ST_travel 156t; studiojh 17t, 128; tawatchaiprakobkit 86-87; Tuayai 49b; tupikov 137t; TwilightShow 20t; Julien Viry 24tl; 28tl; visualspace 33b; zkruger 249crb.

Nam June Paik Art Center: 49cl.

National Museum of Korea: 53bc, 94-95bl, 95t, 95b.

Shutterstock.com: ALNET 144bl; Amankgupta 187t; Anney_Lier 35cl; ARTYOORAN 104; Sarasap Boonrak 161; Chalamkhav 146-147b; Chan008 118; SUJITRA CHAOWDEE 227cb; chojj 261; Erik Clegg 76bl; cstrike 39br; LEE WA DA 138; DreamArchitect 113; Chanchai Duangdoosan 140-141tr; f.maliki 211b; f11photo 208; F16-ISO100 95c; Finn stock 62; Jaione Garcia 189crb; An Sung Hwan 162-163; Yeongsik Im 179cra; inter_view 101; JackPark 134b; jayaibe 125br; Johnathan21 255bc; tae young Jeong 195b; Tanwa Kankang 253c; Nghia Khanh 132-133b; khankhankhan 184; SUDONG KIM 125cr; Panu Kosonen 51tr; Chintung Lee 116b; John Leung 11br; M.Jin 37cla; mastapiece 124tl; MyPixelDiaries 126; CJ Nattanai 98; NOONKKOT 189br; nop popeye77 31br; NothingIsEverything 28-29tc; Olezzo 10-11bc; PangJee_S 37br; Photo Atrium 122-123tl; photo_jeongh 179tl; Pinkcandy 47b; Pitak ga 121; Pvince73 238cra; redstrap 84-85; ROHE Creative Studio 26crb; Dmitry Rukhlenko 139; Isarint Sangmanee 236b; Panwasin seemala 8cl,199; Shepps 189bl; YOO DAE SOUNG 180; ST_Travel 120 174; Stock for you 16b, 19t, 22t, 50tl, 75tr, 79c, 80, 108, 123br, 159tr, 164, 167br, 169, 179tr, 190-191br, 197br, 220, 234cl, 239, 240-241, 243 249clb, 263;

The Green foto 26bl, 34-35tc; Thejipen 255crb; Tom PJ 237t; trabantos 112, 195t; untungsubagyo 177cl; Sayan Uranan 81; PREECHA WIBOONDUANGJINDA 234-235br; yochika photographer 51cl.

Unsplash: David Ford 68clb; YMA 18b, 202.

Cover images:
Front and spine: **Getty Images / iStock:** PictureLake; *Back:* **Alamy Stock Photo:** Oscar Espinosa cb, Jon Arnold Images Ltd / Gavin Hellier cl; **Dreamstime.com:** Nattanai Chimjanon c; **Getty Images / iStock:** f11photo t, PictureLake b; *Front Flap:* **Alamy Stock Photo:** NAMHWI KIM cra; **Getty Images:** Insung Jeon t, © Jong-Won Heo bl, NurPhoto cla; **Getty Images / iStock:** ST_travel br

Romanization
The Korean in this book is presented in Hangeul script, the official writing system of South Korea. For phrases with no appropriate literal translations, liberal translations or common loanwords have been used. The pronunciation for Korean words given is shown in Revised Romanization, the most common method of expressing Hangeul characters in the English language. In some instances, however, exceptions to Revised Romanization have been made for clarity, such as for the names of well-known locations.

Korean names
Family names come before the first names in Korea, a convention followed in this book. Hyphens are used in names where required. However, exceptions to both rules have been made in the case of personal preferences. Depending on the geographical region and the individual, the same family name can often be spelled many different ways; this book adheres to the most common spellings.

Use of Korea
"Korea" is used to represent South Korea throughout this book, unless it is unclear whether the text is referring to North Korea or South Korea, when this custom will be broken for sense purposes.

First edition 2025

Published in Great Britain by Dorling Kindersley Limited,
20 Vauxhall Bridge Road, London SW1V 2SA

The authorised representative in the EEA is
Dorling Kindersley Verlag GmbH. Arnulfstr.
124, 80636 Munich, Germany

Published in the United States by DK Publishing,
1745 Broadway, 20th Floor, New York, NY 10019

Copyright © 2025 Dorling Kindersley Limited
A Penguin Random House Company
25 26 27 28 10 9 8 7 6 5 4 3 2 1

All rights reserved.

No part of this publication may be reproduced, stored in or introduced into a retrieval system, or transmitted, in any form, or by any means (electronic, mechanical, photocopying, recording, or otherwise), without the prior written permission of the copyright owner.

DK values and supports copyright. Thank you for respecting intellectual property laws by not reproducing, scanning or distributing any part of this publication by any means without permission. By purchasing an authorised edition, you are supporting writers and artists and enabling DK to continue to publish books that inform and inspire readers.
No part of this publication may be used or reproduced in any manner for the purpose of training artificial intelligence technologies or systems. In accordance with Article 4(3) of the DSM Directive 2019/790, DK expressly reserves this work from the text and data mining exception.

The publishers cannot accept responsibility for any consequences arising from the use of this book, nor for any material on third party websites, and cannot guarantee that any website address in this book will be a suitable source of travel information.

A CIP catalog record for this book
is available from the British Library.

A catalog record for this book is available
from the Library of Congress.

ISSN: 1542 1554
ISBN: 978 0 2417 3327 1

Printed and bound in Malaysia.

www.dk.com

MIX
Paper | Supporting
responsible forestry
FSC™ C018179

This book was made with Forest Stewardship Council™ certified paper – one small step in DK's commitment to a sustainable future.
Learn more at **www.dk.com/uk/
information/sustainability**

A NOTE FROM DK

The rate at which the world is changing is constantly keeping the DK travel team on our toes. While we've worked hard to ensure that this edition of South Korea is accurate and up-to-date, we know that opening hours alter, standards shift, prices fluctuate, places close and new ones pop up in their stead. So, if you notice we've got something wrong or left something out, we want to hear about it.
Please get in touch at travelguides@dk.com